READ TILL IT SHATTERS
NATIONALISM AND IDENTITY IN MODERN THAI LITERATURE

READ TILL IT SHATTERS
NATIONALISM AND IDENTITY IN MODERN THAI LITERATURE

THAK CHALOEMTIARANA

PRESS

ASIAN STUDIES SERIES MONOGRAPH 10

Published by ANU Press
The Australian National University
Acton ACT 2601, Australia
Email: anupress@anu.edu.au

Available to download for free at press.anu.edu.au

ISBN (print): 9781760462260
ISBN (online): 9781760462277

WorldCat (print): 1048423687
WorldCat (online): 1048423614

DOI: 10.22459/RS.08.2018

This title is published under a Creative Commons Attribution-NonCommercial-NoDerivatives 4.0 International (CC BY-NC-ND 4.0).

The full licence terms are available at
creativecommons.org/licenses/by-nc-nd/4.0/legalcode

Cover design and layout by ANU Press

This edition © 2018 ANU Press

Contents

Foreword vii
Craig J. Reynolds

Author's introduction. 1

1. The first Thai novels and the Thai literary canon 11
2. Racing and the construction of Thai nationalism. 75
3. Adventures of a dangerous Thai woman:
   Huang rak haew luk (1949). 111
4. A civilized woman: M.L. Boonlua Debhayasuwan 137
5. Are we them? The Chinese in 20th-century Thai literature
   and history 155
6. Reading lowbrow autobiographies: The rich, the gorgeous
   and the comical 211

Previously published works. 235
Index 237

Foreword

Craig J. Reynolds

In this volume of literary studies, Thak Chaloemtiarana pretends with disarming modesty to be little more than an enthusiastic reader in search of a good story. His tastes are broad and include early Thai novels that masqueraded as translations from European languages. Of Sino-Thai heritage, he has an enviable command of fiction and memoires about Sino-Thai identity, and he enjoys crime fiction, literary biography, salacious stories and lowbrow, trashy pocketbook autobiographies. Huffy academics might raise an eyebrow at his tastes, but, in these essays, Thak exploits his reading habits to unobtrusively challenge the conventional boundaries of more than one academic discipline.

Professor Thak, a political scientist, is best known for his study of Field Marshal Sarit Thanarat that began life as a PhD thesis and became a prize-winning book. It was reprinted many times and reissued with a new postscript in 2007.[1] As he explains in his introduction to this volume, he wandered into Thai literary studies through force of circumstance. For a dozen years after he left the Dean's Office at Cornell University in 1998, he was Director of the Southeast Asia Program, a position that also required him to teach. Impatient with the current trends in comparative politics, he decided to branch out, exploit the eclectic reading habits that had absorbed him in his spare time, and offer a graduate seminar in Thai political literature. Subsequent seminars included readings in New Historicism, translation, and postcolonial theory. He looked at literature not for its formal properties as art, but for its insights into the struggles of literary artists to express emergent nationalism and Thai identity as the country faced the challenges of Western imperialism and colonialism.

---

1 Thak Chaloemtiarana, *Thailand: The politics of despotic paternalism* (Ithaca: Cornell Southeast Asia Program Publications, 2007; revised edition).

His first publication in this unfamiliar field appeared in a 2003 festschrift for the late Benedict Anderson, his thesis supervisor, confrère and occasional squash opponent. Anderson must have been as pleased with Thak's study of one of the early military government's most popular authors and nationalist ideologues as he was at beating Thak at squash, which he did consistently. Thak had plenty of work to do, because, when he began his venture into the exciting period between 1900 and 1928, there were few serious studies of Thai literature. Several English essays followed, the fruit of conferences and other academic gatherings.

To celebrate Thak's 70th birthday, Thai colleagues translated the essays and published them in 2015 in a single volume with an extensive introduction. The impetus for the Thai volume was to encourage university students of politics and other disciplines to take literature seriously and learn what it could teach them about modern Thai political culture. The essays have never appeared together in English, and the Asian Studies Editorial Board of ANU Press, seeing the value of Thak's scholarship and iconoclastic approach to Thailand's modern literary history, has seized an opportunity and issued the collection in English. The essays as originally published have been edited to suit their place in a single volume.

Thak's self-directed travel through 20th-century Thai literary history is not as improvised and accidental as it might at first appear. 'Making New Space in the Thai Literary Canon', an article he published midway through this journey, captures perfectly what he came to realise was his project. He would rediscover Thai literary works pushed to the margins and rehabilitate them, and he would explore in popular literature the dilemmas and contradictions of Thai modernity, nationalism and Sino-Thai identity. Bilingual in Thai and English, he began his academic career as an insider teaching politics in a Thai university in the mid-1970s. After he left Thailand for the United States, he became an outsider looking in. He had never taught literature in a Thai university, and he had never paid much heed to what the Thai academy regarded as the literary canon. He had not been schooled in the way literature was taught in Thailand, so he was not obliged to analyse literary works for their aesthetic value. He was not expected to use disciplinary concepts and theories, and he did not have to puzzle out the formal structure of novels and short stories in terms of plot, character, setting and language.

Thak is not the first Thai scholar to question the Thai literary canon and challenge its cultural authority. In the early 1980s, the historian Nidhi Eoseewong disrupted the Thai literary establishment with a bold study of early Bangkok literature, proposing that it demonstrated a liveliness and an ability to evolve new forms in the changing environment. In the late 19th and early 20th century, the literary traditions of the court and the people began to diverge. The liveliness and creativity of the earlier period soon faded as royal absolutism exerted its authority to define what constituted literary excellence, a process that stifled the study and enjoyment of Thai literature and left behind 'a lifeless corpse' in Thai textbooks. As Nidhi put it:

> Early Bangkok's upper class literature of such power, liveliness, and intellectual creativity met its final death. It turned into a pretentious, derivative literature for half a century and then disappeared from this world, leaving behind a lifeless corpse in textbooks which the Ministry of Education has to force students to study with great reluctance.[2]

Late in the absolute monarchy, the Thai literary canon became fixed when the sixth Bangkok king, Vajiravudh (r. 1910–25), gave his blessing to the Royal Society of Literature established in 1914. The society identified works in various literary genres produced in court circles that would stand as exemplars of Thai literary excellence. A seal was awarded to certify this excellence. In this endeavour the king was aided by his uncle, Prince Damrong Rajanubhab, who, from 1915, directed the Wachirayan Library and reclassified all the books and manuscripts in the collection into three categories: history, literature, and textbooks and treatises. In the years that followed, other writers, editors and publishers further refined the meaning of literature, which, according to one author, should be polite, serious and possessed of a clear moral compass. According to such strictures, literature should not and could not be vulgar, backward or useless. The Royal Society of Literature was dissolved when King Vajiravudh died in 1925, but successor institutes of one sort or another that passed judgement on what constituted good literature continued into the civilian and military periods well through the early 1940s. A Thai critic of the way the aristocracy wielded its cultural authority refers to 'the discourse of genius' that has forever beset discussions of the royal elite and its accomplishments.[3]

---

2   Nidhi Eoseewong, *Pen and sail: Literature and history in early Bangkok*, ed. Chris Baker and Ben Anderson (Chiang Mai: Silkworm Books, 2015), 146.
3   Thanapol Limapichart, 'The Royal Society of Literature, or, the birth of modern cultural authority in Thailand' in *Disturbing conventions: Decentering Thai literary cultures*, ed. Rachel V. Harrison (London: Rowan & Littlefield International, Ltd, 2014), 37–62; Thosaeng Chaochuti, 'Through the literary lens: Vajiravudh's writings and Siam's negotiations with the Imperial West' in Harrison, *Disturbing conventions*, 77.

Thak's pioneering forays into Thai literary studies have already spurred new research into the works he brought to light. Rachel Harrison re-examined the early Thai novels of Khru Liam and showed how they 'disturbed the literary conventions of the day, rendering the author a victim of "dismissive criticism" and expelling his works to a long-term position at the margins of cultural acceptance'.[4] The Thai literary scholar Phrae Chittiphalangsri has also taken the study of Khru Liam's *The divine nymphs* one step further by demonstrating how translation injected dynamism into the canon as the Thai literary repertoire evolved.[5] I would hope that literary scholars will take up Thak's observation about 'nascent feminist ideals' in this early literature and the ethical, strong and smart women portrayed in Luang Wichit's *Sea of love, chasm of death*, discussed in Chapter 3, and in the novels of M. L. Boonlua Debhayasuwan, discussed in Chapter 4.

What strikes me about these essays is what they reveal about their author, Thak Chaloemtiarana, and his hobbies. Sad to say, he has not been able to work his love of fly fishing and guitar playing into his literary studies, but in Chapter 2, 'Racing and the construction of Thai nationalism', he does draw on his knowledge of high-performance auto racing. He sports a few trophies from his victories at Watkins Glen in upstate New York and other racing venues, and he continues to be a high-performance driving instructor in the Porsche Club of America. His essay on the racing princes, Birabongse Bhanudej and Chulachakrabongse, celebrates their escapades on the world racing circuits when Thailand was a little-known country thought to be somewhere between India and China. The princes' mastery of Western machinery was a singular accomplishment, because in the 1930s Thais did not build motor cars, let alone high-performance racing machines. Prince Bira won the undercard race of cars with small displacement engines in the 1936 Monaco Grand Prix. The Thai flag was flown and the national anthem played for the first time at an international sporting event. Bira went on to win the coveted Road Racing Gold Star awarded by the British Race Drivers' Club in 1936, 1937, and 1938. The successes of the racing princes showed that Thailand had mastered Western machinery and was equal to the West on the racing circuits.

---

4   Rachel V. Harrison, 'Mummies, sex and sand: Bangkok gothic and the adventure fiction of "Victorian" Siam' in her edited volume, *Disturbing conventions*, 82.
5   Phrae Chittiphalangsri, 'The emerging literariness: Translation, dynamic canonicity and the problematic verisimilitude in early Thai prose fictions' in *Translation and global Asia: Relocating networks of cultural production*, ed. Kwan Uganda Sze-pui and Wong Lawrence Wang-chi (Hong Kong: The Chinese University Press, 2014), 207–40.

FOREWORD

In observing from afar Thailand's tumultuous politics, inequalities and censorious laws against political dissent, Thak Chaloemtiarana can be no less sure of his footing as an insider outside than are his compatriots and fellow scholars, both Thai and foreign, living inside the country. So it is that he wrote affectingly of his fellow graduate student, Dr Boonsanong Punyodyana, who, in the midst of the increasingly violent politics of the mid-1970s, was felled by an assassin's bullet in the lead-up to the massacre at Thammasat University on 6 October 1976. Thak has memorialised his friendship with Boonsanong and paid tribute to his bravery for embracing socialism in conservative Thailand, thus betraying the interests of his own class. Boonsanong's death saddened all his friends. As Thak wrote:

> It had a sobering effect but it also galvanized our resolve to do what is right. I was among his many friends, admirers, and students who attended his over-flowing cremation ceremony. Boonsanong's death was a life changing lesson for those of us he left behind. We may not be as brave or as daring as Boonsanong, but in a small way, we have learnt to be true to our convictions. Many of us tried to affect meaningful social and political change from within the government. I tried that but only briefly. Frustrated by that experience, I opted for the easy way out and decided to spend the rest of my career within the safe confines of the academy. I gave up my position at Thammasat and the Prem government to return to Cornell to teach students about convictions and how to seek truth … The convictions I still hold about social justice and human dignity inspired by Boonsanong are renewed every time I use one of the melamine plates or that one bowl he had left me. After these many years, I still think of him, his smile and his booming voice.[6]

Thak knew Boonsanong when they were both young and the future before them looked bright and promising, but Thak, unlike Boonsanong, never had a liking for Thai party politics. His passion is for understanding Thai political culture.[7]

Craig J. Reynolds
Canberra
February 2018

---

6   Thak Chaloemtiarana, 'Ramlukthung bunsanong bunyothayan [In Memory of Boonsanong Punyodyana]', *Matichon weekly*, 30(1541) (26 Feb.–4 Mar. 2010): 32–3.
7   In writing this foreword, I have benefited from comments by the Thai literary scholar, Chusak Pattarakulvanit, in his introduction to Thak Chaloemtiarana, *An jon taek wannakam khwamthansamai lae khwampenthai* [*Read till it shatters: Literature, modernity and being Thai*] (Bangkok: Aan Publications, 2015), [21–41] and from Nicholas Farrelly's 'Interview with Thak Chaloemtiarana', *New mandala*, 19 October 2007, accessed 19 February 2018, www.newmandala.org/interview-with-thak-chaloemtiarana/.

Author's introduction

Readers who are familiar with my early work may wonder why someone trained to study Thai politics has wandered off to encroach upon as tightly guarded a field as Thai literary criticism. In fact, this intellectual and disciplinary retooling late in life is the result of three rather ordinary circumstances.

First, although I had studied political science, taught it, and written about it during the first part of my professional career, disciplinary advancements overtook the original inclinations of why I wanted to study politics. My training and preferences viewed politics as part and parcel of the give and take of social interactions animated by peculiar cultural influences; and it is also about the interactions of political actors. I was always fascinated by how political science engaged other disciplinary fields that helped us understand how societies structure their 'allocation of values', how they structure authoritative institutions, how political succession or change are achieved, how political legitimacy is achieved, and how conflicts are resolved. Among the disciplines that influenced my own work besides political science were anthropology, language and literature, history, art, and, more recently, cultural studies. But as political science, especially as taught in the United States, moved further and further away from what I would call the substance of politics to try to justify political science as real science by focusing on theory, methods and prediction, I became more and more disenchanted with the discipline.

Second, I have always been partial to literature and how one can learn about the human condition (including politics) through reading literary works. Even during my high school years spent at a boarding school in Hong Kong, I loved reading fiction and in fact had the highest mark in English literature in my senior year. But instead of pursuing literature in college, I, like others, chose a more 'practical' subject to study. I was led to believe that political science and international relations would pave the way for a career as a diplomat or, at worst, a professor. The American war in Vietnam and my own resistance to that war made me question and eventually reject the idea of representing Thailand as a diplomat. What if I did not agree with my government? How could I carry out my duty as a representative of a government I cannot support? These questions led me to consider my fallback position, that is, teaching at the university where I could express my ideas and opinions protected by the principle of academic freedom. My professors, especially George Kahin, demonstrated how one could 'speak truth to power' freely and without intimidation by the authorities during the Vietnam War years.

Therefore, instead of joining the Ministry of Foreign Affairs to follow in the footsteps of my father, I became a faculty member at Thammasat University's Faculty of Political Science prepared to 'speak truth to power'. My career at Thammasat coincided with the brief 'open' period between 14 October 1973 and 6 October 1976, the Thanin reactionary regime, and the early part of Prem Tinsulanonda government. One of the first courses I taught was the team-taught 'Foundations of Thai Civilization'. This course was taught for years by M.R. Kukrit Pramoj. However, many of us newly minted faculty members, led by Charnvit Kasetsiri, decided that it is time to teach that course by challenging Kukrit's royalist conservative view of Thai society. We wanted to make incoming freshmen think critically about what constitutes Thai civilisation, uncoupled from the yoke of historical orthodoxy that all good things flow downwards from the top. In fact, democratic ideas would stand that orthodoxy on its head.

Among our team were Charnvit Kasetsiri, Sombat Chantornwong, Chonthira Klad-yu, Banthorn Ondam and other 'progressive' faculty members. My own contribution to the class was to focus on Thai politics. I chose to give lectures on political legitimacy. To change the old culture of students writing down whatever the professor says in class and to regurgitate them during exams, I forbade anyone in class to take notes. The freshmen students were told to just listen carefully and to write notes after the class was over. Also on purpose, I let my beard and hair grow, wore striped bell-bottom pants and Dr Scholl's wooden clogs, and smoked a cigar when I entered the auditorium where the class was held. I told my bewildered students that they did not have to call me *ajarn* (professor/lecturer) until the class was over and to judge for themselves if I was worthy of that honorific.

Not only was my attire and physical appearance an affront to my senior colleagues at Thammasat, but my instruction to the freshman class to honour their teachers only if they were worthy indirectly undermined the sanctity of the *ajarn*. In those days, male faculty members wore white long-sleeved shirts with a necktie, and proper shoes. I did none of that. For the final exam, I asked students to start thinking about how to answer the question: 'There are many ways to think about Thai history and civilisation. Which version would you prefer and why—Prince Damrong, Luang Wichit, or Jit Phumisak?' Some of my senior colleagues later accused me of creating chaos on campus because the students formed study groups to discuss possible answers and even approached some professors to ask for their opinion. Instead of the usual multiple choice examination questions, I assigned my students to write an essay. Little did I know that reading hundreds of essays would take weeks to mark.

After the 14 October 1973 upheaval, students were free to read the many books that were banned by the Sarit regime. I also took the opportunity to use some of those formerly banned books in class, especially to help teach Thai political history. Textbooks are fine but they are dull and do not fully give a sense of reality. Ironically, prose fiction or novels can help liven up the past. Of particular note, I used Kulap Saipradit, *Lae pai khang na* [*Looking towards the future*], in class when we discussed political change. For this purpose, I did not assign Kukrit Pramoj, *Si phaendin* [*Four reigns*]. Kulap's novel is about the struggle for a democratic form of government, while Kukrit's novel is about the fall of absolute monarchy and the important role played by the Thai kings and nobility. However, academic freedom and the ability to freely 'speak truth to power' were cut short by a military coup and the appointment of the reactionary government of Thanin Kraiwichien that followed the bloody 6 October 1976 incident.

The Thanin government warned us not to speak ill of Thai society or risk being arrested. We were also prohibited from teaching or writing about 'ideologies'. I was teaching a course on Chinese politics and a senior seminar that focused on different paths towards political regimes based on the work of Barrington Moore. I also taught a course on 'Society, the Military and Politics'. This government dictum meant that I could not teach any course at all. Even today, chills go down my back when recalling a faculty meeting where our Rector told us that there was still academic freedom but 'if the police arrest Ajarn Thak for what he says, it is his problem, not Thammasat's'. It is not just professors who need protection for 'speaking truth to power'; all Thai citizens should have the right to think and to express their opinions freely, especially towards those who are in positions of authority. Sadly, Thai history tends to repeat itself.

The third and final reason why I shifted my disciplinary focus from political science to literature had to do with the shift in my academic career. After leaving Thammasat to return to Cornell in 1981, teaching jobs for Southeast Asian specialists were not readily available. There were jobs in Australia and short-term teaching jobs at small colleges in America, but I did not want to leave Cornell and its excellent Southeast Asia Program. My return to Cornell was funded by a grant from the Social Science Research Council. When that ran out, I was lucky to find a position in the Dean's Office in the College of Arts and Sciences. I started out as an assistant dean and eventually became an associate dean in charge of admissions. My duties included academic advice to students, academic disciplinary action and the language house program. Concurrent with that position, I was given an adjunct appointment in the Department of Asian Studies, which allowed me to teach the area studies course 'Introduction to Southeast Asia'. During my years as associate dean and teaching one course a year, there was no time to do much research or to write. My scholarship was put on hold for most of those 15 years. This situation changed in 1998 when a crisis of faculty leadership occurred in the Cornell Southeast Asia Program.

Universities in America experienced unprecedented expansion during the mid-1960s when abundant federal funds poured into universities for research and for graduate studies. As a result, an unusually large number of new professors were hired during that time. They eventually came to represent the largest cohort of faculty members in American universities. This group of faculty members acted as a bottleneck in the academy, preventing the hiring of the next generation of faculty. For example, only one among my group of graduates in the early 1970s found a teaching job in the United States. Most of us ended up in England, Australia and Asia. By the late 1990s, faculty members hired in the mid-1960s began to retire or had died. Because this group occupied most of the tenured positions available, only a handful of new junior faculty members were hired during those 30-odd years. This meant that departments were top-heavy with senior full professors, a few associate professors and even fewer assistant professors.

The Cornell Southeast Asia Program also faced this same crisis—that is, the senior professors who took turns as director had retired or were about to retire. There were no assistant professors, and only three associate professors who could take over directorship of the Program. Because of this leadership crisis, I was asked to leave the Dean's Office and to assume the directorship of the Southeast Asia Program. Because I had been an associate dean of the college and was familiar with the various department chairs, other senior faculty members and senior members of the university administration, my dean, provost and faculty colleagues felt that I would be in a good position to help negotiate with the various academic departments to replace retiring Southeast Asianists with new hires. This was not easy because, after the Vietnam debacle, few universities wanted to invest in Southeast Asian studies. With the support of the University Provost and the Dean of Arts and Sciences, I was successful in replacing all of the retirements with young faculty members. But it would take many years before the new professors could be tenured and promoted to full professor so they would be in line to take over the directorship. So instead of the two years I had agreed to serve as director, my term lasted 12 years. My retirement in 2010 forced younger colleagues to consider taking over leadership of the Program. Unlike in Thailand where deanships or directorships are seen as plum positions, few faculty members in the United States want to give up their scholarship for administration. Most faculty members view administration as a duty to serve their peers, and are happy to return to teaching, research and writing.

Leaving the Dean's Office also meant that I became a full-time regular member of the Department of Asian Studies. The department focuses on Asian literature, language teaching and religious studies. Area studies courses are also under that department. However, the graduate field of Asian studies is only at the MA level. PhD students have to be in the graduate field of Asian literature, religion and culture. To fit into the intellectual culture of the department, I had to teach myself a new discipline. I had always liked literature and therefore the switch seemed natural. However, as an outsider with no academic training in literary studies, I had to do a lot of reading, to learn a new vocabulary and a new set of theories, and eventually to design new courses to teach.

In short, retooling late in my career was the result of a frustration with modern political science, my love for literature and the need to become intellectually compatible with colleagues in my new department. Although my appointment as Director of the Southeast Asia Program meant splitting my time between administration and teaching, for career advancement I was still required to produce academically, that is, to write about Thai literature. Teaching and service do not count much towards salary increases or promotions. Research and publications far outweigh all other activities. My last academic appointment before joining the department was associate professor, a position I attained at Thammasat University in 1980. To be promoted as professor in a new field and to be taken seriously by colleagues in Asian Studies, I had to publish. The rule in American research universities is that the faculty members are hired to teach, do research and publish. The split is 50-50. Corny and pretentious as it may sound, faculty members are supposed to conduct 'cutting edge' scholarship that will 'push back the boundaries of ignorance'. Therefore, I must admit that the production of scholarship is partly driven by less-than-noble reasons. Self-preservation, status and money provide incentives, but luckily I actually like working on modern Thai literature.

The first article on Thai literature that I tried my hand at writing was written to honour Ben Anderson on his retirement. The essay was an analysis of Luang Wichit's *Huang rak haew luk* [*Sea of love, chasm of death*] published in James Siegel and Audrey Kahin's edited collection, *Southeast Asia across three generations*.[1] Again, the genesis of that article was serendipitous. The four-volume republication of the novel was a present from Wilasa, a gifted Cornell structural engineering graduate who happens to be the granddaughter of Luang Wichit. I was reading the novel when I was asked to contribute to Ben Anderson's retirement volume. Because it was my first article on Thai literature, I relied on the opinion and assistance of some friends. Gerry Cox, a professor of English literature and a colleague in the Dean's Office, helped to edit the essay and to teach me how to write critically and clearly. The other expert on Thai literature was Rachel Harrison of SOAS (the School of Oriental and African Studies, University of London). The two were instrumental in building up my confidence to write about Thai literature.

In fact, Rachel has helped in other ways, especially in the publication of two of my essays that were products of the conference 'Ambiguous Allure of the West', held at Cornell in November 2004. The essays on Khru Liam's *Nang neramit* [*Divine nymphs*] and *Khwam mai phayabat* [*The non-vendetta*] and were first published in *Southeast Asia research*,

---

1   James Siegel and Audrey Kahin, eds, *Southeast Asia across three generations* (Ithaca: Cornell Southeast Asia Program Publications, 2003).

15(1) (March 2007) and 17(3) (November 2009), respectively.[2] The third essay of that series, 'Making space in the Thai literary canon', which reflects on how modern Thai prose fiction could help illuminate Thailand's encounter with, and resistance to, colonialism was published in the *Journal of Southeast Asian studies*, 40(1) (February 2009). This article was developed from a keynote address given at the conference on Thai studies in Madison and at Chulalongkorn University in December 2007. I have consolidated and re-edited these three articles into Chapter 1 of this book.

The article on the depiction of the Sino-Thai in Thai literature was written for a conference at Kyoto University in January 2012. Although the English version appears in the *Kyoto journal of Southeast Asian studies* (December 2014), the Thai translation was published first in *Aan*, 5(1), (July–December 2013). The review article of Susan Fulop Kepner's book, *A Civilized Woman: M.L. Boonlua Debhayasuwan*, was first published on the *New mandala* website, 21 November 2013, and subsequently in *Aan*, 5(3) (May–August 2014). The two other chapters in this volume on Prince Bira and on lowbrow autobiographies were developed out of talks delivered at the Cornell Kahin Center. The article on the racing Thai princes appeared in *Sojourn*, 31(2) (July 2016).

The racing career of Prince Bira has long been an interest of mine. I learned about his exploits from my father. As a young man inspired by the racing successes of Prince Bira in the 1930s, my father and another friend raced an MG at events held in Bangkok. Since then, my father was always interested in fast cars. Naturally, I inherited that interest and have always had a sports car in my garage. In fact, I still have several today. One of these cars has been painted 'Bira blue' and sports the name 'Hanuman' as a tribute to Prince Bira's race car. I am embarrassed to admit that I like to drive fast cars on race tracks and have been doing this for over 25 years. The article on Prince Bira was motivated by my fascination with how the racing achievements of the two Thai princes could be viewed through the lens of modernity, identity, orientalism and nationalism.

Readers will notice that common themes animate my writing. These themes reflect my early training as a political scientist and my recent fascination with literary criticism and postcolonial theory. I am still

---

2 For the full publication details of all of the author's essays discussed here, see 'Previously published works', this volume.

trying to grasp the full meaning of nationalism, influenced by the work of my graduate school mentor Benedict Anderson, gender, modernity and identity as they relate to our understanding of Thai society, its people(s), culture(s) and nationhood.

Several Thai colleagues began to notice that my articles were encroaching on a rather conservative discipline in the Thai academy and that my untrained foray into that domain was iconoclastic and challenged received wisdom. In particular, Ajarn Thanet Wongyanawa, the editor of *Ratthasatsan* whom I had met at the 'Ambiguous Allure of the West' conference in Ithaca was first to ask permission to translate and publish the three articles that grew out of that conference. These Thai articles appeared in *Ratthasatsan*, 28(2) (May–August 2007); 29(1) (January–April 2008); *Ratthasat 60 pi* 2 (2009). It seems ironic that after shunning political science, my articles on literature would appear in a journal about politics, a journal housed at the Thammasat Faculty of Political Science, my academic home from 1968 to 1980.

Importantly, other colleagues encouraged me to continue to write about Thai literature. Among these I would like to thank Suwanna Kriangkraipetch, Chalong Soontravanich, Thongchai Winichakul, Thanapol Limapichart and Michael Montesano. Of the five, only Suwanna is trained as a literary critic, the others are historians. I admit that my approach to studying literature combines those disciplines plus my own training in political science. The adage that 'teaching is learning' is particularly true in my case. Teaching a seminar on modern Thai fiction allowed me to test new ideas, to sharpen my thinking, and to learn from my students. Although they may not realise it, I learned more from them than they from me. For this, I would like to thank my former students, now good colleagues and friends, Tyrell Haberkorn, Richard Ruth, Worrasit Tantinipankul, Alexandra Denes, Samson Lim and Bryce Beemer. I also appreciate the helpful comments for revision by anonymous referees of this volume in English as well as the editing assistance of Maria Myutel and the copyediting and indexing by Beth Battrick. Throughout the production process, Emily Hazlewood and the ANU Press team gave professional advice on a complex manuscript, and I thank the Press for the publication subsidy that made the book possible.

Another serendipitous encounter that led to the publication of my articles in Thai occurred when I met Ida Aroonwong, Chusak Pattarakulvanich and May Ingawanij at a conference at Cornell in October 2012. The three are active writers for *Aan* journal where Ida is editor. That friendship subsequently led to invitations to publish articles on Thai literature in *Aan* journal. In 2014, Ida convinced me to publish my articles on Thai literature in one volume. Because my work is in English, Ida had my articles translated or retranslated by Phonglert Phongwanan. The title of that book, *Aan jon taek* (*Read till it shatters*), published by Aan Publications in 2015, is a reference to the Thai version of literary deconstruction, that is, to break apart the whole in order to understand the individual pieces and how they fit together. Ajarn Chusak Pattarakulvanich also wrote an insightful critical introduction to the Thai volume.

This English volume is the brainchild of Professor Craig Reynolds. He believes that there is value in my writings about Thai literature and that putting them in one volume will facilitate access and use as a text in the classroom. I am very grateful for his confidence, support, friendship, and especially for the generous foreword he has written.

Thak Chaloemtiarana
Ithaca, New York
February 2018

1

The first Thai novels and the Thai literary canon

Modernity in Thailand is commonly associated with the reign of King Chulalongkorn (r. 1868–1910), who modernised Thailand by appropriating many advancements made in the West. The general discourse on 'modernity', *khwam than samai* or *samai mai* in Thai, which mean 'being in step with the present era, or the new age', is closely related to the Thai obsession with *khwam jaroen* or 'prosperity and progress'.[1] This prosperity can be manifested by material wellbeing or intellectual prowess. For the state, prosperity is reflected in the material things—buildings, transportation, public works, etc.—that were more highly developed in

---

1   *Siwilai* resounds of the English 'civilised', which the Thai appropriated to represent high international culture mostly based on English aristocratic culture. *Khwam jaroen* has connotations of industrial artefacts of modernity—good roads and transportation, running water, electricity, brick buildings, radio and television, etc. *Khwam than samai* includes both cultural, behavioural and material artefacts of modernity based on a model of a secular and industrialised society. To the Thai, there is a *khwam than samai sakon*, or universal modernity that is not necessarily tied to the West. Japan by the turn of the 20th century, for example, is an example of a modern society for Thailand to emulate. And so is colonial India—the official dress code for males appearing in state ceremonies in Thailand today can either be the *chut ratcha pataen* uniform based on the 'Raj Pattern of British colonial India' or *sut sakon*, which is the 'universal Western suit'. Thai identity is not compromised when it is clothed in a universal form of modernity. Also see Thongchai Winichakul, 'The quest for *siwilai*: A geographical discourse of civilizational thinking in the late nineteenth and early twentieth century Siam', *The journal of Asian studies*, 59(3) (August 2000): 528–54.

the West after its industrial revolution. Modern Thai literature is also dated to this period, and, as the National Identity Board has recognised, Thai literature also partakes of this modernisation process.[2]

In the West, following Cervantes' *Don Quixote* (1615), the novel came to reflect socio-historical reality that represented a clear departure from the symbolism and allegory found in literature of the Middle Ages. As a new way of writing/thinking, the plot of the novel became grounded in a specific historical context, with a real geographical location. In fact, the historical rise of the novel is a history derived from, and directed to, the rise of the middle class. And in contrast to the long tradition of the novel in the West, the novel in Thailand was altogether new. The first novel introduced to an emerging literate middle class was a translation of Marie Corelli's *Vendetta* (1886), which was published in 1902.

It is clear that, by the reign of King Mongkut, the Thai court had concluded that the centre of the civilised world had shifted from China and India to Europe. But, unlike the influence or allure of India and China, the two major hegemonic powers that flanked Thailand, the allure of the West was more dangerous, ambiguous and problematic. India and China never exercised direct political or military control of states in Southeast Asia, except perhaps in the case of Vietnam.[3] But European imperialism threatened to impose political, economic, intellectual and military domination of Thailand as indeed had happened elsewhere.

---

2   The National Identity Board, *Treasury of Thai literature: The modern period* (Bangkok: Prime Minister's Office, 1988), 5. Literary scholars also endorse this idea, see Suphanni Warathorn, *Prawat kan praphan nawaniyai thai* [*History of the Thai novel*] (Bangkok: Thai Textbook Project Foundation, 1976), 24–39.

3   The Thai court participated in the Tribute Economic Regime from the Sukhothai period up to the early Bangkok period (13th–19th centuries). The Thai courts sent tribute missions to China, symbolically accepting the superiority of the Chinese court. Thai tribute gifts of local raw material, such as aromatic woods, deer hide, antlers and spices, were exchanged for silk, jewellery and precious ceramics. In this unequal exchange, the Thai court came out richer. Parenthetically, it should also be noted that the Thai also replicated this system locally and demanded 'tribute' from its vassal states such as Pattani. One should view the new European economic regime of laissez faire and free trade as replacing the Tribute Economic Regime. But, in the case of the new regime, it came hand in hand with military and political threats. What was mostly cultural hegemony on the part of China was replaced by Western imperialism that had already imposed direct economic, political and military control over Thailand's neighbours. The Thai court had to find ways to participate in this new trade regime without falling prey to direct colonialism. David Wyatt, *Thailand: A short history* (New Haven: Yale University Press, 1982), 56. For a detailed account of Thai trade with China, see Sarasin Viraphol, *Tribute and profit: Sino-Siamese trade, 1652–1853* (Cambridge: Harvard University Press, 1977), doi.org/10.2307/j.ctt1tfjb0r.

1. THE FIRST THAI NOVELS AND THE THAI LITERARY CANON

To understand fully the adoption and adaptation of the novel in Thailand as part of a larger survival strategy, it is also necessary to understand the political forces faced by Thailand and the defensive strategies that its leaders took. The Bowring Treaty of 1855 with Britain, which opened Thailand to the new free trade economy, is quite problematic. On the one hand, one can view the treaty regime as a humiliating imposition on Thailand's sovereignty. But from the Thai perspective, the acceptance of extraterritoriality that was part of this treaty can be seen as a price to be paid for participation in the new trade regime, as well as the cost for maintaining control over its own citizens.[4] The court's strategy also included social engineering and intellectual improvement. The court believed Thai society should look modern/civilised to the West, so there would be no excuse for the West to colonise it. At the same time, it should

---

4   In fact, the opening up of the Thai market and the trade in rice in large quantities to feed the British colonies enriched the coffers of the Thai court. In addition, adopting the new political paradigm provided by the West allowed the Central Thai court in Bangkok under Rama V to consolidate its power over its provincial rivals. As a pragmatic strategy for maximising local power and survival, acceptance/submission to Western demands was logical and unavoidable. The Thai court was also careful in portraying itself as an 'equal' of European royalty. In dealing with outsiders, the court made sure that, for domestic consumption, the royals were to appear as 'royals' in their interaction with the West. After the turn of the 20th century, Thai kings did their best to make themselves appear as members of the international family of royalty. For example, Queen Saowapha, Rama V's consort, made it a point to show foreign visitors her intimate knowledge of her distant 'relatives' in Europe. See Maurizio Peleggi, *Lords of things: The fashioning of the Siamese monarchy's modern image* (Honolulu: University of Hawai'i Press, 2002), 32. Kannikar Sartraproong's excellent study of Chulalongkorn's visit (*pai thiaw*) to Singapore and Java tells us that the Thai officials wanted to make sure that the British and Dutch authorities treated the Thai king (and therefore Thailand) as a monarch and not as one of the 'local princes'. The colonial authorities did their best to put the Thai monarch in his place, but the local Malay papers used his visit to criticise the colonial authorities (especially in Batavia) for not inviting local leaders to some of the activities, and for not whitewashing government buildings to prepare for the king's visit. To assert his position as equal to Queen Victoria, Chulalongkorn, who was still a teenager, sent her the following telegram:

> *We* have left Bangkok on the 9th or 10th to see *Our Provinces*, and we have arrived at our most gracious *Majesty's colony* at Singapore, the first time that a *King of Siam* has landed on an English Country. His Excellency the Administrator has received us with the highest honors, and *made us most comfortable at Government House*. We are delighted to see the Country and people prospering so well under Your Most Gracious Majesty's rule. We repeat *Our* grateful thanks to Your Majesty for your friendly reception of *Us*, and we wish you long life, health, and prosperity in every respect.

Telegram from the King of Siam to Her Majesty, Dispatches from the Secretary of the Straits Settlements, COD/12, 01-06-1871 (emphasis added), quoted in Kannikar Sartraproong, *A true hero: King Chulalongkorn of Siam's visit to Singapore and Java in 1871* (Bangkok: Tana Press and Graphic Co. Ltd, 2004), 218. Kannikar's meticulous study uses English, Dutch, Malay and Thai sources to compare and contrast the various accounts of the visit. This excellent study shows the intent of the Thai court, and the stakes involved. For another account, see Imtip Pttajoti Suharto, *Journeys to Java by a Siamese king* (Ministry of Foreign Affairs of Thailand, 2001). Also see Lysa Hong, 'Extraterritoriality in Bangkok in the reign of King Chulalongkorn, 1868–1910: The cacophonies of semi-colonial cosmopolitanism', *Intinerario: European journal of overseas history*, 27(2) (2003): 25–46.

learn about Western culture and language in order to understand better the people they had to deal with. This policy can either be seen as a pragmatic strategy of the weak, or as what others have called auto-colonialism, self-colonisation or crypto-colonialism.⁵

Coming to terms with Western culture by appropriating what is seen as helpful to national survival, Thailand did its best to maintain some control over its own affairs, and to find ways to maximise profit from trade. Adopting Western clothing, architecture, music and artistic tastes may have made the Thai people appear more Western, and therefore 'civilised' (*siwilai*), but the core of Thai beliefs and character remained essentially unchanged. For example, Christianity never replaced Buddhism as the predominant religion. Nevertheless, adopting Western modernity had its drawbacks—the allure of modernity compromised and changed local social and ethical values.

As survival strategy, the Thai ruling elite began to send their children to Europe to learn the ways of the West and therefore become more effective leaders who understood the West—not just speaking their language, but understanding their culture and mindset. In fact, there were more Thai who were familiar with the West than Westerners who knew anything about Thailand. Because the West was the new hegemonic power centre, the new Mandala,⁶ it was best that the Thai public should know something about this new threat to Thai identity and Thai culture. I think that from the Thai point of view, 'knowing' the West, is to 'conquer' the West— to make Western knowledge part of Thai knowledge.

Many of these students, particularly those who studied in England, were exposed to European literature. Most, of course, were exposed to the readily available popular novels. Before the age of film, novels offered an altogether seductive initiation into the ways of the world. The young Thai

---

5   In his opening remarks at the 'Ambiguous Allure of the West' conference held at Cornell University, 5 November 2004, Peter Jackson proposed that 'semi-coloniality' might be a useful concept to explain Thailand's relationship with the West. Jackson argues that it was Thailand's own elite emulating the Western colonisers that helped changed Thailand into a society that resembled colonies in the region. In addition, the Thai elite also used colonial policies and practices to consolidate their power. He referred to Kasian Tejapira's idea that the Chakri monarchy was an 'auto-colonial' power. Jackson also referred to Michael Herzfeld's notion of 'crypto-colonialism', see note 9 below.

6   See Oliver W. Wolters, 'Among the Mandalas', in *History, culture, and region in Southeast Asian perspectives* (Ithaca: Cornell Southeast Asia Program Publications, 1999), 126–54.

students studying in England would have read Victorian novels not only to improve their grasp of English, but to explore imaginatively this new world of Western culture.

Although postcolonial literary scholars debate whether the indigenous novel is written 'to mimic', 'to ridicule' or 'to resist' the colonial masters, such an analysis does not apply neatly to the Thai case. There is no question that the Thai novel is directly influenced by the European literary tradition, but the nature of that influence is complicated and ambiguous. Thais tended to look at translation not in the literal sense but as a version of the looting accompanying conquest. Nor were Thais reticent about admitting that they were looting good ideas from the West. In other words, the influence of Western literary ideas was not part and parcel of direct colonial rule where education and cultural influence is the official policy of the foreign power. The influence of the West in Thailand was self-induced, not as a form of submission but as a weapon for resistance. With official support from the court, Thai authors freely borrowed from the West with ease and without anxiety. They were not submitting to the West but doing what Rama V had urged in a speech to prize-winning students at Suan Kulap School in 1886. To wit:

> There are few of us who are authors and knowledgeable about other countries that can transfer knowledge from their texts to make it our own … But we have hopes that when our students learn enough they will strive to write books that will be useful. In addition, those who have studied abroad should be diligent in translating texts from foreign languages into Thai in order to support and to spread education.[7]

The king and the promoters of the new literature took a thoroughly pragmatic attitude. How best to learn about the West if not through appropriated and 'translated' Western forms? Translated articles with Western content also educate the Thai public about the foreigner in a controlled way to keep them part of a Thai construction of the *farang*

---

7   Quoted in Suphanni, *History of the Thai novel*, 32. In the first editorial of the magazine *Lak witthaya*, published in 1900, Jaophraya Thammasakmontri urged writers to consider the prose narrative form to express modern ideas. Translations were also encouraged as a defensive strategy to prevent Thailand from falling victim to colonisation. For a discussion of the use of translation in the colonial context, see Tejaswini Niranjana, *Siting translation: History, post-structuralism, and the colonial context* (Berkeley: University of California Press, 1992). Postcolonial studies focus a lot of attention on translation as control and as resistance. Also see Vincent Rafael, *Contracting colonialism: Translation and Christian conversion in Tagalog society under early Spanish rule* (Durham: Duke University Press, 1993). Rafael argues that translation and mistranslation is the Tagalog Filipino's way to cope with and to participate in the colonial process.

Other. This counter-hegemonic strategy parallels colonial translation of colonised texts that is part and parcel of the colonisation process that portrays the colonised as inferior.

Rather more than straightforward translation is involved here. The Thai intellectuals acknowledged and even proclaimed that they were 'stealing knowledge' or 'plagiarising' from the West. They clearly felt no shame about this theft. To the Thais, appropriating the novel from the West was in fact seen as a 'clever' mastery of the West, and not as the bankruptcy of indigenous genius. Western influences were not seen as impositions because Thailand had not been colonised. Having escaped direct colonisation, the Thai elite focused on appropriating what they saw as good, and perhaps less on 'rejecting' what can be seen as bad, outside influences. Rejection and exclusion of what is seen as bad outside influences do appear within the context of the novel, but more as a way to control the boundaries of culture through the use of satire and ridicule.[8]

Also in this regard, the debate over the dichotomy between what is *than samai* (modern) and what is *siwilai* (civilised and Western) is moot in the Thai case. The outward appearance of *siwilai* and *than samai*, albeit based on the West, would not compromise local identity so long as it was done consciously—and it was. *Than samai* connotes modernity or the best of the era—in science, technology, industry, education, statecraft, business, etc. It is not necessarily seen as Westernisation per se.[9] In fact,

---

8   Stephen Greenblatt, 'Culture' in *Critical terms for literary study*, ed. Frank Lentricchia and Thomas McLaughlin (Chicago: University of Chicago Press, 1995), 226. In a sense, many of the translators took liberties to insert a Thai voice or perspective. For example, in a clever use of translation, the first novel to appear in the Thai language in 1902, *Khwam phayabat*, a translation of Marie Corelli's *Vendetta*, elevates Thai culture to an international level comparable to English culture. The translator assumes the persona of the author and superimposes the Thai over the English to 'provincialise' Italy. Mae Wan [pseud.], *Khwam phayabat* [*The vendetta*], in *Cremation volume of Khunying Nuang Surintharacha* (Wat Thepsirin, Bangkok: 6 June 1967). The idea of provincialising the West is adapted from Dipesh Chakrabarty 'Postcoloniality and the artifice of history: Who speaks for "Indian" pasts?' *Representations*, 37 (Winter 1992): 1–26, doi.org/10.2307/2928652.
9   Michael Herzfeld's talk 15 April 2004 at the Cornell Kahin Center takes a slightly different view of Thailand as a semi-colonial state. The reference is based on his paper 'The absent presence: Discourses of crypto-colonialism', *The South Atlantic quarterly* (Fall 2002). Herzfeld poses the idea of 'crypto-colonialism' where non-colonised states such as Thailand and Greece were also subjected to colonial influences or hegemony but felt too awkward to complain about the effects of colonial influence. Thai nationalism is a complex process of appropriation and resistance. The Thai elite encouraged the embracing of standards of civilisation that originated from the West; admittedly, an example of influence. However, appropriation and accommodation are the hallmarks of Thai identity, where hegemonic influences exist side by side with what is said to be Thai, an essentialist view of Thainess that is based on values derived from Buddhism. See 'Dialogue between Nai Mun Chuchart and Nai Khong Rakthai broadcast over the radio between 1941–1942', in Thak Chaloemtiarana, ed.,

the Thais have appropriated selectively from outside civilisations but, at the same time, de-privileged their hegemony by not directly emphasising the originating source.

Now, it might be argued that obscuring or hiding the actual foreign source of a cultural form should be interpreted as an interesting cultural strategy within a semi-colonial context of power. From this point of view, hiding the foreign source of a cultural form does not make it any less a form of cultural mimicry. But the situation is perhaps not so easily resolved, for the Thais were simultaneously publishing translations and adaptations of European novels and short fiction. And, far from concealing their Western origins, the magazines in which these works appeared proclaimed the cultural mindset of the Thais about modernity.

Several Thai literary magazines published either translations or adaptations from European novels and short stories. The goals of these magazines were to encourage the composition and translations of prose fiction and to spread this new form of entertainment to an expanding literate public clamouring for more works in Thai.[10] But note what these magazines were called by the intellectuals who founded them. One representative

---

Thai Politics, 1932–1947: Extracts and documents, volume 1 (Bangkok: Social Science Association of Thailand, 1978), 260–316. In the dialogue between Nai Man and Nai Khong aired over the radio in the mid-1930s, the English were held up as models of the modern and civilised. Thais were urged to emulate the English and not the African who are depicted as the least civilised. But at no point did the elite advocate embracing Christianity. Michael Herzfeld's example that the Thai used Western forks and spoons to eat but adapted these to their own practices can either be seen as evidence of crypto-colonialism or the Thai ability to embrace hybridity.

10   Suphanni, *History of the Thai novel*, 47–50, 63–80. The modern term for the novel is *nawaniyai* (new tale). Wibha Senanan Kongkanan, *The genesis of the novel in Thailand* (Bangkok: Thai Watthana Panich Co., 1975), 39–44. Wibha believes that the term *nawaniyai* was probably coined by Si Burapha's *Klum suphap burut* [*The gentleman's group*] in 1928. The term *nawaniyai* did not appear in the Ratchabanditsathan dictionary until 1982. The term *nawaniyai* is an improvement over *nangseu an len* (books to read for fun), which is the common term used to describe the genre. S. Plai Noi asserts that the journal *Thalok witthaya* was published in 1900 for a few years by Wan Thalok Witthaya, and that it reappeared in 1912. According to him, Khru Liam was the sole writer of the magazine that appeared in 1912. See S. Plai Noi, *Khru Liam phu khian nawanijai thai khon raek khwam mai phayabat* [*Khru Liam the first Thai novelist who wrote khwam mai phayabat*] (Bangkok: Dokya, 2002), 82–3. Suchart Sawatsi even speculated that *Khwam mai phayabat* was serialised in that journal. Luang Wilatpariwat mainly wrote as 'Nai Samran' [Mr Happy] in that magazine. But he also used other pen names such as 'Kaew Kung' [Glass Shrimp], 'Rang Jiep' [Absolutely Farang], 'Khun Thong' [Minah Bird], 'Pakka Kaew' [Glass Pen], 'Kluea Kaew' [Crystal Salt], 'Malaeng Mum' [Spider], 'Maew Europe' [European Cat], 'Suriwong Songfa' [Lightening up the Sky], 'Sithanonchai' (a famous court figure from the Ayutthaya period), 'Nai Talok Khon Thi Song' [The Second Comedian], 'Hong Thong' [Golden Swan], 'Nok Krathung' [Krathung Bird], 'Editor', 'Gaw Gaw' (the first letter of the Thai alphabet), 'Nok Noi' [Little Bird], and 'Nok Nori' [Nori Bird]. Suphanni, *History of the Thai novel*, 65.

is *Lak witthaya* [*Stealing knowledge* or *Plagiarism*] edited by Phraya Thammasakmontri. Although it lasted only a few years after it began in 1900, the founders of *Lak witthaya* included Prince Phitayalongkorn, Jaophraya Thammasakmontri and Phraya Surintharacha.[11] Some scholars claim that Crown Prince Vajiravudh and Khru Liam were also members of the editorial board. Another is *Thalok witthaya* [*Exposing knowledge*] edited by Luang Wilatpariwat or 'Khru Liam' or 'Nai Samran'. The third is *Thawee panya* [*Increasing wisdom*] of Crown Prince Vajiravudh.

The name *Lak witthaya* by itself is interesting and significant.[12] It could have easily been *lak witthaya* with a low tone on *lak* meaning 'principles of knowledge'. It could even have been *rak witthaya* or 'love of knowledge'. Instead, the magazine took the unabashed name 'to steal or plagiarise knowledge', presumably from the West. There was no pretence about 'mimicking' or about denying any debt to European achievements. There was no shame in appropriating something of value. Perhaps the fact that Thailand was not a direct colony of any Western power allowed the Thai elite to view themselves as moral equals of the West and therefore there could be no considerations of inferiority or superiority between Thai and European literature. For the Thais of this period, imitation does not seem to be accompanied by the anxiety of influence. The Thai public is not fixated on the origins of what constitutes Thai culture. In fact, to many Thais, the *Ramakian* is considered Thai and not a copy or a version of the Indian epic, the *Ramayana*. Even though the Thai 'appropriated' foreign literature, the act of translating from another culture into the Thai language is regarded as transforming the original work into a Thai one. In fact, Thai culture has been formed through a process of appropriation, translation and adaptation—the invention of a writing system; the adaptation and translation of Indian, Indonesian and Chinese literatures; and the adoption of Buddhism and Brahmanism, are some examples.

The impact of modernity, including its critique, can be glimpsed from several of the early Thai novels, in particular, the first novel written in Thai by a Thai author that is about Thai society. This novel—Khru

---

11   Officials were given titles and names by the king until the overthrow of absolute monarchy in 1932. In ascending order, these are Khun, Luang, Phra, Phraya and Jaophraya.

12   *Lak witthaya* can also be translated as 'Theft of knowledge'. Its editorial staff included Prince Bidyalongkorn (pseudonym No Mo So), Crown Prince Vajiravudh, Jaophraya Thammasakmontri, Phraya Surintharacha (pseudonym Mae Wan) and Luang Wilat (pseudonym Khru Liam). Mattani Rutnin, *Modern Thai literature: The process of modernization and the transformation of values* (Bangkok: Thammasat University Press, 1988), 21.

Liam's *Khwam mai phayabat* [*The non-vendetta*]—was published in 1915. But before we examine Khru Liam's novel, it should be noted that it was written to parody the first novel that was marketed in Thailand in the Thai language. That novel was Marie Corelli's *Vendetta*, translated by Phraya Surintharacha, one of the very early Thai scholars sent by the court to study in England.

The candid and complex ways that the Thai engaged with the West are reflected in the appropriation of Western literature through translation. Here again, *Lak witthaya* is especially significant as the publisher of the Thai translation of Marie Corelli's *Vendetta! Or the story of one forgotten, a novel* (1886). Marie Corelli (1855–1924) was a prolific and bestselling writer in Victorian England. The Cornell University Echols Collection contains 48 titles under Marie Corelli's name. Also, as indication of the Thai fascination with her work, of the 48, six are Thai translations of her novels. Marie Corelli is the pseudonym of Mary 'Minnie' MacKay, who imagined herself as hyper-feminine, struggling against the prejudices of male literary critics. Despite outselling her male rivals by a large margin, she never gained the respect of literary scholars. She was seen as an author of popular fiction. On average, each novel sold over 100,000 copies, to the chagrin of her 'highbrow' competitors. For example, H.G. Wells and Arthur Conan Doyle sold about 1,500 each of their novels. She was read by the booming middle class, and perhaps in this one can draw a parallel that explains why she became so popular also in Thailand and elsewhere in Asia. At one point, the *London mercury* asserted that 'Miss Corelli, in her heyday, was read by the entire middle-class'.[13] Corelli's novels were also a favourite of Queen Victoria and hundreds of thousands of readers in Europe, in America and in Asia. Her works contributed more to English hegemony in Asia than most of her contemporary literary giants like H. Rider Haggard and Arthur Conan Doyle.

Corelli's *Vendetta* was translated by Phraya Surintharacha, a man, who used the feminine pseudonym 'Mae Wan' (literally meaning 'Mother Wan' or 'Madame Wan'), perhaps to indicate that the original author was a woman. The novel was published in 10 instalments under the Thai title *Khwam phayabat* and was completed in April 1901. The instalments were then collated and published as a book in 1902. It became Thailand's first full-length novel and was highly influential. Not only did the novel

---

13   The *London mercury* quotation is from Annette R. Federico, *Idol of suburbia: Marie Corelli and late-Victorian literary culture* (Charlottesville: University Press of Virginia, 2000), 169.

revolutionise the Thai language with its simplified spelling and use of English punctuation,[14] it exposed the Thai reading public to a new form of narrative.

Before the modern novel appeared, classical Thai literature concerned itself mostly with the lives of the Thai nobility and aristocracy. Although some of the major literary compositions commissioned during the early part of the Ratanakosin period were based on foreign literature—Chinese, Indian and Javanese—they were mostly epics or didactic literature. In contrast, *Khwam phayabat* is about the present and the mundane, and the exciting daily happenings in the lives of people with whom the reader can easily identify—just what we would expect a novel to deal with. But the novel also draws on romance. The story is set in Italy, a foreign and exotic place to the Thai as well as to the English. The novel contains passionate love affairs, adultery, tragedy, betrayal, secrecy, adventure, excitement and revenge.

That being said, Mae Wan's text cannot be considered just a literal translation of Marie Corelli's *Vendetta*. What we may call cultural norms are open to question, or, indeed, to reinterpretation. Mae Wan took the liberties of inserting his own thoughts, asides and explanations of European behaviour (e.g. kissing of the hand). He also excised most of Corelli's criticism of the state of European morality and ethics[15] and substituted his own comments. For example, at the beginning of the novel where the main character, Count Fabio Romani, tells the reader that he is writing from the grave, that is, he is 'already dead', Mae Wan draws the Thai reader in by adding comments about the disposal of the corpse, especially in regard to how the Thai way of cremation is superior to the European way of burial. Mae Wan remarks that 'dead' means that the person has been sent to the *Wat* (Buddhist temple) and that he has already been cremated. He writes that the disposal of the corpse in this manner is clean and 'safe', using the English word spelt in Thai, meaning that cremating a corpse is the safest way to ensure that the person is really dead and gone. This assertion is, however, disingenuous: if Count Romani had been 'cremated', there could not have been a story. In Corelli's original, he was, in fact, buried alive and was able to escape to later plot revenge against

---

14 Suphanni, *History of the Thai novel*, 153.
15 W. Winichaikul, *Pak kai wannakam* [*Literature from the pen*] (Bangkok: Dokya, 1994), 10.

his wife and her lover.[16] The retention of English words gives the novel an air of authenticity and intimacy. To the newly educated readership, most of whom would have studied English in school, or have studied abroad, those English words have entered into their popular vocabulary as signs of modernity, *siwilai* and sophistication. The insertion of English also allowed the Thai reader to identify with the English narrator who expressed disdain towards the Italians.

Mae Wan also inserts the Thai voice and asserts Thai cultural superiority by asking the reader why other cultures do not emulate the superior Thai practice of cremation. In this rewriting of the narrative, the West is decentred because European fruits become Thai fruits, and 'South American forest' is turned into 'forests in the north of Siam'. In this way, the writer establishes a rapport with the reader and, in addition, places the Thai on par with the English and thus superior to the Italians in the story. In fact, the ending in the Thai version differs from the original because, after the story's hero achieved his revenge, he disappears not into the jungles of South America, but sets sail to live in Thailand.

Most literary historians assume that *Khwam phayabat* achieved great success following its publication in 1902, and it may indeed be true that it was read so widely and so avidly that no copies of its first printing remain. In fact, I am unaware of the existence of a copy of the first edition because even the National Library of Thailand does not have a copy of the original printing. But it is noteworthy that after the first printing appeared in 1902, the novel seems not to have been reprinted until 11 years later in 1913. The Cornell University Library copy of this novel is a reprint of the 1913 edition, published as a cremation volume of Phraya Surintharacha's wife in 1967. Because the 1967 cremation volume edition is based on the second edition of 1913 rather than a later one, I am assuming that no new editions were published and sold during those 54 years.

---

16   For the story to work, the Count must be buried alive and not cremated. His friend Guido, who was having an affair with the Count's wife, buried the Count when he had fallen ill with cholera. The Count managed to escape from his tomb to exact his revenge by killing Guido in a duel and later revealing himself to his wife who is tragically killed by a slab of stone falling on her. Mae Wan adds a Thai Buddhist interpretation to Nina's death by saying that her *karma* had caught up with her.

Even though it seems not to have gone through many editions, scholars agree that *Khwam phayabat* is the first significant novel to appear in the Thai language.[17] As a result, Marie Corelli became an iconic author to the educated Thai. A sign of her acceptance as one of the canonical authors for the new educated class appears in Si Burapha's *Luk phuchai* [*The real man*], published in 1928. In *Luk phuchai*, Si Burapha suggests that the lead female character is not only well-read, but a sophisticated, modern Thai woman because her library holds works by Dickens, Walter Scott, the Greek philosophers, Thai journals such as *Lak witthaya* and *Phadung witthaya*, and Rama VI's *Dusit samit*—and Marie Corelli.[18]

As the first modern 'Thai' novel, Corelli's *Vendetta* established a set of conventions for Thai writers to work with. First, it became possible to envision a large and sweeping setting that included exotic and foreign places. Second, authors could begin to describe the places in the novels with enough details (be they real or make believe) to allow the reader to imagine and to see clearly where the story takes place. Third, the characters could become more real, plausible and familiar, and not just kings, princes and princesses. Fourth, plots could be more exciting and fast-moving and full of tension without relying on the occult. Fifth, authors could begin to scrutinise and challenge changing social behaviour and cultural values. And lastly, issues of gender, sexuality and adultery could now be raised. Although sexuality is not alien in traditional Thai literature, the fact that it is written in prose and uses everyday language and not metaphor is tantalising. As we shall see later, the later Thai novel that was written to negate the moral of *Vendetta* uses language that goes a step further, to include mundane and vulgar language. In this later text, eroticism is no longer metaphoric but literal.

The novel, with its portrayal of the modern, also became a way to spread the culture of modernity. A modern public concerned with being up-to-date will demand and presumably reward modern forms of entertainment. Novels at once satisfy that demand while providing a means of criticising aspects of modernity. Deviating from traditional subject matters that focused on Buddhist and religious themes, the new literature explored the impact of modernisation and Westernisation on Thai culture, politics, women's rights, gender behaviour and morality. What we see reflected in

---

17 Suphanni, *History of the Thai novel*, 54–5; Marcel Barang, *The 20 best novels in Thailand* (Bangkok: Thai Modern Classics, 1994), 60; Wibha, *The genesis of the novel in Thailand*, 39.
18 Si Burapha [pseud.], *Luk phuchai* [*The real man*] (Bangkok: Dokya, 1975), 213.

this Thai mirror held up to nature is a complex interweaving of traditional Thai values and those deemed to be modern and potentially subversive. The *siwilai* project initiated by the Thai elite brought material modernity and new ways to corrupt the morals of young people. Women who have traditionally been insulated from corrupting behaviour are now equally exposed. Open sexuality subverts traditional notions of chastity and modesty. And the impact of Western culture plays out not only on issues of form but also content of the new, modern Thai novel.

Contemporary scholars of Thai literature have known of the publication of Khru Liam's *Khwam mai phayabat*, but they could not read it: all copies were lost. It was only rediscovered in 1997 and reprinted in 2001.[19] Although many scholars conceded that *Khwam mai phayabat* is almost certainly the first Thai novel, the orthodox interpretation has been that it was written to contradict Marie Corelli's Gothic ideas about revenge in *Vendetta*.[20] The interpretation of the Thai novel's title has been reified as a 'Thai' novel because it negates the European 'Other' by emphasising

---

19 The version used for this chapter is Nai Samran, *Khwam mai phayabat* [*The non-vendetta*] (Bangkok: Double Nine, 2001). This version is the novel's second printing. The typeset and format are reproduced as close as possible to the original. There is also a controversy over its second printing as two publishers have vied for that credit. The other 'second printing' is reproduced by the Dokya Group, which marketed their version of the novel in October 2002. The second copy of this novel was found at the home of Krum Suranan. This copy was signed by the author when he was a monk in July 1923, eight years after its initial printing. Interestingly, the Thai word 'novel' or *nawaniyai* was not used by Khru Liam. Instead he used the term *pralom lok khwam riang*, which translates as 'a composition to soothe the world'. He contends that his book is the first of its genre and that it is a genuine '*novel Thai*'—using the English term. Although no longer in common usage, according to the *Ratchabanditsathan Thai dictionary* (1954 edition) novels that focus on romance and sex were known as *nawaniyai pralom lok*. These novels are said to 'please the world or worldly passions'. This is ironic because, in strict Buddhist sense, the concept *pralom lok* is a negative one—that is, it caters to the desires of the flesh. The other irony is that in his desire to make the novel 'Thai', Khru Liam went against the grain of novels of that period where sex is proscribed by Victorian modesty. Coincidentally, Lorraine Patterson writes in her thesis on Cambodian novels, that the novel in Khmer is also '*pralom lok*'. The first Cambodian novel is said to have appeared in 1938, many years after Khru Liam's novel. Lorraine Patterson quotes from Khing Hoc Dy and Mak Phoeun in her chapter 'Cambodia' in *Southeast Asia: Languages and literature: A select guide*, ed. Susan Herbert and Anthony Milner (Honolulu: University of Hawai'i Press, 1989), 57. Seng Ly Kong, who teaches Khmer at Cornell University, verifies that the Khmer literal translation of *pralom lok* is the same as the Thai. If this true, it suggests that the purpose of the novel is to entertain the reader with romance and sex. The discussion above shows the persistence of Thai erotic culture in the face of Victorian era sexual prudery. It is a good example of Thai agency and selectivity in the face of Western imperialism. The Thais did not copy everything or get rid of all aspects of their culture that may have conflicted with Western values.

20 Bunchuay Somphong said that *Khwam mai phayabat* was written to 'match' Mae Wan's *Khwam phayabat* and to counter Western ideas of revenge with Buddhist teachings of forgiveness. Quoted in Chuay Phunpherm, *Chiwit lae ngan khong khru liam* [*The life and works of Khru Liam*], in the introduction of *Sao song phan pi* [*The two-thousand-year-old maiden*] by Nok Nori, one of Khru Liam's

the value of Buddhist non-vengeance and non-anger. This novel is a fascinating example of appropriating a Western cultural form in order to enunciate an anti-Western position. But, because the negation takes place within a framework at least partly Western in origin, the negation itself is only partial.[21]

The fact that a copy sat on the shelves of a book collector, and that its owner and perhaps others who may have read it had failed to come forward to talk about it, raises one question: What is the novel about?[22] We may not be able to know why it was forgotten or ignored, but we can come to it with fresh eyes. When we do so, the novel reveals itself to be problematic, almost elusively so.

To begin with, the publication date of this novel is itself elusive. In mentioning the novel's existence, Suphanni relies on an insert discovered in another book published by Nai Samran in 1915 or 1916 advertising the publication of *Khwam mai phayabat*.[23] The insert announced that *Khwam mai phayabat* is written to impress the Thai reader and that it is an original novel written by a Thai author who does not have to rely on *farang* ideas. The novel is about good and evil and about affairs that will soothe the heart. The advertisement promises that the language used will be sweet-sounding and will reflect the heritage of the Thai language. The advertisement also promises that the novel will have pictures and notes. It boasts that the new novel in two volumes will cost no more than Mae Wan's *Khwam phayabat*.

---

pseudonyms. This book is the republication of Khru Liam's translation of H. Rider Haggard's *She*. The translation was republished in 1990 by Dokya (Nok Nori, *Sao song phan pi* (Bangkok: Dokya, 1990)).

21 I want to thank Peter Jackson and Rachel Harrison for this insight. Rachel agrees that *Khwam mai phayabat* demonstrates the complex dynamics of adoption, absorption, influence, mimicry, resistance, appropriation, intertextuality, anxiety and ease/confidence.

22 Khru Liam's contemporaries admitted in his cremation volume in 1966 that they remembered reading *Khwam mai phayabat*, but no one said anything of substance about the story itself. The only reference to the plot is given by Bunchuay Somphong, who said that the novel is based on the Buddhist notion of forgiveness that allowed the wronged husband to win back his adulterous wife. Bunchuay Somphong in *Wilatpariwatranusorn*, quoted in Thammakiat Kan-ari, 'Khru Liam poetchak nawaniyai thai rueang raek duay "khwam mai phayabat"', *Silapa watthanatham*, volume 5 (May 1984): 111. The quote suggests that the husband was a *phon ek* or military 'general', which is untrue. Perhaps it is a misprint and the word should have been *phra ek*, or the leading man. Also see excerpts quoted in Ajin Jantharamporn, *Nakkhian thai nai 'wong wannakam'* [Thai writers in the 'literary circle'] (Bangkok: Dokya, 1997), 9–52.

23 Suphanni, *History of the Thai novel*, 57.

Although the insert was found in Nai Samran's *Nang neramit*, which appeared around 1916, Suphanni erroneously dated *Khwam mai phayabat* as appearing during King Chulalongkorn's reign and therefore contemporary with the first publication of Mae Wan's *Khwam phayabat* in 1902. This mistake was also made by Ajin Jantharamphorn, who also asserted that the novel appeared during Rama V's reign. However, he was correct in naming the novel's publication date—1915, which coincides with King Vajiravudh's reign.[24] Had the literary scholars made the connection that the *Khwam phayabat* in question is in fact the 1913 second edition, they would have known that *Khwam mai phayabat* was a contemporary of the former's second printing and not of its first. King Chulalongkorn died in 1910.

The other clue that scholars missed is that the novel appeared soon after the promulgation of the Literary Act in 1914, and that fact has some interesting implications. The preface of the novel obliquely refers to the Literary Act's purpose of promoting indigenous works in Thai by Thai authors. The author proclaims:

> This story is an imaginary story composed by a Thai. It is a genuine Thai story, not an abridged story, not a translation, and not an adaptation of some other story. It is the inaugural copy of a book in the family of *pralom lok khwam riang* which is a real Thai *novel* which should be appealing to the Thai readership whom I pity. Now they can read a genuinely Thai *pralom lok khwam riang*.[25]

To bypass for the moment the novel itself and jump ahead to the postscript, Khru Liam reveals there that the idea for the novel was actually an opportunistic commercial venture. *Khwam mai phayabat* reflects, in fact, converging events. Khru Liam admits in his postscript that he was commissioned to write a novel with the predetermined title *Khwam mai phayabat* by a book publisher, presumably the owner of the Thai Printing Company that later published the novel. The timing of the

---

24   Ajin Jantharamphorn, *Thai writers in the 'literary circle'*, 52. Ajin also claims erroneously that Khru Liam's novel was published during the reign of King Chulalongkorn in 1915 and that it coincided with the publication of Mae Wan's novel. Suchart Sawatsi admits that he too had written about the novel without ever having read it and that he based his conclusions on the (erroneous) assertions of other literary scholars. Suchart went as far as giving credit to Khru Liam's magazine *Thalok witthaya* for publishing instalments of the novel, not realising that it was over 700 pages long and would have taken several years to publish the whole novel in serialised form. We know now that Khru Liam wrote the novel in one sitting—that is, he completed the novel in 22 days writing for six hours a day. See Suchart's introduction in the novel's Dokya edition, 107.
25   Nai Samran, *Khwam mai phayabat*, foreword.

novel also coincided with the recent republication of *Khwam phayabat* in 1913, as well as with the promulgation of the *Literary Act 1914*. That Act intended to curb the proliferation of mediocre works of translation and with them the importation of grammatical forms from the West into Thai. It also urged Thai authors to produce good Thai literature.[26] Although Khru Liam does not mention the publisher by name, he admits that his employer supplied him with paper and pencils. He was also told that he could write any kind of story as long as it was not a *farang* (that is, a Western) one.[27]

Thus charged, Khru Liam wrote a story about the contemporary Thai society that was rapidly changing around him. Even though the language Khru Liam used is colloquial and even vulgar Thai, some borrowed English words still appear. The use of English words does not make the novel less Thai, because it reflects the common usage of language of Thai society at that time. However, Khru Liam did not follow the advice of the Literary Act to refrain from the use of Western grammatical forms and punctuation—again a reflection of the popular Thai belief that if something is useful and better, why not appropriate it?[28]

---

26   The Act can be interpreted as Rama VI's attempts to 'nationalise' the emerging literature, and to exert some quality control on these new literary forms now that they have taken root. The law lamented the fact that translations of bad novels were sold and that the Thai language was contaminated by Western syntax and grammar. For details of the *Literary Act 1914*, see *Ratchakitchanubeksa*, vol. 31, 310–311, also quoted and translated in Wibha, *The genesis of the novel in Thailand*, 72, 73. Wibha concludes that the law had little impact. However, she does not make the connection between the law and the appearance of *Khwam mai phayabat* the following year.

27   Nai Samran, *Khwam mai phayabat*, 720. It is possible to interpret this requirement as 'resistance' against *farang* novels and the West. But one can also argue that the publisher is responding to Rama VI's call to move beyond translations to original works. Khru Liam's novel is indeed an original work about contemporary Thai society and culture. However, this novel was not a market success, which led to the second original novel written by a Thai author in Thai. That novel, *Nang neramit*, imitates the Western novel form as well as content. Therefore, the resistance to the West is once again only partially successful because the Thai readership demanded stories of adventures by Westerners in far and exotic places. It is only in the late 1920s that Thai novels based on Thai stories came into their own in the market place. In 1929, *Luk phuchai* [*The real man*] (Si Burapha), *Sattru khong jao lon* [*Her enemy*] (Dok Mai Sot), and *Lakhon haeng chiwit* [*The circus of life*] (Mom Jao Akat Damkoeng) sold in sufficient numbers. These novels are now considered the first real 'Thai' novels worthy of canonisation. See David Smyth, ed., *The canon in Southeast Asian literatures* (Richmond: Curzon Press, 2000), Chapter 13.

28   The novel's foreword uses two commas, two full stops, and quotation marks. Rachel Harrison points out that it is not objectively the case that Western grammatical forms and punctuation are useful and better in the Thai language—and the usage of such has not persisted. She thinks that this is a marker of further ambiguous attitudes to the West that are distinctly rooted in the context of those times, i.e. that Western punctuation and grammar were seen, in the early decades of the 20th century, as 'useful and better' and therefore to be appropriated, even while other aspects of 'Western-ness' were not (personal communication with the author).

1. THE FIRST THAI NOVELS AND THE THAI LITERARY CANON

Perhaps referring to the misunderstanding and the flap over the interpretation of *Sanuk nuek*, Khru Liam asks the readers to be tolerant if they find that he is using real names and real places.[29] He even makes fun of this by saying that 'the factual is more fun than fiction'. By implication, he is saying that his novel is also 'real' in many ways. Khru Liam boasts that he finished the novel in 22 days by following a strict regimen of writing five pages per hour for six and a half hours each day. All this was done while the author held down another job. Khru Liam wrote as if he were running a marathon: the novel is 730 pages long![30]

---

29 The first major controversy over prose fiction appeared after the establishment of the Wacharayanwiset library, founded by King Chulalongkorn early in his reign. The library published the monthly *Wachirayanwiset* journal. The members of the executive committee were responsible for producing and writing articles for the journal. In 1886, Prince Phichitprichakorn, a half-brother of the king and a prominent legal scholar, wrote what could have been the first instalment of an original Thai novel titled *Sanuk nuek* [*Fun-filled thoughts*]. The story was about several young monks discussing their plans to leave the monkhood and what they would do after leaving. The monks are from Wat Bowoniwet where Prince Phichitprichakorn had been ordained. Because he was familiar with the temple and the surrounding area, he provided very realistic descriptions of the location of his story. His description of the temple grounds was so accurate that Abbot Somdet Krom Phra Porawet (who was incidentally both the Supreme Patriarch and the king's uncle) thought that the incident was real. He was worried that the story would reflect poorly on his administration and promptly lodged a complaint with the king. King Chulalongkorn had no choice but to reprimand his brother for upsetting their uncle. The king was worried that his uncle, who was quite old and frail, would become fatally ill from the anguish caused by the story, which was circulating among readers in the palaces, government offices and the monasteries. The king did, however, explain in his letter to the abbot that Prince Phichitprichakorn's article imitated the *nowel farang*, of which thousands and thousands have been written and published around the world. Literary scholars, in deference to the king, have identified Chulalongkorn's analysis of *Sanuk nuek* as the first example of Thai literary criticism. Unfortunately, the controversy raised by the first instalment put an end to this effort and *Sanuk nuek* never became a full-length novel.

30 When Khru Liam presented a copy of the novel to Mae Wan (Phraya Surintharacha), his classmate from his English school days, he acknowledged his debt to Mae Wan for writing *Khwam phayabat*. At that meeting, Mae Wan marvelled over the fact that it took less than a month for Khru Liam to finish his novel, compared to European authors who might take a year to finish one. Many Thai authors pride themselves for being prolific and fast writers. To many, writing is like exercising—the more you practise, the faster you get. Such a production schedule meant that the writer had to finish writing the novel in one long continuous process to make the story flow smoothly. This production process and timetable ensured that a book could be finished and marketed in a very short time. It is also a concession to the still limited technology where typesetting is done by hand, and, because of the limited types available, after pages are printed, the type settings were broken down and the types reused for the next instalment. Considering the lack of time to edit, it is amazing that some of the early novels are as good as they are. This sort of literary production, that is, fresh and instantaneous, has its roots in writing and singing competitions such as writing *klon sot* (fresh verses). Many Thais are trained to produce poetry or poetic songs at the drop of a hat. For example, note the pride expressed by Luang Wichit Wathakarn when he wrote his monumental novel *Huang rak haew luk* also in record time. Luang Wichit talks about writing as if it were calisthenics. See Thak Chaloemtiarana, 'Move over Madonna: Luang Wichit's *Huang rak haew luk*', in *Southeast Asia across three generations*, ed. James Siegel and Audrey Kahin (Ithaca: Cornell Southeast Asia Program Publications, 2003), footnote 1, 5.

Khru Liam had been writing fiction for some time, and had already translated novels by H. Rider Haggard (best-known is *She*), scientific texts on health and cinematography, and movie plots and dialogue. But this effort is his first original full-length novel.[31] He also admits in the postscript that, although he had avoided writing about adultery in the past, he focused on this subject at the request of a writer friend. This writer was the victim of his wife's infidelity, and he had been pestering Khru Liam to write a story about how modernity had corrupted Thai women. Khru Liam confesses that, once he got started on the subject, he realised that this issue was so important that he could not stop writing about it. The resulting novel exposes the decadence of the Bangkok high society, condemning both men and women who depart from traditional values and thus fall prey to the allure of modernity.

Khwam mai phayabat is perhaps best understood by placing it in the context of Marie Corelli's *Vendetta/Khwam phayabat*. The novel begins with the Buddhist quotation that *non*-revenge is sweet, a clear statement of resistance to Western predilections. The author quotes the Pali proverb, 'We can win against his anger with our non-anger; we can win over his evilness with our good deeds'. The novel claims to be 'Thai' by invoking Buddhist values while simultaneously rejecting the Western proverb so central to *Vendetta*, 'revenge is sweet'.[32] The narrator, Nai Jian, argues that the sweetness of revenge is only fleeting and that bitterness and anguish will eventually take over. Revenge is pitiful, cowardly and shameful. Revenge leads to more hostility. The really brave gentleman (*suphap burut*) is one who can control his heart and forgive those who have wronged him.[33]

---

31 Examples of his books are cited in Dr Wichitwong Na Pompetch, *Nakkhian sinlapin lae sangkhom thai* [*Writers, artists and Thai society*] (Bangkok: Saeng Dao Press, 1999), 33, 35. Khru Liam also left a large body of fiction, and even pornography [*rueang kamarom*], that has not been published.

32 It is Rama VI who associates Buddhism with what is unique about Thai nationalism. Interestingly, following the 11 September 2001 attack on the Twin Towers, the Thai band *Carabao* performed a song asking the rhetorical question of whether the Thai should support the all-powerful America or the Arabs who had nothing but the Koran. Their answer was similar to Khru Liam's as they quoted the same Buddhist teaching of forgiveness.

33 The modern Thai concept of the gentleman (*suphap burut*) is Western because sometimes the English term 'gentleman' is used interchangeably in the early novels. The *suphap burut* has higher standards than the *phu di* (upper class), which is a class concept. The *suphap burut* resists the corruption of the *phu di*. Nai Jian is a *suphap burut* while his tormentors are corrupted *phu di*. This differentiation appears in later novels such as *Luk phuchai* [*The real man*], in which the hero Manote from a working class family ends up as the 'real man' because he was a *suphap burut*. Interestingly, George Mosse in his book *Nationalism and sexuality* made very much the same point about European masculine gender culture in the 19th century, with the rising bourgeoisie criticising the effete masculinity of the established European nobility (George Mosse, *Nationalism and sexuality: Respectability and abnormal sexuality in modern Europe* (New York: Fertig, 1985)).

To convince the reader of the merit of Buddhist non-anger, the narrator goes on to say that his happiness, wealth and high social standing are the result of his non-vendetta and his victory over *mara* (evil). However, even forgiveness is painful because it brought tears to his eyes.[34]

The novel begins at the end of the saga. Nai Jian is the unlikely hero of the story. He spent three years in England. He is 30-ish, not handsome, overly sensitive and unassertive. He has not been successful at his job, having worked for several government ministries. His mother wants him to get married and suggests that he visits a lovely woman, Prung, who lives outside Bangkok. She is 22 and full of life. They marry and live on her parents' plantation. After a short and blissful honeymoon, Prung convinces her husband to move back to Bangkok so she can enjoy the benefits of modernity. Soon after, Jian's wife is corrupted by the Bangkok social life and she leaves him for a lover. He saves the young girl Praphai from a dirty old man and in gratitude she becomes his mistress. After Prung's lover abandons her, she returns to ask her husband for charity. He forgives her and eventually takes her back as his wife.

From the opening pages of the novel, the reader is drawn in and perhaps even scandalised by the graphic descriptions of erotic behaviour. Romance is not idealised but seen in tandem with sex. Before the meeting with his adulterous wife, Jian is described as sitting alone crying. He is crying because he was thinking about the evil that roamed the world and the evil that made his wife leave him for another man. He is crying also in self-pity that his wife has cheated on him. Upon seeing his anguish, the teenage girl comes to console him and to sit by his side. Nai Jian is unaware that he is crying, but upon seeing this young dark-eyed beauty (Praphai) he begins hugging and kissing her—a startling and rather unexpected reaction. The narrator says:

---

34 It is possible that manly tears in a novel comes from English or European models. In Johann Wolfgang von Goethe's *The sorrows of young Werther* (1774), Werther believes that the essence of life is governed by his feelings. When he is sad or disappointed he has no trouble throwing himself on the ground and weeping bitterly. See translation by Burton Pike, *The sorrows of young Werther* (New York: The Modern Library, 2004), 67. In addition, Count Romani in *Vendetta* also cries when he thinks of his lovely wife. I have been unable to verify whether Thai men of Khru Liam's generation were apt to shed tears in public, whether this behaviour is specific to Khru Liam, or whether there are literary antecedents. Khru Liam's description of men crying in his novel, and himself crying during the writing of the novel, seems unusual as it does not fit the ideal of Thai masculinity. Tamara Loos believes that the novel is similar to those that appeared in the 1920s and 1930s (including the writing of Rama VI) in that they are 'sappy, sentimental and nostalgic' and the excessive crying of the protagonists is part of the sensitivity that could characterise the drama of young men's lives in these kinds of novels (email correspondence, 29 April 2004).

> I lost my senses and grabbed her body in an embrace. Her flesh is so soft. She is barely twenty and I am twice her age. She with the dark eyes and great beauty is witness to my non-revenge. I continue to embrace her and *to kiss her so many times that I lost count*. She cries out but it is not a scream. Then she lays her face on my body and sobs. Her tears fall and soak my flesh. Then, she says to me while sobbing 'Oh, dear sir, please forgive my father.'[35]

Nai Jian tells her that he has already forgiven Praphai's father and his own cheating wife a long time ago. With this reassurance, she puts her arms around his neck in gratitude and thanks him, promising that she will serve him for the rest of her life. As a reward for her pledge of loyalty, he kisses her again.

After this episode, Praphai tells Jian that Mae Prung wants to see him to ask for a donation that will pay for her ordination. Nai Jian, who has not seen her for over a year, at first refuses, but Praphai convinces him to meet his former wife. Nai Jian is shocked by what he saw. He can hardly recognise the woman with whom he was once madly in love. Without intending to be cruel, he blurts out, 'Is this what is left of you, Mae Prung?' She has come to ask for his forgiveness and peace of mind. Jian tells her that he bears her no ill will and that he is willing to pay for her ordination to become a nun. Mae Prung confesses her infidelity and reveals that she recently got pregnant but her lover forced her to have an abortion before leaving her. Instead of blaming his wife, Jian blames his own karma and his wife's evil lover. Mae Prung is so touched by his generosity that she swoons and faints. But before he summons for help, Nai Jian takes his wife into his arms and looks at her closely.

> I touched the body of the woman I once loved. Her flesh used to be so soft but now she is all bones. She used to be so vivacious. Now her face is darkened by suffering. I embrace her with a heavy heart and remark loudly all the while sobbing 'Oh Mae Prung, how can this happen to you?'... As I continue to sob, I lay my face on her bosom.
>
> Upon hearing someone approaching, I steal another hard look at Mae Prung's face and *I kiss her on the lips* for old time's sake, having missed kissing her for a long time.[36]

---

35 Nai Samran, *Khwam mai phayabat*, 6–7, emphasis added. All translations throughout this book are the author's, except where otherwise stated.
36 Nai Samran, *Khwam mai phayabat*, 21, emphasis added.

1. THE FIRST THAI NOVELS AND THE THAI LITERARY CANON

I would suspect that to the contemporary Thai reader this first chapter was exciting, different and salacious, if not scandalous. I am unaware of any Thai classical romance that starts in this manner. In addition, the description is not in metaphor but in everyday language—perhaps inaugurating a new and modern sensibility. And although it is not unusual to find explicit love scenes in classical Thai romantic literature, those romantic trysts tend to be between kings, princesses, the nobility and mighty warriors. The sexual exploits of the common man are barely featured. It is easier to imagine romance and sex between handsome kings and beautiful princesses, or between mythical beings such as Hanuman and the mermaid, but it is a stretch to imagine a person like Nai Jian as a romantic object of affection.

Jian shows his lust for women by kissing both his young mistress and his unconscious wife.[37] This emphasis on sex appears elsewhere throughout the novel. Describing his first meeting with Mae Prung, Nai Jian

---

37   Krom Silapakorn, *Sepha rueang khun chang khun phaen* [*The tale of Khun Chang Khun Phaen*] (Bangkok: Department of Fine Arts, 1950), 89. In the chapter where Plaikaew (Khun Phaen) makes love to Nang Phim, the word *jup* appears. Khun Phaen kisses Nang Phim on the cheeks and on her breasts. Khun Phaen also seduces Nang Phim's sister and does the same with her (i.e. kiss her breasts) (122). The word to describe the kiss here is *jup*, a word that implies planting one's lips on another person's body. The word *jup* is derived from the sound made while sucking on something. The Thai version of a kiss is *horm*, for example, *horm kaem*—kissing the cheek—is inhaling or smelling another person's fragrant scent. Although the Thai version is also intimate, it lacks the eroticism of a European kiss. Kissing on the lips is not openly practised in Thai culture, as it suggests sexual desire. Although the first Thai cinematic kiss took place in 1932, it was not generally accepted or performed on film until recently. See Scot Barmé, *Woman, man, Bangkok* (Lanham: Rowan and Littlefield, 2002), 212–13. A kissing scene appears in the first Thai talking film *Long thang* [*Gone astray*], released in 1932. A still photograph of the kissing scene appears in Barmé, 212. The scene takes place in a nightclub in Bangkok where three men are drinking beer and whiskey and are entertained by two high-class prostitutes. In *Lilit phra lor* [*The tale of Phra lo*], there is a passage in the 252-stanza *chuey chom chu pak pon*, which has been interpreted as kissing on the lips, that is 'the lovers praise each other and present their lips to each other and touching lips to lips'. See Phra Worawetphisit, *Khumue lilit phra lo* [*A handbook of lilit phra lo*] (Bangkok: Chulalongkorn University, 1960), 287. The word *jup* can be found in D.J.B. Pallegoix, *Dictionarium linguae Thai* (Paris: Jussu Imperatoris Impressum, 1854), 101, and in D.B. Bradley, *Dictionary of the Siamese language* (Bangkok: Khurusapha Press, 1971; reprint edition), 151. This word is also found in Laotian, a language that could be considered less adulterated Thai. Wiraphong Meesathan, *Potchananukrom lao thai* [*Lao–Thai dictionary*] (Bangkok: Mahidol University, 2000), 6. A Laotian–French dictionary published in 1912 also identifies the Laotian *jup* as *baiser* (French: 'to kiss'). Theodore Guignard, *Dictionnaire Laotien-Francais* (Hong Kong: Imperimerie de Nazareth, 1912), 83. It is possible that the Lao word is derived from Thai. But if such is not the case, the word can be an indigenous one in old Thai. *Jup* also appears in *Phra aphaimani*, which was written by Sunthorn Phu in the late 18th century. The love scenes in classical literature are graphically described in *bot sangwat*, where physical contact such as kissing and caressing are described. Intercourse, however, is described in metaphor such as a kite fight between the large male star kite and the smaller female kite that pursues the male to capture it. The imagery is interesting in that it is not logical to Western thinking that the star kite should be the male instead of the female. The smaller kite has a long tail and could easily be interpreted as the male sperm chasing

admits to an instant attraction to her. She, too, seems ready to work her charms on him. The description of Prung is almost entirely focused on her physical beauty, and the trope of the female exploiting her physical sexuality appears throughout the novel. For example, after a brief and even superficial courtship, the not-so-coy Mae Prung quickly offers herself to Jian as a ploy to speed up their marriage.

At their second meeting, Mae Prung teases Jian by whispering in his ear that 'the wedding should be arranged quickly. But you can have me even before the wedding, my body is yours just like this bouquet of flowers'.[38] Although Jian did not take advantage of her at that point, he agrees with his friend's crude remark that he could have had Mae Prung any time he wanted. His friend tells Jian *ao mai tong wiwa ko dai saduak*, which means 'she can be taken easily even without marrying'. The word *ao* is also a vulgar term used to describe 'having sex'.

The next time Jian visits her, Mae Prung lures the timid Jian to the back of the orchard surrounding her house and invites him to sit next to her on the same bench. Without his knowledge, Jian's friend has given Mae Prung a love poem that Jian had composed. When confronted with the poem, Jian becomes embarrassed, but it is the woman who initiates the intimacy. Mae Prung tells Jian that they are far away from prying eyes. She then moves closer to him and touches his shoulder. In Thai culture, the act of 'touching' is seen as an invitation for more intimacy. And when their hands touch, chills go up and down Jian's body. Jian then describes his own feelings:

> I am shocked. Is Mae Prung engaged in magic or is she using powerful mantras …? Why is she sitting so close and even touches my shoulder? Why is she sitting shyly here *as if to claim a kiss*?[39]

Jian becomes bolder, so he embraces her (*kot*) and then kisses (*jup*) her. She does not resist.

---

the large female star kite or womb. But in this instance, the female is chasing the male. See the seduction of Phra Aphaimani by the Sea Ogress in National Culture Commission, *Phra Aphaimani* (Bangkok: The Interest Co., 1998) 30–2. Given the kite fight as a representation of male and female social interaction, one is not surprised to find stories in classical and modern Thai literature where the man is pursued by the woman.

38 Nai Samran, *Khwam mai phayabat*, 51.
39 Nai Samran, *Khwam mai phayabat*, 59, emphasis added.

1. THE FIRST THAI NOVELS AND THE THAI LITERARY CANON

Mattani Rutnin asserts that Thai middle-class morality suppresses sexuality in the early Thai novels.[40] If this is correct, then the erotic passages like the one above suggest that *Khwam mai phayabat* does not fit the norm expected of early Thai novels and, therefore, would be rejected by most middle-class readers. The fact that we know that the novel was not a great market success may or may not support Mattani's observation. My own sense is that *Khwam mai phayabat* employing familiar Thai tropes— women having soft flesh, slender arms and tantalising breasts—found in classical literature is, therefore, not new. What may be unpalatable to Thai readers is the frank criticism of Bangkok high society.

Khru Liam's construction of the Thai male also breaks new ground.[41] Khru Liam does not idealise Thai masculinity but writes about the emerging Thai male as being both good and evil. In fact, aside from Jian, the other Thai males in this novel are unsavoury characters. Khru Liam appears to be chastising the Thai male for his decadence, for having been lured into debauchery by modern Bangkok. His examples of the Thai male suggest that moral values have declined and that overindulgence in sex and alcohol have become rampant in Bangkok society. The Thai obsession with modernisation and their exposure to capitalist conspicuous consumption have degraded Thai morality.

---

40 Mattani, *Modern Thai literature*, 32. I am not sure if this observation is correct. The focus on sex as human behaviour is not that foreign in Thai culture. In fact, sexuality is viewed as natural human behaviour. I have already mentioned how sexuality is dealt with in classical literature. In addition, one has only to visit and to view temple murals to witness open depiction of sexual activity which include both normative sexual behaviour (men fondling women's breasts and having intercourse), as well as homosexual sex. The paintings also show rabbits, birds and horses copulating. See Niwat Kongphian, *Cherng sangwat: Kamarup nai phapkhian tam prapheni thee mee siang wannakhadee thai* [*Of carnal knowledge: Pornography in traditional paintings that resonate in Thai literature*] (Bangkok: Silapa Watthanatham, 1998).

41 Models of popular Thai masculinity in literature include Phra Lo in *Lilit phra lo*, Khun Phaen in *Sepha rueang khun chang khun phaen*, and Phra Aphaimani in *Phra aphaimani*. Phra Lo is a male character believed to be from Phrae or Lampang who lived in the 12th century. He is said to be the model of the tragic male lover. Khun Phaen is a character who allegedly lived in Ayutthaya at the end of the 15th century. The poetic form, written during the early Rattanakosin period, is said to have been based on a folk tale. Khun Phaen is a good soldier, a lover who has no qualms about seducing another man's wife. Phra Aphaimani is one of Sunthorn Phu's greatest works. It is speculated that he wrote it while in prison during the reign of Rama II. The story is a voyage of fantasy and the hero is based on a Sinitic model of the ideal man—a scholar and artist. It is said that Sunthorn Phu also based his story on the Arabian tales of travel by ship to faraway lands. See Sittha Phiniphuwadol and Nittaya Kanchanwan, *Khwan ru thuapai thang wannakam thai* [*General knowledge of Thai literature*] (Bangkok: D.K. Book, 1977), 100–2, 198–201, 222–4. One of the few studies of literary models of masculinity is Wibha Senanan Kongkanan, *Phra ek nai wannakhadi thai* [*The leading man in Thai literature*] (Bangkok: Thaiwatthanapanich, 1995). Her study suggests that the three characters above represent ideal types of Thai masculinity and romantic leading men.

One specific dilemma faced by many Thai men educated abroad had to do with deciding between two types of women: the traditional woman, or the modern woman; one representing traditional Thai values and the other decadent but alluring Western modernity. All of the now-canonised early novels—Mom Jao (Prince) Akatdamkoeng's *Lakhon haeng chiwit* [*Circus of life*]; Kulap Saipradit's *Luk phuchai* [*The real man*] and Dok Mai Sot's *Sattru khong jao lon* [*Her enemy*]—published between 1928 to 1929 also agonised over this dilemma. The main characters of these novels were returning students (*nakrian nok*) who faced the dilemma of finding the ideal wife. In the end, all the men reject marrying a foreigner or a modern liberated Thai woman. Even Dok Mai Sot, who is female, agrees that her American-educated heroine is just too Westernised for the Thai man, even if he is himself a *nakrian nok*.

Although Jian studied in England, he, too, preferred the more traditional Thai woman. He is, however, an unusual prototype for a Thai man. Jian's strength is not physical but moral. He is the virtuous man who follows the teachings of the Buddha. Although he is attracted to sex just like the other men he criticises, his lust is acceptable because it remains within the confines of marriage. Unlike the other men, he resists the temptation to take advantage of Praphai and Prung before they become his wives. His ability to resist temptation comes from the love for his wife and his religious beliefs. These strengths, in spite of his constant tearful whining, are attractive to women. The author is perhaps trying to 'modify' or to 'create' a new male culture where manliness is synonymous with virtuous morality. And to make this point even more forceful, even the whiny and physically weak man such as Jian can win sexual favours from beautiful and desirous women.

Jian lusts only in his heart and he is not, therefore, a male sexual predator. As a good man, he easily wins the hand of the lovely Prung and lives happily in the countryside. After this rural interlude, his life changes after he agrees to move back to his mother's house in Bangkok. Crossing the canal to Bangkok symbolises the crossing from a pristine and traditional Thai life to the modern one represented by the city. The crossing is as transformative for the woman as going abroad to study is transformative for the man. Through his relatively virtuous and rural protagonist, Khru Liam levels a stern criticism at the modern hedonism of Bangkok high society. He describes a dinner party that Khun Phak throws for Jian in honour of his new assignment to a post in the provinces. Aside from Jian, Khun Phak invited eight other guests—all of them male. And even before the arrival of Jian, who is the featured guest, several of the men have already begun drinking heavily. Several have taken their jackets and shoes off and are laughing and talking loudly. By the time the men settle down to dinner, more jackets, shoes and even shirts have come off. The meal features soup, fried chicken, fresh venison stew, beef tongue, *farang* sausage, salad and pickled vegetables from abroad. Dessert consists of ice cream, fruits and something called 'jelly'. Although Jian is impressed that these expensive and unusual European dishes were served in his honour, he is uncomfortable with the amount of alcohol already consumed by the other guests. One should note here that both these varieties of food, as well as this excessive consumption of expensive 'whiskey', are linked to the West.

> Jian is increasingly uneasy in this setting, especially when the drunken men begin to grab the women who served them. He becomes horrified when two women voluntarily take off their blouses. Jian describes them as '*wearing just their inner shirts*, with belts tied around their round waists and *breasts that stood at attention in our honor*'.[42]

The women must have been used to this situation because they are quite efficient in taking off their clothes. Jian is scandalised by the sight of the old Khun Phra hoarding one of the girls just for himself. She too adroitly disrobes and is soon sitting on the old man's lap. The two are soon kissing and eventually retire to another room to carry on their coupling on a couch. Before Jian can make a quick exit, one of the drunken guests gives a speech and presents him with a going-away present. It is a package of condoms. Jian throws the package on the floor and says that he did not need such devices to protect himself from venereal diseases. But he decides to be gracious and announces that the remaining partygoers can better use the condoms. This brings loud approving laughter and a mad struggle for the package.

Khru Liam, of course, is having it both ways when he places a virtuous protagonist in titillating scenes of debauchery. This same technique is obvious when he and his friend Nai Khabuan follow Mae Prung to a hotel where she is conducting an affair with the wealthy Khun Phak. The hotel functions as a setting where the Thai can consume the West and behave as Europeans, that is, become un-Thai. The hotel is therefore a site where the confines of Thai culture are loosened and neutralised. The sophisticated

---

42 Nai Samran, *Khwam mai phayabat*, 257, emphases added.

Thais go there to consume European food and wine, to smoke cigars, to speak English with the guests and among themselves, to relive foreign experiences and to indulge themselves fully in a totally modern milieu.[43] But when Jian goes into the hotel and sees his wife embracing her lover, the experience is too much for him. Altogether characteristically, he faints.

Prung's active sexuality is not atypical. All three female characters in *Khwam mai phayabat* exploit their sexuality to get their way from men, though they also become victims of unwanted sexual attention and assaults. What we see then in the novel is the transformation of the traditional woman—innocent girl, good daughter and faithful wife—into the 'modern' female. This transformation, of course, is fraught with pitfalls. The novel appears to suggest a concern on the part of the (Western-)educated Thai male that Thai women are unprepared to cope with the glitter and temptations of modernity that could easily corrupt them.

The novel also suggests the representation of women as beautiful objects to be displayed and to be paraded about for others to see. They are said to be for 'show', a borrowed word that is now part of the Thai lexicon. The idea that certain objects, especially objects that represent modernity and sophistication, or beautiful and valuable possessions, are acquired just for show is as contemporary today as it was when the novel was written 90 years ago. This 'show' culture applies to objects that act as signifiers for modernity and high-class culture.

Even nowadays, it is not uncommon when visiting Thai homes to see expensive whiskey and brandy bottles (as well as cheap souvenirs from abroad) displayed prominently on shelves. Their corks may have long dried up and the alcoholic content may have evaporated, but the evidence of high-class sophistication still remains on those shelves for all to see, even if never to be consumed.

---

43   Although some educated people of Bangkok may use hotels as sites of modernity, these institutions might not satisfy the *nakrian nok* who think that the hotels in Bangkok are merely parodies of the real hotels they know in Europe. S.N.J. Antonio, *The 1904 traveller's guide to Bangkok and Siam* (Bangkok: White Lotus Press, 1997), 15, suggests that Bangkok is a 'veritable city of hotels'. However, the guide continues to advise that not all are good and many Europeans soon are taken in as house guests by the Thai. This raises the question, who, then, stays in those hotels?

What this novel reveals about Bangkok society at the turn of the 20th century is that beautiful women were treated as objects to be put on show.[44] This emphasis on 'show' is heightened when Jian organises a version of a coming-out party to 'show' Prung to his Bangkok friends and acquaintances. Her coming-out party transforms her from the country girl across the canal into a sophisticated Bangkok belle. The transformation is both external and internal. Not only has her clothing changed, but she is ready to consume and enjoy the promises of modernity. In the negative sense, her internal transformation can be described as the Thai *jai taek*, which literally translates as 'heart falling apart', a term that is not quite the same as the English one of a heart breaking. In the Thai meaning, the core of a person's value, which resides in the heart, is open to corruption by bad external influences when the heart itself breaks open.

Khun Phak does indeed corrupt her, as we have seen. She is attracted to Khun Phak's material wealth and the tantalising life of a liberated woman free to pick her friends and associates. Her transformation and move to the 'darker side' are facilitated by the sudden death of the infant baby that she had with Jian. No longer tied to the traditional confines of woman as mother, she becomes free to indulge more fully in the life of bourgeois leisure—opportunities presented to her by Khun Phak. By showering her with expensive jewellery, Khun Phak eventually seduces Prung.

To understand this novel, it is important to remember that in Thai culture, only the woman is regarded as committing adultery. Women who stray beyond the bounds of matrimony are labelled as *mi chu*, or adulterous. Men, on the other hand, are said to commit *nork jai mia* or 'going outside his wife's heart', an act that is not regarded as being as wrongful as adultery. The novel does not show much confidence in Thai women, for it questions their ability to cope with the new freedom that modernity provides. A modernity that pries women away from traditional social structures such as the family, their role as mothers, and as wives undermines traditional Thai culture and values. Women with their new-found liberty are in danger of losing themselves as Thai women. They can be easily corrupted by worldly and material temptations. Women are therefore more likely to use female sexuality as an instrument or means towards ends. And by doing so, they contribute to their own downfall because they are treated as ornaments to be acquired for 'show' and for

---

44 Similarly, in Kulap Saipradit's *Luk phuchai*, written 15 years later, the woman is still described as a 'priceless ornament' (*phuying pen aphon an lam kha*), Chapter 10.

sexual pleasure. Infidelity and adultery soon follow. Khru Liam's novel is thus an indictment of bourgeois decadence that must be curbed by anchoring Thai society onto Buddhism and the sanctity of the family unit. Thai men can gain strength from Buddhism. Women, on the other hand, must rely on the family unit to give them strength.[45]

The novel also levels indictments against the male libido. The novel's message is that, although it is the nature of a man to lust after women, lust should be controlled by a belief in Buddhist morality and, if a man is married, by the husband's concern for the feelings of his wife. Khru Liam is not against polygamy, because at the end of his novel Jian is married to two women. Khru Liam's ideal man is far from a 'man's man', but he is a man of great virtue. The novel's hero is not the epitome of manliness or *khwam pen luk phuchai* advocated in the other novels. The man is supposed to be quiet, thoughtful, circumspect, strong, level headed, unemotional, generous, decisive, loyal to friends and physically strong. Khru Liam's Jian is the antithesis of the *luk phuchai*. Nai Jian is whiny, timid, emotional, weepy, physically a weakling and indulges too much in self-pity. Even his name is not manly because it means 'a long time', or 'to leave'. Jian may be an unattractive male protagonist, but in the novel he wins the favours of two beautiful women because of his virtue.

---

45 For Thai women raised in traditional ways at the turn of the 20th century, and especially those who grew up in royal and aristocratic households, the ideal woman is still someone who fits the poet Sunthorn Phu's construction. The woman always plays second fiddle to the husband and she is to endure his transgressions quietly. Women also should not take on the behaviour of men but should be true to their feminine upbringing. To wit:

Koet pen ying hai hen wa pen ying	Born a woman one should be a woman
Ya tot thing kariya atchayasai	Do not abandon your feminine ways
Pen ying khreung chai khreung ya phueng jai	Do not be happy in being half woman half man
Khrai khao mai sanrasern mern arom	Ignore those who disagree
Mae phua duert jao chong dap rangap wai	Hold your passions even if your husband is angry
Ya pho jai kheun siang thiang khrom	Don't be too glad to raise your voice to argue
Khao pen fai rao pen nam khoy phram phrom	He is fire and we are water to sprinkle gently
Mae radom kheun thang khu cha wuwam	If we both escalate sparks will fly

(from *Cremation volume of Phiengthong Devakul Na Ayuthaya* (Wat Mongkut, Bangkok: 11 July 2004)). Khun Phiengthong was born in 1917. The selections of Sunthorn Phu's poetry that she lived by were found in her memoirs. In traditional literature there are poems known as *suphasit son ying*, or wise sayings for women. Sunthorn Phu penned several of these, which have become standards for feminine behaviour. See Sittha Phinitphuwadol and Nittaya Kanchanawan, *General knowledge of Thai literature*, 227–8.

1. THE FIRST THAI NOVELS AND THE THAI LITERARY CANON

The novel's ending is also quite clever. Although the novel begins with a flashback, that scene is not the final episode of the story. It is only a foundation upon which the story of Prung's downfall as wife and mother is built. Khru Liam uses the story's final twist to impart a lesson to his readers. The novel is both a critique of modern Bangkok society and a didactic story about the pitfalls of modernity. After forgiving his wife for her infidelity and supporting her desire to become a nun, Jian is now at peace, we are led to believe, and that is the last we will hear about Mae Prung. She is also described as physically spent, and no longer desirable as a woman. But Khru Liam wants us to believe that karmic reward need not be postponed to the next life or future lives, but that one can immediately reap the rewards of one's meritorious deeds. Jian's new wife/mistress Praphai rehabilitates Mae Prung and offers her once again to Jian to reward him for being virtuous.

Forgiveness and reacceptance by her husband transforms Prung into the beautiful woman that she was before she was discarded by her lover. This act of full repentance by the corrupt woman restores her to her proper place in society. She becomes physically attractive again to her husband. This reconciliation and rekindling of desire is confirmed by the fact that Prung is made pregnant again by her husband, reconfirming the notion that the woman's role in reproduction as mother is central to the notion of the Thai female. We should remember that Prung was a good mother and wife up to the time of her first child's unexpected death. Her final pregnancy is, however, her redemption. Once again, she is fulfilling her traditional role as wife and mother. The new wife, Praphai, also fulfils her role as a good Thai woman. She, too, becomes pregnant at the same time. The good end happily and the bad unhappily: to paraphrase Oscar Wilde, this is how we know that fiction is fiction.

Although *Khwam mai phayabat* was the first Thai novel, it seems to have been too radical a departure from the translated European novels so popular at the time. It failed to sell. A possible reason for this failure is the persistent fascination with the West as a site of the modern and the *siwilai*. The top-down policy to modernise/Westernise Thailand seemed to have worked well, so much so that there was real consumer demand and fascination for translated stories about the West. The fact that, in the end, Khru Liam capitulated (for financial reasons) and wrote a follow-up novel *Nang neramit* [*Divine nymphs*] (published in 1916) is once again instructive. In that novel, Khru Liam pretends to be an Englishman writing about an English mystery adventure. That novel shows glimpses of H. Rider Haggard's *She*, a novel that Khru Liam translated some time during the early 1900s. Instead of Africa, the story takes place in Egypt. In fact, the privileging of Western novels over Thai novels lasted until 1928–29 when three major Thai novels—*Luk phuchai, Sattru khong jao lon, Lakhon haeng chiwit*—were published, which captured the public's imagination. But even these three novels were about Thai characters living, working and studying in the West, who eventually returned to Thailand to cope with tensions between the two cultures. Instead of Western main characters, the new characters were *nakrian nok*, or foreign-trained students—a hybrid of the modern elite who is both Thai and European.

In the postscript to his novel *Nang neramit*, published under pseudonym of SR, or (Nai) Samran, the same pseudonym he used in *Khwam mai phayabat*, Khru Liam writes:

> After my novel *Khwam mai phayabat* did not sell that well, I realized that one has little power to change people's belief that the Thai could not write well, that they lacked the ability to write an engaging story. Because of this, I have composed a *farang* novel about divine nymphs. I have also composed other *farang* novels as well, more than stories that I translated. Friends who have been told know that these are my original compositions. In fact, many know that *Nang Neramit* is composed by the same author of *Khwam mai phayabat*.[46]

It appears that *Khwam mai phayabat* was written before its time, so it failed to have a strong impact on Thai society. Only now, in hindsight, can one appreciate the novel's significance. Although it is possible to claim that *Khwam mai phayabat* was written to 'compete' with *Vendetta* as a representation of the West, it could also be seen as a form of resistance to the West. But it should be taken into account that this resistance is itself conveyed through a medium appropriated from the West, that of the novel. It is a truism of literary study that form and content cannot be separated. Borrowing a Western form to emphasise what it really means to be Thai is daringly original, but the financial failure of *Khwam mai phayabat* and the success of *Nang neramit* suggest that Thai readers still

---

46   Nai Samran, *Nang neramit*, 400. Only a partial manuscript of this ancient novel could be found; the author's copy of this manuscript may be found in the Echols Southeast Asia Collection, Cornell University Library, call number PL4209.W535 N36 2005. All page numbers for this manuscript refer to that copy.

expected to read novels about places and people other than themselves. They wanted to be entertained and to learn about the Other, be they places or people.

If this separation of form and content were not problematic enough, Khru Liam is also attempting to redefine what it means to be Thai during a time when traditional values were coming into question. But his criticism of cultural decline, especially with regard to the corruption of Thai femininity and the exploitation of young girls by modernity, is not a direct condemnation of the West. Khru Liam is also concerned with the 'allure of modernity' as a universal phenomenon. With modernity come opportunities for infidelity, for perverted sexual behaviour, and for the exploitation of women. Ultimately, Buddhist forgiveness and virtue overcome the ill effects of modernity and the negative influence of the West. And therefore, far from being merely just another purloined copy of the Western novel, Khru Liam's *Khwam mai phayabat* is also quintessentially Thai.

Nang neramit [*Divine nymphs*] (1916): Imitation or Thai

To reiterate, the primary strategy used by the Thai elite during the 19th century in order to resist colonisation was to learn more about the West.[47] The Thai elite has used this strategy for centuries to appropriate what is best from other cultures, particularly Indian, Chinese and Khmer culture—Indian and Khmer science, religion and administration; Chinese trade and political practices.[48] The new European hegemonic power(s) was also different in that it was multi-centred—England, France,

---

47   See, for example, David K. Wyatt, *The politics of reform in Thailand: Education in the reign of King Chulalongkorn* (New Haven: Yale University Press, 1969); William J. Siffin, *The Thai bureaucracy: Institutional change and development* (Honolulu: East–West Center Press, 1966); Abbot Low Moffat, *Mongkut the King of Siam* (Ithaca: Cornell University Press, 1961). Thai history taught in Thai schools continues to promote a royalist history that credits King Mongkut and King Chulalongkorn for saving Thailand from colonisation by 'modernising' its administration, education, culture and technology along the European model.
48   Thailand converted to Buddhism from India and Sri Lanka, adapted Khmer script, incorporated Hindu and Khmer science of government and court language, participated in the Chinese tribute trade system, and adapted the Chinese tribute concept to use with Thailand's own subordinate states. For an excellent study of the formation of Ayutthaya (Ayudhya), see Charnvit Kasetsiri, *The rise of Ayudhya: A history of Siam in the fourteen and fifteen centuries* (Kuala Lumpur: Oxford University Press, 1976).

Portugal, Spain, Holland and the United States. In addition, the scale of the threat of Western imperialism was becoming alarming as more and more states surrounding Thailand fell under the direct control of European countries.[49] Facing this enormous threat of colonisation, and still smarting from the loss of Ayutthaya to the Burmese armies in 1767, the Thai were determined to find a strategy that would preserve their autonomy at all costs.

The new free trade international economic regime promoted by the colonial powers replaced the centuries-old Sino-centric tribute system of trade. It appears that the Thai leaders did not want to be left out of the lucrative commercial trade with the West. Therefore, the concession of certain legal jurisdiction over foreign nationals within Thailand's territory seemed to be the price of doing business. This trade filled the coffers of King Chulalongkorn's treasury, which allowed him to fund the modernisation of education, administration and infrastructure.

The concession of sovereignty does not necessarily mean that the Thai leaders felt spiritually or intellectually inferior to the Europeans. The West and its superior technology (seen as signs of modernity) were not just to be feared, but to be emulated. The best features of this 'modernity' were to be appropriated and made Thai. The Thais had a thoroughly pragmatic attitude. The West was—and remains—yet another source for Thai cultural improvement.

Without question, Khru Liam is the author both of *Khwam mai phayabat* and of *Nang neramit*. It is most likely that Khru Liam has also authored many other novels that are passed off as translations. It also appears that the novel-reading public did not have much faith in the ability of a Thai author to write a good novel, nor was it ready for a real Thai novel that focused on their own daily lives: readers, it appears, would rather have read a *farang* novel, written by a *farang* to allow them to fantasise about the Other. In *Nang neramit*, Khru Liam subverts this popular notion by delivering what his audience wants—a *farang* story of adventure in exotic

---

49 The British took control of Penang in 1786, Singapore in 1819, Burma in 1885, Sarawak, Brunei and North Borneo in 1888; the French colonised Cochin China in 1866, Cambodia in 1867, Annam and Tonkin in 1887, and Laos in 1893; the Dutch government took over the administration of Indonesia from the East India Company in 1799; the United States colonised the Philippines in 1898 after it defeated Spain, which had held that colony for over 350 years.

Egypt ostensibly written by a *farang* author. The joke is on the readers who, after reading 400 pages, are told that they will never find the English original because there is none!

Furthermore, in this postscript Khru Liam is quite candid about his own willingness to write whatever the public wants to achieve financial success:

> An author can always write whatever he wants, but the tastes of his readers tend to force him to write things that will sell easily. So if I want to recover my investment I have to find a story that many buyers want. Because of this, it is not my fault that I have to write this story to recover my investment ...
>
> This is the first story composed by a Thai as a novel that is as expansive a story as a *farang* story. However, you might find the plot to be quite short because as someone with limited capital, I had to make it short.[50]

Compared to *Khwam mai phayabat*'s 730 pages, *Nang neramit* is relatively short, a mere 399 pages long. Despite these limitations, Khru Liam was intent upon entertaining his readers by transporting them to a foreign and exotic land, promising a story of adventure, intrigue, magic, battle scenes, romance, ghost stories and a heavy dose of eroticism—all commingled with Buddhist values. Thus, in both of his early novels, Khru Liam inserts Buddhist values into the plot, perhaps to draw in his Thai readers and to make the stories more accessible.

Although I cannot say for certain whether many other novels were published immediately after *Khwam mai phayabat*, I believe that it is safe to say that *Nang neramit* can be considered the second authentic Thai novel, that is, an original novel composed by a Thai author in the Thai language. The fact that it imitates the *farang* novel should not make it less authentically Thai. Khru Liam is doing what authors before him had done, that is, write about another culture as if it were his own. Parenthetically, Khru Liam is emulating his European models: Corelli and Rider Haggard. The former, an Englishwoman, writes about Italy in her novel *Vendetta*; the latter, an Englishman, writes about Arabs and Egyptians in Africa in his novel *She*. Why then should Khru Liam, a Thai, not write about the English in Egypt in his novel *Nang neramit*? The only

---

50 Nai Samran, *Nang neramit*, 400.

twist here is that Khru Liam was compelled to make his readers think that *Nang neramit* was a translated English novel of adventure and mystery, something that could have been written by Rider Haggard.

Nang neramit is nevertheless a genuine Thai novel about some English, Egyptian, Arab and Negro[51] characters in Egypt. As an early Thai novel, it should be considered a transitional Thai novel that would bridge the gap between the first real Thai novel *Khwam mai phayabat*, and the three successful novels that appeared in 1929—Kulap Saipradit's *Luk phuchai* [*The real man*], M.C. Akatdamkoeng's *Lakhon haeng chiwit* [*Circus of life*] and Dok Mai Sot's *Sattru khong jao lon* [*Her enemy*]. Literary scholars have canonised those three novels as the first authentically Thai novels.[52]

Indeed, that the characters of *Nang neramit* are *only* foreign suggests that the Thai readership would rather be transported to another world to learn about those Others. But the story about exotic Africa and mysterious Egypt is not that foreign to Thai readers—and that also is due in large part to Khru Liam. Close upon the heels of Mae Wan's translation of *Vendetta*, Khru Liam also translated Sir H. Rider Haggard's *She*, giving it the title *Sao song phan pi* [*The two-thousand-year-old maiden*]. Khru Liam used 'Nok Nori' as his pseudonym for that translation, which appeared in the journal *Thalok witthaya*.[53] Thus, the Thai public was already familiar with Africa and Egypt because of this and other translated novels.

It should be noted here that *Sao song phan pi* was also reprinted in 1916, the same year that *Nang neramit* was published. This meant that the Thai public was able to compare the two novels side by side. Of course, the perceptive ones will note that *Nang neramit* was a 'Thai novel' about Africa and Egypt, and *Sao song phan pi* was a Thai translation of an English novel about Africa and Egypt. Because it would seem that, as Khru Liam

---

51   Khru Liam refers to black Africans as 'Negroes' (*nikro*), the term in Thai usage in his day. There continues to be racial prejudice in Thailand against black Africans as primitive. This term is maintained in this discussion as a reflection of the attitudes that informed Khru Liam's writing, as this is a significant part of his Thai rewriting of the novel.
52   See Smyth, *The canon*, Chapter 13.
53   It is unclear when Khru Liam first translated *She*. Most likely it was not much later than the appearance of Mae Wan's *Khwam phayabat*. According to S. Plai Noi, *Sao song phan pi* was reprinted in 1916, 1934, 1944 and 1991. See S. Plai Noi, *Khwam mai phayabat*, 88. It is also possible that the 1944 copy is, in fact, another translation of *She* by Chaiwat (pseudonym of Charoen Chaichana), published in 1943. Chaiwat used Khru Liam's Thai title. A copy of this latter translation is found in the Chulalongkorn University Library. And, most recently, Sotsai [pseud.] retranslated *She* under the title *Amata devi* (Bangkok: Praphansarn Press, 2004). It is interesting that neither Chaiwat nor Sotsai acknowledged the pioneering translation of the novel by Khru Liam.

1. THE FIRST THAI NOVELS AND THE THAI LITERARY CANON

hastily wrote *Nang neramit* to recoup his lost investment in *Khwam mai phayabat*, he must have had in mind his translation of *She* and he inevitably borrowed freely from that novel.

Rider Haggard's *She* is about the immortal sorceress Ayesha, or 'She-who-must-be-obeyed', commonly referred to as just She, who has been waiting for her dead lover for over 2,000 years. Ayesha—a white woman who rules over a tribe of Africans—has achieved immortality after immersing herself in a sacred fire. The story concerns a handsome Egyptian high priest who ran off with his lover, an Egyptian princess, to find refuge in Ayesha's realm, only to fall victim to her amorous desires. When the priest refuses to murder his wife the princess, as ordered by the sorceress, She kills him in a fit of rage. Of course, She immediately regrets her action and proceeds to preserve her lover's dead body in a special crypt. In fact, She still has access to her lover's physical being, but not his soul. Through the ages, She continues to visit the body and to sleep at night by its side hoping that one day he will return from the dead. She believes that she has found him again when the young English hero Leo appears in her realm.

Leo is seeking adventure in Africa, following some instructions left to him by his late father. The reason Leo looks just like Ayesha's dead lover is not coincidence. The Egyptian priest in fact is Leo's distant ancestor. Ayesha tries to convince Leo to enter the magic fire so that both he and she can be immortal. But when She re-enters the fire of life for a second time, she immediately ages and dies. Although the novel is a romance, pure and simple, it provided the reader with a wealth of information about Africa—its people, its climate, its culture, its geography and its plant and animal life. The novel is a vivid portrayal of this alluring and exotic place. It is most certain that the insatiable Thai reading public found the idea of 'knowing' Africa and romantic European culture intoxicating and different. It is a parallel experience to drinking imported Scotch whisky and drinking the pungent local rice liquor. The ability to read about and discuss topics related to other cultures were signs of modernity and sophistication. Why should anyone be concerned about the social ills of Bangkok society depicted in Khru Liam's first novel?

Unlike novels written by colonial subjects to mimic the West, Khru Liam's *Nang neramit* written in 1916 appropriates the English as his own characters, exploiting them for purely commercial reasons. One is aware of Francophone literature and Anglophone literature—literature written about former colonies by colonial subjects in the language of the

Metropole. This hybridity seems to be a natural product of colonialism. In the Thai case, the Thai novel is less of a hybrid—the novel *Nang neramit* exploits both the form and appropriates the characters by pretending to be a translated novel. Discerning readers, of course, will find out when they finish reading and glance at the postscript that Khru Liam has played a trick on them.

Nang neramit tells the story of the adventure of a young English scholar, James Billford, on vacation in Egypt. During his explorations of ancient ruins and caves, he and his friends come across mummies that appear to be so well preserved that they look alive. These well-preserved mummies were those of young females. It turns out that a Muslim Arab high priest has discovered a way to revive mummies whose sole existence was to sexually please men, especially the priests. These mummies are so alluring that if a man touches them, he would be forever lost in lust. And the more these revived mummy nymphs have sex with men, the more lustful and the more desirable they become. The story also involves a struggle between the English forces in Egypt trying to rescue Billford's fiancée, abducted by the priests and the Arab armies that were followers of the priests.

Two questions we might want to ask are, first, whether *Nang neramit* presents a caricature of the Thai author's understanding of English and Egyptian characters, and second, whether the plots and stories resonate for the Thai audience. My contention is that most of the Thai readers will accept that the *farang* and *khaek* (Arab) characters in the novel appear odd enough to be genuinely foreign, that the detailed descriptions of the various places in England and in Egypt give the novel an air of authenticity. Yet there is a particular usage of English that has been appropriated into Thai to indicate to the Thai reader that perhaps the author is not a *farang*, but a Thai who is translating a *farang* novel. The plot, however, appears to be somewhat too fantastic and improbable to be a *farang* plot. The ending especially is rather comical and unserious, something that usually appears in Thai popular fiction. Although the magical aspects are present in both *Nang neramit* and in *She*, Khru Liam inserts into *Nang neramit* stories about insatiable sexual appetites and the role of women as objects of desire. But unlike his first novel, *Khwam mai phayabat*, where Thai women are victims of male desire, in *Nang neramit*, they are revived Egyptian women.

Khru Liam's adaptations from *She* are also unmistakable. Both novels have English heroes, that of *She* being Ludwig Horace Holly, who studied mathematics at Cambridge; that of *Nang neramit* being James Billford, who studied classics at Oxford. Both heroes went to North Africa; both dealt with the occult. One met up with a sorceress, the other with a grand wizard. Both stories focus on the immortality of women.

Yet the way Rider Haggard and Khru Liam depict women is altogether different. The sorceress in the novel *She* is still full of lust, thoughts and feelings of endless desire. The sorceress Ayesha is still looking for her long-departed lover and is scheming to get him back even after 2,000 years. Her love is obsessive. She is a jealous lover who, in a fit of rage, has killed the man she loved. Despite her beauty, no man can trust a woman like her. In contrast, Khru Liam's own version of the immortal woman in *Nang neramit* appears to be an imaginative construct of the Thai male's sexual fantasy. The divine nymphs in *Nang neramit* are devoid of their own desires. Their bodies are like empty vessels that exist as *rupatham* (objective truth) that only absorb the lust of men as content—that is, *namatham* (subjective truth)—and reflect those feelings back at men who are their lovers. These concepts resonate for the Thai audience familiar with Buddhist concepts of form and abstraction. The divine nymphs have no emotions except those given to them by their lovers. If rather obviously limited as individuals, they are altogether trustworthy as lovers and sexual partners. The revived female mummy nymphs are devoid of *namatham*, and only exist as *rupatham*. Any *namatham* is acquired from lovemaking and involves only amorous and lustful emotions.

Khru Liam himself was both a Thai Buddhist and trained in England. Therefore, the author/narrator is a hybrid of sorts. In *Nang neramit*, Khru Liam inserts his Buddhist philosophy into the story right from the opening pages by speaking through James Billford.[54] James launches into a full discourse about life and existence. He points out that human existence is composed of two dimensions—*rupatham* and *namatham*. It is most likely that in life these two dimensions are conjoined, but following death, the two are separated. It is quite possible, scientifically that is, to revive the dead if a way was found to reunite the two. These terms are familiar to the Thai readers who understand the concept of *rupa* and *arupa*—being and non-being, and the idea of the self and the soul.

There are also other familiar Thai markers in the novel. For example, Khru Liam's description of the ashram would also sound familiar to Thai readers. It was as if he was describing a Thai temple. He also used Buddhist

---

54   Nai Samran, *Nang neramit*, 3–4.

terms to describe this Islamic compound—*kuti* (monks' quarters), *lan wat* (temple courtyard). And to provide comic relief, which is a common trope in Thai literature and drama, Khru Liam makes fun of Muslim men and the Thai male's fear of circumcision. In the novel, Captain Craig asks if the cult followers must adhere to *latthi khao sunao*—the Muslim practice of circumcision. As the narrator, Khru Liam goes on to remark that perhaps Arabs do not get sick because of this practice. I assume that he is referring to venereal diseases. One should remember that Khru Liam was hired by the Ministry of Health to translate English medical texts. It is very possible that he could not resist adding this medical advice for his readers.

I want to discuss some of the major themes that appear in the novel. Khru Liam is known for writing openly about male and female sexuality, Buddhist religious concepts and the occult. In *Nang neramit*, he highlights the malleable sexual Other (revived Egyptian mummies), the stereotyping of Arab and Negro male sexual appetite and prowess, the binary of male sexual drive and female responsiveness, and how sexuality can be conditioned by the objective and the subjective self. We will discuss this by loosely following the plot of the novel to witness how these themes appear in context.

Sexuality and race

In *Nang neramit*, the English explorers visiting Egypt find a coffin inside a pyramid containing the body of a beautiful female mummy probably dead for over 4,000 years. From her dress and jewellery, she appears to have been the young queen of a Pharaoh. It is amazing that she looks as if she had just died: her face looks fresh but is cold to Billford's touch. In one of the many bizarre incidents in this novel, Billford cuts off the mummy's head as a souvenir. This grisly action would probably have been too risky for a Thai hero to take, for it would have tempted or aroused the anger of *phi* (spirits of the dead). But by having a *farang* as the hero, Khru Liam was able to add this twist to his plot. In fact, in the novel, Billford proclaims 'we are *farang*, we are not afraid of *phi*'.[55]

Many incidents later, the Englishmen explore some caves near the ashram of a wizard reputed to have the power to raise the dead. They have been told that the lights emanating at night from the wizard's ashram are called

---

55 Nai Samran, *Nang neramit*, 86.

'the rays of he who represents god' and that they are used to resurrect female mummies, making them into divine nymphs (*nang neramit*). It is the wizard, in fact, who revives only female Egyptian mummies, to be given to his disciples just for their pleasure. It is this wizard who later reconnects the Queen's head to her body and revives her to her glorious splendour. He wants the Queen for himself. But of course, in spite of being in love with the Englishwoman, Vivian, Billford cannot help but lust after the Queen.

In these caves, the Englishmen and their trusted Negro servant find treasure, perhaps looted from crypts and pyramids. On the side of the cave walls are ledges where lifelike statues are placed. The explorers get goosebumps when they realise that the realistic statues are, in fact, mummies who were already used and 'traded in' for newer models. At one corner in the cave, they are surprised to find a carpet on the ground with a pile of women's clothing at the side. On the carpet is a pile of human bones, as if someone has made love to the pile of bones. The mummies consist of men, children and lots of women. Strangely, the young female mummies appear to be beautiful young women who look almost alive.

One particular mummy, a very pretty woman who is partly nude, attracts their attention. As the explorers are marvelling at how well preserved she is, they notice that blood is pumping through her veins, and that her lips, skin and even nipples are quite pink. Then they notice that the mummy is actually breathing!

The explorers soon hear footsteps and see a Negro man (an Ethiopian) come into the cave. He goes straight to the breathing mummy, lifts her down from her perch and takes her away to make love to her in the dark. The men notice that when the woman opens her eyes, there is no sparkle in them. In contrast to her originally limp and quiescent state, she is soon actively responding to the lust of her dark partner—her white skin contrasting with his coal-black skin.

The stereotyping of the black man as a virile beast is unmistakable here. Khru Liam, like many Thais of his generation who studied in England, internalised the inherent racism of the West. While the Negro is vilified, the Arabs are depicted as having higher culture and knowledge, as they were the master of the Negro, yet they are *khaek* (a term used to describe

Arabs, Indians and Muslims) and are not to be trusted.[56] In the story, the Negro is lost in lust and does not even hear the arrival of a pair of Arab priests (*toh khaek*) and a team of six Negroes carrying three stretchers bearing three beautiful nymphs. The bearers proceed to lead the nymphs back to their places on the ledge. Once there, the nymphs close their eyes and go into a state of suspended animation.

Soon the priests become aware of the Negro making noisy love with one of the nymphs in the darker reaches of the cave. They catch him and lash him with their whips. Then they order another Negro to lead the nymph back to her place on the ledge. Upon touching her, he, too, is unable to control his lust and begins to make love to her. In the end, the Arab priest has to intervene. Realising the power of the nymph's *namatham*, which is saturated with sexual desire, he leads the nymph back to a stretcher by his whip to avoid touching her. Three other mummies from the collection are also selected. These three beautiful female mummies are rather stiff and lifeless. On their way out, the priests complain that 'these [Negro] men do not know how to be gentle with the women. They would have destroyed and wasted them. We should raise the punishment for their transgressions'.[57] Even the Arabs are shown sharing the stereotype of the black African male as a lustful beast. Similar to most objects, the essence (*rupatham*) or the physical being of the nymphs would be destroyed, that is, reduced to dust, if they are overly exploited or used up. That is, once expended, the body (re)turns to dust.

After the Arabs leave with the mummies, the explorers take a closer look at the recently returned mummies, who are still breathing. One of the Englishmen, Captain Craig, touches one and is immediately overwhelmed by sexual desire. James literally holds him back. Not long after, one of the Negro men sneaks back into the cave, takes down one of the nymphs and begins making love to her lustily on the carpet. The man leaves, not wanting to see the nymph reduced to a pile of bones.

This particular section of the novel reflects Khru Liam's fascination with sex, which to him was not necessarily pornography. His first novel, *Khwam mai phayabat*, also contains sexual orgies. But those orgies were realistic ones, ones that imitated what we can presume was actually happening in

---

56   A popular Thai riddle asks: 'If you come across a cobra and a *khaek*, what should you do?' The answer is 'You would beat the *khaek* first'.
57   Nai Samran, *Nang neramit*, 250.

hotels, in the private rooms of restaurants, and in secret love nests of the rich in Bangkok society in the early 20th century. In that novel, Khru Liam suggests that those orgies were organised by immoral Thai men in an increasingly immoral Thai society under the influence of modernity and urbanisation. And as we know from Khru Liam's own account, that novel did not please the Thai reading public. In *Nang neramit*, however, Khru Liam cleverly allows his readers, especially his male readers, to fantasise about sex in a detached and guiltless way.

The men in this novel are all but helpless once they touch the divine nymphs: they are spellbound and cannot help themselves. The male lust for sex is guiltless in this case because they are responding to female lust. And, perhaps ironically for the reader today, their lust is all-consuming— but with a twist: excessive sex reduces not the male who instigated the contact, but the female into a pile of bones. The sex industry today has created love dolls and other sexual devices. But none of these artificial sexual playthings can compare with Khru Liam's divine nymphs!

The idea of 'wasting a woman' and 'reducing her to dust' is an intriguing one. At what point is too much of a good thing not wonderful, as Mae West would have it, but too much? Is this a comment on the belief that men require lots of women to satisfy their sexual cravings, a common sentiment of Thai men who, in spite of having loving wives, still keep mistresses and minor wives? Metaphorically, the ability to pick and choose and to 'turn in' one woman for another seems like the perfect fantasy for the male. Perhaps Khru Liam is trying to satisfy the (Thai) male's fantasy of the perfect sexual partner—a partner whom he never tires of and who in turn never tires of him. Interestingly, Khru Liam inserts an idea of sexual moderation and the fragility of the woman as a sexual object, that is, if there is too much sex, the female sexual object will be reduced to a pile of bones.

A common belief among Thai men is that 'good' women may not be exciting sexual partners: they tend to be passive because their minds are elsewhere, thinking about the family, their children, parents, servants, etc. 'Good' Thai women are not supposed to exercise their sexual agency.[58] It is

---

58 According to Rachel Harrison, Thai women fulfil their role as women by being mothers and wives. Their own sexuality never surfaces. This is true in social behaviour as well as in literature. It is not until Thida Bunnag penned several novels that allowed Thai women to exercise sexual agency that this assumption began to break down. However, most of the women whose stories are told do not necessarily fall within the category of good traditional women. Also see Rachel Harrison,

also not uncommon that wives arrange minor wives for their husbands to lessen the burden of their own sexual responsibilities, especially after ageing. It is widely believed, moreover, that a woman's ardour may wane after menopause, but a man remains sexually active until old age.

These common Thai beliefs give point to much of the action in Khru Liam's *Nang neramit*. Not only are the young Arab priests full of lust, but the ancient grand wizard himself still engages in sex with his beautiful creations. Male sexual lust is treated as universal in the novel because it affects all males in the novel: the Arabs, the Englishmen, the Ethiopians and the Negroes.

The occult

Like *She*, *Nang neramit* features an exotic locale and explores the occult. Yet, much as in *Khwam mai phayabat*, Khru Liam also incorporates tropes and themes altogether familiar to a Thai audience. In classical Thai literature, the appearance of *phi* (ghosts, spirits), magic potions, the sacred, the occult and even sex between humans and demons or gods are familiar tropes. Even though the concept of the separation of the body reflected in the idea of *rupatham* and the soul that is subsumed under the concept of *namatham* is not exclusively Thai or Buddhist, a Thai readership is prone to more seriously believe in the separation of the two dimensions.

The assertion of the presence of 'subjectivity' as distinct from 'physicality' is also easily understood, as it is the foundation of the belief in the existence of *phi* or ghosts and spirits. To give the story an exotic twist, Billford asserts that the *khaek*, which is a Thai category for Indians, Arabs, Egyptians and Muslims, have found a way to preserve the *rupatham*, that is the physical body, and free it from its *namatham*. The belief in *phi* is a cornerstone of Thai culture inherited from the past and relating to the prevalence of animism.[59] There are both good and bad *phi*. It is also necessary to please, feed and placate these spirits who exist almost everywhere—in caves, in trees, in stones, in mountains. Those who have died a horrible death

---

'The Madonna and the Whore: Self/Other tensions in the characterization of the prostitute by Thai female authors', in *Genders and sexualities in modern Thailand*, ed. Peter A. Jackson and Nerida M. Cook (Chiangmai: Silkworm Books, 1999).
59   On the subject of Thai ghosts and spirits see Phraongjao Sisaowaphong, *Nangsue waduay amnat phi lae phi loak* [*Text on the power of phi and haunting by phi*], B.E. 2464 [1921] (Digital Rare Book, Tha Chang Book Store).

(*phi tai hong*) still roam about, scaring people. It is not uncommon, even today, to hear people say that they have seen *phi* or were frightened by experiences of haunting (*phi lok*). For example, stories like these appeared in Thai newspapers after the 26 December 2004 tsunami disaster. People have reported numerous ghost sightings that, to many Thai readers, are real phenomena. This may also explain the popularity of *nang phi* (ghost movies) until this day.

Over time, these roaming *phi* become weak and lose their power. They turn into peaceful souls before returning to the cycle of birth and rebirth. James Billford, speaking for Khru Liam, says that the *namatham* can be reunited with the *rupatham* before the former disappears, allowing a corpse to be revived. But Khru Liam adds an interesting twist to this Buddhist idea of incarnation, by suggesting that the Arab grand wizard is able to revive dead people with a blank *namatham* (negating *karma* acquired from past lives), which is only receptive to storing feelings of lust and sexual desire. Essentially, Khru Liam inserts Thai world views into *farang* minds.

Eventually, the wizard explains to the Englishmen that the resurrected divine nymphs are pure physical beings (*rupatham*) with empty minds (*namatham*). They only feed off a man's emotions. If the man who they are with is romantic, they too will be romantic. If he is angry, they will also be angry. Because their minds are blank, they can store men's emotions and radiate those emotions back to those near them. If a man touches a divine nymph, he will feel the full force of her emotions accumulated over time like an electrical charge. This charge can get stronger and stronger the more times she is made love to. This is why, over time, the nymphs become absolutely irresistible to any man if touched. If the men are careful and do not over-indulge in sex with a divine nymph, she is good for about seven days. Too much sexual activity, and her body will become overheated: the flesh will fall away, leaving only her bones. After seven days of careful use, the nymphs are sent back to the cave to cool off and to recover.

Khru Liam seems to be playing to the male desire for 'pure sex'—sex without guilt, and sex without attachments. It is purely physical and mental eroticism. The man will no longer have to question his partner's ardour during lovemaking because she only reflects his own lust and those of other partners she has had before. In fact, the nymph, after a period of time, will have more lust and eroticism in her than one man because she has stored in her *namatham* the lust of several men, or several sessions of lovemaking. As the wizard explains to the Englishmen in highly sexist terms:

> women are full of obscene thoughts [*lamok*] and they are full of desire [*kilet*] ... They smear our hearts with sin. They lie, cheat, and mislead. They are elusive, and have debasing thoughts even when they give their bodies to their male sexual partners. But our divine nymphs partake with us our love in innocence. They will not die. They do not give us any other emotion except love.[60]

Khru Liam makes the same point again when the wizard enjoins a young priest to treat his divine nymph with care:

> This nymph is yours. Think pure thoughts when you make love to her and she will know only pure sex. Forget all of your miseries before making love and she will incubate only pure love. Soon she will only release that pure love for you to enjoy and you will discover that there is nothing as sweet as pure sex. Most people have sex with women who are both physical beings [*rupatham*] and emotional beings [*namatham*]. Women's emotions are full of desires and evil. But by having sex with a divine nymph who is only a physical being, we men can place only our emotions in them, and that is pure physical love.[61]

After a woman dies, her *namatham* or subjectivity dies with the body. All the base and evil thoughts disappear. When the body is revived and takes in the desires and lust of man, the new female can respond shamelessly to her man's sexual desires.

The divine nymphs are not just beautiful and perpetually young, but they are always ready to have sex with men. Men need not fear rejection. In the novel, female sexual agency is also exercised by these divine women. Surely, this is another Thai male fantasy—that all beautiful women would want to sleep with them, and that all women would be physically and emotionally responsive during sex. The divine nymphs as ideal women are neither good nor bad; they are neither shameful nor shameless. They are just beautiful women who respond to man's every sexual need: divine nymphs, indeed, fit for any Thai male's fantasies.

---

60 Nai Samran, *Nang neramit*, 304.
61 Nai Samran, *Nang neramit*, 315.

But sexual fantasy should appeal to all men regardless of their race, religion or culture. This generalisation is expressed in the novel, which has a very unusual ending. In trying to rescue Vivian, Billford's sweetheart who has been abducted by the priests, clashes between the English expeditionary force and desert Arab forces loyal to the priests take place. The fighting only ends after a volcano erupts, which revives all of the female mummies who wander into the battlefield. It does not take long before all the soldiers are making love with the nymphs and not war with each other. Both the English and the Arabs are soon too weak to continue fighting. And after a long spell of lovemaking, the divine nymphs are all reduced to just bones and the soldiers separate and go their own ways. Billford is not immune to the attraction of the divine nymphs because he, too, falls prey to the lust he has for the Queen. It is only when she has turned into dust that he comes to his senses and returns to Vivian. The two eventually marry, move back to England and live in high style by selling off the jewellery they have taken from the mummies.

In conclusion, *Nang neramit* suggests that Thai readers of the new literature brought in from the West still expected to read stories about places and people other than themselves. They wanted to be entertained and to learn about the Other, be they places or people. The opening of this novel, inspired by Rider Haggard's *She*, seemed to have resonated with the Thai readership. It is unclear how well *Nang neramit* sold, or how popular it became. It is also unclear whether it sold just as many copies as *Sao song phan pi*, which also appeared in 1916. My hunch is that *Nang neramit* was not as popular as *Sao song phan pi* because, unlike the latter, which was subsequently republished and retranslated in 1916, 1944 (1945?), 1991 and 2004, *Nang neramit* disappeared from the public eye, never to be reprinted. I only 'discovered' this novel after a long inquiry to friends and book collectors. A tattered copy was finally located in April 2005.

Even though *Nang neramit* is definitely more sophisticated and more appealing to the Thai reader than his 'authentically Thai' novel *Khwam mai phayabat,* it is still inferior in significance to the latter. One can argue that *Khwam mai phayabat* was a novel before its time, and that it failed as a novel at the time of its publication because it was too realistic, too didactic and too harsh a criticism of the very people it was supposed to appeal to—that is, the emerging modern social classes in the capital city. That novel, too, begins with an explanation of Buddhist beliefs of forgiveness and non-revenge. In that story, the hero was a man much like Khru Liam, who was about 30 and a failed student who had to cut short his studies in England. The hero, Nai Jian, was an ordinary and weak man, unlike the handsome James or the swashbuckling Captain Craig. The Thai hero finds himself a beautiful wife only to lose her to rich high society rivals in the rapidly modernising Bangkok. Even though he makes good towards the end by gaining the gratitude of a much younger woman and even gains back his repentant wife, his success did not seem to resonate with the reading public.

There is no sense of adventure or the exoticism of foreign places in that first Thai novel. It is almost as if Khru Liam's first novel was too 'modern', too 'realistic', and too 'Thai' for the public, which did not want to read about the reality of a morally corrupt Bangkok society. Traditional Thai literature is both entertaining and didactic. *Khwam mai phayabat* is didactic but not entertaining. *Nang neramit* is primarily entertaining as it allows the reader to be transported into a foreign land, to see life and adventure through foreign eyes. That novel allowed the Thai to imagine faraway places, and to imagine the lives of Englishmen, Egyptians, Arabs and Ethiopians. Yet *Nang neramit* mimics a Western form of entertainment, not a mimicry of colonial masters. In this sense, by allowing the Thai to look at the West and at Egypt and Africa as exotic and mysterious places, in *Nang neramit* Khru Liam *reverses* the Western gaze that looks at Thailand as an exotic and strange place.

It would be much later that the Thai novel would place Thai characters on the world stage. Perhaps this is why literary scholars date the emergence of the Thai novel to the year 1929, when three authors penned novels that portrayed Thai characters in Thai, European and American settings. *Khwam phayabat* had only European characters but whose hero escaped to live in Thailand; *Khwam mai phayabat* only had Thai characters living Thai lives; *Nang neramit* had only Others living outside of Thailand. None of these really included Thai characters in the broader canvas that connected Thailand to the rest of the world. Perhaps this is one reason why Kularp Saipradit's *Luk phuchai,* Dok Mai Sot's *Sattru khong jao lon,* and Mom Jao Akatdamkoeng's *Lakhon haeng chiwit* are canonised as the first (successful) Thai novels. The Thai main characters in these novels lived and studied overseas before returning to live in Thailand. They are also learned, sophisticated (know about the West), and idealistic.[62]

---

62   Of the three, *Lakhon haeng chiwit* is said to be the best example of the first Thai novel. It is a story of an aristocratic student who leaves Thailand to study in England. He eventually becomes a journalist writing for a major English paper. He travels to many countries in Europe and to America; his girlfriend is English, but he refuses to marry her because he wants to return to Thailand to

1. THE FIRST THAI NOVELS AND THE THAI LITERARY CANON

If we ask *why* Khru Liam's novels failed or succeeded, we can give only tentative answers. Perhaps Khru Liam's early works appeared before their time. The Thai reader wanted to read about the West and other exotic places such as Egypt, Arabia and Africa, as described by Western authors who knew those places intimately. The lesson Khru Liam learned was that they were not interested in reading about social realism in Bangkok society. He also learned that a Thai novel about Egypt and Africa would sell better than a Thai novel about Thailand. But even providing such exotic locales would not divert the Thai readers' thirst for real English novels, even if they were translations. Again, it is only after M.J. Akatdamkoeng's placing of sophisticated Thai characters on the world stage that the Thai novel became accepted as genuine. The ambiguous allure of the West through the novel ended only when the novel form was separated from its English content and adapted to authentic Thai material. In what can be best understood as 'clever' mastery of the West, the *rupatham* of the novel is finally joined with the *namatham* of Thai characters and plot to make the novel an accepted Thai literary genre.

Making new space in the Thai literary canon

As someone not trained in literary studies and teaching in America, I propose to contest the Thai literary canon from the margins— disciplinarily and geographically. This chapter has examined three early Thai novels that have not been included in the Thai literary canon. In my assessment, these three novels represent important examples of the Thai novel that helped the Thai public deal with the West during the turn of the 20th century.

My own interest in politics and the novel began in the mid-1970s when I used Kulab Saipradit's *Lae pai khang na* [*Looking to the future*] (1955) in a class at Thammasat University. The novel describes the political awakening of a boy from Isan, Thailand's poorest region, privileged to study at an elite school in Bangkok. There, he meets students from all classes and ethnicity and a favourite teacher who would later become involved in the overthrow of absolute monarchy. The novel focuses on the years immediately following the 1932 coup, showing how the good

---

promote monogamy. The other two novels also have similar themes of the main characters studying abroad and returning to Thailand to modernise the country. All three are didactic and entertaining. They succeeded where *Khwam mai phayabat* and *Nang neramit* failed.

intentions of the leaders turned sour when the new democratic regime itself became authoritarian and repressive. The novel was to be in three parts, corresponding to human life cycles: formative years, mature years and declining years. However, Kulab was unable to finish the last volume after his self-imposed political exile in China following the Sarit Thanarat coup in 1957.

I used *Lae pai khang na* to help contextualise the cultural and social milieu surrounding the 1932 coup that ended absolute monarchy in Thailand. During the late 1960s and into the 1970s, heated debates occurred frequently on campus between faculty members, who resisted the proliferation of what was seen as trashy leftist novels read by the students, and other lecturers, who were willing to discuss what the students were already reading. The schism took on political and disciplinary dimensions when the Thai language faculty argued that they were the true protectors of not just 'good' Thai literature, but also the nation, religion and the monarchy. Those who did not agree with them were labelled left-leaning *rua hang yao* (long tail boats): lecturers out to destroy Thai culture and the Thai nation by encouraging students to read seditious novels and books that celebrated socialism, communism and social justice.[63]

The (re)discovery of Thai novels as good sources for social criticism was the work of radical students and some young Thai literary scholars who were looking for ways to critique the inequities of Thai society. Student activists and other young literary critics republished many novels that

---

63 On 19 February, 1975, faculty members in the Thai Language Department at Thammasat University organised a panel discussion, '*Wannakam hai arai dae sangkhom*' [*What does literature give to society?*], as a counterattack against radical students who were accused of trying to destroy Thai literature by reading trashy leftist novels instead of classical Thai literature. The students rejected traditional Thai literature as instruments of the ruling and oppressive *sakdina* (feudal) classes. Tomayantri, a conservative writer and one of the panellists, attempted to explain *sakdina* in a positive light but was booed by the students. I had been one of a handful of lecturers who had assigned students to read recently resurrected 'leftist' literature. For example, my open-book examination question asked freshmen in the 'Thai Civilization Foundation' course to consider the connection between ideology and history when reviewing the works of Prince Damrong, Luang Wichit and Jit Phumisak. Students were asked which history they preferred and why. Students across campus organised study groups to discuss the exam, much to the dismay of some conservative faculty members who accused me and the students of promoting leftist politics on campus. *Rua hang yao* refers to the modern, sleek, fast and flashy boats equipped with powerful Japanese car engines connected to a long drive shaft to the propeller (thus, 'long tail boat'). I assume that these boats motoring up and down the Chaophraya River along the Thammasat campus and the progressive faculty members on campus are seen as dangerous to the preservation of order and tradition. The tension between those in favour of the novel and those against teaching the novel started in the 1960s. See David Smyth, 'Towards the canonizing of the Thai novel', in Smyth, *The canon*, 174–5.

were banned during the previous dictatorial regimes. In addition to *Lae pai khang na*, students were reading, for example, Seni Saowaphong's *Pisat* [*The demon*], the many works of Asani Pholachan, and Jit Phumisak's *Chomna sakdina Thai* [*The real face of Thai feudalism*].⁶⁴

Many years later, beginning in 2000, I began teaching a graduate seminar on the Thai novel at Cornell University. These seminars analysed selected Thai novels in light of Hayden White's theory of tropes, the New Historicism of Stephen Greenblatt, and translation theory, especially postcolonial translation theory.⁶⁵ In one seminar, we read in the vernacular several of Kulab Saipradit's novels such as *Luk phuchai* [*The real man*] (1928), *Khang lang phab* [*Behind the painting*] (1937) and *Lae pai khang na* [*Looking to the future*] (1955) to try to understand why his novels are considered by many to be politically radical and socially relevant. In another, we read and compared Mae Wan's *Khwam phayabat* [*The vendetta*] (1902) with Corelli's *Vendetta*, and Nai Samran's (pen name of Luang Wilatpariwat, popularly known as Khru Liam) *Khwam mai phayabat* [*The non-vendetta*] (1915). What I discovered is that, although Kulab's *Luk phuchai* (1928) was one of the three canonical novels designated as the first authentic Thai novels, Phraya Surintharacha's *Khwam phayabat* and Luang Wilatpariwat's *Khwam mai phayabat*, which predated them, were not. I became intrigued by two fundamental questions: 'How is the canon constructed?' and 'What limitations does a canon impose upon the study of literary transmission and the significance of other literary works ignored by the canon?'

---

64   The standard text on the social and political role of the Thai novel is Trisin Bunkhachon, *Nawaniyai kap sangkhom Thai* [*The novel and Thai society*] (Bangkok: Samnakphim Sangsan, 1980). Also see Hiramatsu Hideki, 'Thai literary trends: From Seni Saowaphong to Chart Kobjitti', *Kyoto review of Southeast Asia*, 8 (March 2007). Among the young progressive literary scholars were Chonthira Kladyu and Suvanna Kriengkraipetch. A comprehensive list of the books that were reprinted during this critical period can be found in Prajak Kongkirati, *Lae laeo khwam khlueanwai ko prakot* [*And then a movement appeared*] (Bangkok: Thammasat University Press, 2005), 438–42.
65   Hayden White, *Metahistory: The historical imagination in nineteenth-century Europe* (Baltimore: Johns Hopkins University Press, 1973); Catherine Gallagher and Stephen Greenblatt, *Practicing New Historicism* (Chicago: University of Chicago Press, 2000); Jeremy Munday, *Translations studies: Theories and applications* (New York: Routledge, 2001).

The Thai literary canon

David Smyth's preface in *The canon in Southeast Asian literatures* is instructive in answering my questions. Smyth's preface identifies two important features of the canon:

> Traditionally the literary canon is seen as a chronological arrangement of famous authors and major works which 'have stood the test of time' because of their intrinsic merits and which are linked over the centuries by a presumed cultural unity … the term 'canon' is most widely understood to refer to an institutionally recognized list of exemplary works, such as the body of works constituting the national literature of a country, it is also used to denote a system of rules for creating such works.[66]

First, a canonical work must stand the test of time and reflect an 'authentic' cultural characteristic, at least of the predominant culture. Second, the canon identifies works that have become timeless and 'institutionally recognized' as national literature. This implies that canons are constructed by institutions, in this case, by academic literary scholars who research, teach, and most importantly, write and publish about why a particular work is more important than others. This process, in turn, ensures that the selected works will stand the test of time because other scholars will also write and teach these in academic institutions. This observation answers my second question: that is, even though it is assumed that the canon changes as scholars' opinions change, once a canon is institutionalised, it is difficult to dislodge.

Here I will question the established canon, especially the designation of the first 'authentic' Thai novel, to accommodate several, such as the three covered in this chapter, that have not been considered. It is not my purpose to discuss in detail the complexities of canonical construction. I am only responding to the ontological nature of the canon which I believe puts an undue emphasis on the 'big three', namely, Kulab Saipradit's *Luk phuchai* [*The real man*], Mom Luang Buppha Kunchorn's *Sattru khong jao lon* [*Her enemy*] (writing under the pen name Dok Mai Sot), and Mom Jao Akatdamkoeng's *Lakhon haeng chiwit* [*Circus of life*], all published around 1929. This overemphasis, I would argue, elides the importance of novels published before that date, and at the same time funnels scholarly energy

---

66 Smyth, *The canon*, vii.

towards only those novels the canon itself identifies. If the year 1929 demarcates the birth of authentic Thai novels, then anything written before that is less important, or worse, is considered unauthentic.

A recent institutional reinforcement of this canon is the publication of a special volume of the influential *Warasan phasa lae nangsue* [*The journal of language and books*], 35 (2004), dedicated to the 100th birthday anniversary of four exemplary authors. That issue celebrates the *Rung arun nawaniyai Thai* [*Dawn of the Thai novel*], suggesting that the Thai novel began with the works of four authors. In that issue, the novels of Mom Jao Akatdamkoeng, Kulab Saipradit and Mom Luang Buppha Kunchorn (Dok Mai Sot) are once again selected, analysed and critiqued. The focus on the three novels ignores, devalues, precludes and omits the importance of pre-1929 novels. In addition, the celebration of the three novels denies the importance of the transmission of earlier literary traditions upon which the canon is based.[67]

The reinforcement and reiteration of this canon in *Warasan phasa lae nangsue* reflects the work of the two influential scholars writing in the mid-1970s. Suphanni Warathorn published her 1973 Chulalongkorn University MA thesis as 'Prawat kanpraphan nawaniyai Thai' ['The history of the Thai novel'] in 1976. A year earlier, Wibha Senanan published her 1974 University of London PhD dissertation as 'The genesis of the novel in Thailand'. Wibha's book became the standard text in English and was only revised and published in Thai in 1997. Both books gave a convincing account of how the rise of print capitalism in Thailand helped spawn literary magazines, journals, newspapers and books that introduced European-style prose fiction to the expanding literate and increasingly urban public. Suphanni and Wibha also concurred that the three novels

---

67 I am not alone in this assertion. Phichet Saengthong's article on Mom Jao Akatdamkoeng also questions the effects of designating *Lakhon haeng chiwit* as the first Thai novel. He argues that the current canon does not sufficiently cover literary transmission, and the influence of Thai literary traditions on Akatdamkoeng's novels. Phichet believes that Akatdamkoeng's novel became an exemplary novel because it fits the leftist inclinations of literary critics of the 1970s who wanted to use the novel to critique class society in Thailand. He suggests that there is a relationship between the canon and the ideological preferences of its constructors. I agree with Phichet that the division between lowbrow *nangsue aan len* (books that are read for fun), and highbrow *wanakam sathorn sangkhom* (literature that reflects social conditions) is artificial and not very helpful. The social and cultural impact of trashy lowbrow novels on the reading masses may be as important, if not more so, than the effects of esoteric literary works on a handful of literary scholars and their students. See Phichet Saengthong, 'Phatthanakan nawaniyai Thai: korani Mom Jao Akatdamkoeng Raphiphat' ['The development of the Thai novel: the case of Mom Jao Akatdamkoeng Raphiphat'], *Warasan phasa lae nangsue*, 38 (2004): 53–86.

published around 1929 by Kulab Saipradit, Mom Jao Akatdamkoeng, and Mom Luang Buppha Kunchorn warranted special recognition as the first 'authentic' Thai novels. These two texts became the definitive study of the birth and evolution of the Thai novel. More recently, Mattani Rutnin (1988), Marcel Barang (1994), and David Smyth (2000) continued to reinforce Suphanni's and Wibha's pronouncements.[68]

Those literary scholars point out that the three 'authentic' Thai novels depict Thai society realistically through main characters who are Thai, and with central themes that are serious and substantive.[69] As illustration, Wibha asserts that Kulab Saipradit is 'more serious in his imaginative writing than most of his contemporaries whose work normally evolved around the theme of melodramatic love, mystery, or detection'.[70] More importantly, these literary scholars insist that the three novels had developed a distinct Thai identity. It is not clear to me what constitutes 'distinct' in these cases, or why some novels are more imaginative than others. My own reading suggests that all three of the novels are indeed melodramatic love stories, not radically different from earlier novels which were pejoratively labelled *nangsue an len* (books read for fun), or *banthoeng khadi khlueap* (enamelled entertainment). Authenticity, and what is considered to be Thai, is such an elusive and contingent concept that seems to be important only to regimes that define the Thai nation-state. I am more impressed by the fact that the three texts are modern novels written in the vernacular Thai language, and I feel that a debate about authenticity is unwarranted and distracting.

The canon is inevitably constructed by literary scholars, conditioned by their own subjectivity/ideology, influenced by the intellectual climate of their generation. The period in which the canonical novels were published coincided with the impending crisis of the old regime, the rapidly expanding middle class and bureaucracy, exciting social change, the vast improvement of education, and the emergence of writing as a vocation. The end of the 1920s set the stage for the modern Thailand of the middle class, a period that the scholars of the 1970s were more familiar with. In addition, by the end of the conflict in Vietnam in 1975, young people

---

68 Mattani, *Modern Thai literature*; Barang, *The 20 best novels in Thailand*.
69 Suphanni, *History of the Thai novel*, 233–4.
70 Wibha, *The genesis of the novel in Thailand*, 83.

were becoming nationalistic and more socially aware. They advocated economic nationalism and in turn searched for 'authentic' Thai products, including national literature that critiqued the injustices in Thai society.

The renewed focus on the place of literature, especially the novel, from both the conservative and radical camps, resulted in a struggle to define authentic, relevant and good literature. Nationalistic Thai literary critics concluded that the very early Thai novels were just too derivative, too indistinct from the European novels upon which they were based, and therefore, too unauthentic. On the other hand, the young radical literary scholars were also busy excavating and promoting literature with social and political messages in their own attempt to insert these radical voices into the canon itself. In this strange mix, the fate of the very early novels was sealed. They were summarily ignored.

Reconstituting a genealogy of the Thai novel

We have seen that by the end of the 19th century, short stories began to be published regularly. Many of these were translations of English compositions.[71] By the early 20th century, many students who returned from Europe also found publishing outlets in the emerging magazine market. Although we know about the names of these magazines and some of the very early compositions from the accounts in Suphanni's book, it is not possible to fully assess the totality of novels that were written during the first decade and a half of the 20th century. Even the titles cited in Suphanni's book could not be easily found in the national or university libraries. It is more than likely that these are still languishing on private collectors' bookcases, or feeding termites in boxes stored away in closets.

---

71   An excellent selection of some of these early translations and original essays can be found in Nawatri Ying Sumali Wirawong, ed., *Roikaew naew mai khong Thai B.E. 2417-2453* [*The new Thai prose writing, 1874–1910*] (Bangkok: Samnakphim Sayam, 2004). The short stories were published in *Darunowat, Wicharayanwiset, Wicharayan, Lak witthaya, Thalok witthaya, Thawi panya, Kula satri, Samran witthaya* and *Nithranukhro*. This edited volume is an amazing anthology of 40 Thai short stories written mostly during the reign of King Chulalongkorn. Sumali provides a concise tabulated analysis of each short story, documenting names of authors, publisher, length in pages, main characters, plot summaries, writing styles, origin (Thai or translation) and other useful observations. This anthology should be required reading for students interested in Thai modernity, literary transmission, the evolution of modern Thai language, postcolonial theory and intellectual history.

Few examples of the novels of the first period remain in circulation. Printing runs were low and circulation was limited to the elite intellectual class. Suphanni says that most of these early novels were based on Western examples.

Suphanni also identifies two Thai proto-novels—*Nithan thong in* [*Thong-in tales*], and *Darawan*. *Nithan thong in* was a detective story inspired by Arthur Conan Doyle's *Adventures of Sherlock Holmes* series. Self-contained episodes were written by Prince Vajiravudh under the pseudonym Nai Kaew Nai Khwan in 1904. Fifteen episodes were published. *Darawan* was the work of Kromamuen Narathip Praphanphong, using the pseudonym Prasertaksorn. That novel appears to be a proper Thai romance set in Malaya. Aside from Suphanni's excellent analysis, these two early novels have not attracted much interest from other literary scholars. It is puzzling to me why these novels are not included in the canon.

Even more puzzling is the exclusion of *Khwam phayabat*, which has been acknowledged as the first novel to appear in the Thai language. Even though *Khwam phayabat* is a translation, it introduced the Thai public and aspiring authors to the novel form. Neither Suphanni nor Wibha analysed this novel in their influential texts, nor has the novel been mentioned in recent publications that identify/institutionalise important works of literature. Ignoring the importance of this translated novel is, in my opinion, a grave oversight.[72]

I argue that the three non-canonical early novels covered in this chapter should be included in the Thai literary canon, representing the genre of the vernacularised (translated) novel, the original Thai novel, and the hybrid/imitation/bicultural novel that helped prepare Thailand for modernity and political and cultural autonomy. Contemporary Thai literary scholars have dismissed these novels as unauthentic Thai because they are *nangsue plae* (translated book), *nangsue prae* (transformed book) or *nangsue plaeng* (metamorphosed book), which are distinctions without difference.

---

72 Suphanni also lists 18 titles published between 1911 and 1919, but it is unclear whether these novels are original compositions or translated novels and whether they are still available to researchers. Undoubtedly, this period is indeed a lively period for novels that deserves serious attention. Suphanni, *History of the Thai novel*, 151–2. Another popular author whose works have been translated into Thai is H. Rider Haggard. The most famous among his translated novels is *She* (1886), first translated by Luang Wilatpariwat using the pseudonym Nok Nori sometime in the early 1900s or early 1910s, under the title *Sao song phan pi* [*The two-thousand-year-old maiden*]. This translation has been reprinted several times, most recently in 1990. The term *sao song phan pi* is now a common description of women who refuse to age. Few, however, remember how the term originated.

1. THE FIRST THAI NOVELS AND THE THAI LITERARY CANON

Vernacularisation as appropriation

Thai culture over the centuries has benefited from translations of literary works from other cultures.[73] The *Ramakian*, for example, is a Thai rewriting of the *Ramayana* that has been accepted as an exemplar of classical Thai literature. I would not be surprised if many Thai do not realise that the epic is in fact an important scripture in Hinduism. In my own case, it was not until I was an educated adult that I realised that *Nithan isop* [*Aesop's fables*] and *Inao* from the Indonesian Panji tales were not Thai.

Translation from a foreign language into Thai predominantly involves sense for sense and not word for word. The accuracy that is demanded of academic translation is not the concern of most of the early translations. Translators have exercised a wide range of agency in adding to, subtracting from, or changing the stories they translate.[74] For example, the *Ramayana* has been rewritten, reinterpreted, and reformatted, so that as the *Ramakian* it has taken on a new life to celebrate the royals and not the gods as in the original Hindu text. In fact, each Southeast Asian version of the *Ramayana* reflects its own local history and cultural specificity.[75]

Postcolonial scholars like Tejaswini Niranjana and Gayatri Spivak focus on the power relations involved in translation.[76] Niranjana is concerned with how translations 'inform the hegemonic apparatuses that belong to the ideological structure of colonial rule'.[77] This is because domination is carried out by the state apparatus. Spivak, on the other hand, highlights how colonial translation is a way to reconstruct or to rewrite the image of the colonised as an inferior culture. Through the process of interpellation, a term coined by the French Marxist theorist Louis Althusser, the colonised internalise this inferiority and thereby perpetuate the myth of inequality. Vince Rafael in his book, *Contracting Colonialism*, however,

---

73 For a discussion of translation as culture and translation as appropriation, see Susan Bassnett and Andre Lefevre, eds, *Translation, history and culture* (New York: Pinter, 1990). Assimilating foreign text into a target culture and language can also be seen as a domesticating process. While generally a negative concept, when used by the subaltern it can be empowering.
74 The translator's ideology generally wins over all other considerations, be they linguistic or poetic: Andre Lefevre, *Translation, rewriting, and the manipulation of the literary frame* (New York: Routledge, 1992), 39.
75 For a study of plot variations, see Nicanor G. Tiongson, 'The rule of Rama from the Bay of Bengal to the Pacific Ocean', *SPAFA journal*, 10(2) (May–August, 2000): 5–25.
76 Gayatri Spivak, 'The politics of translation', in *The translation studies reader*, ed. L. Venuti (New York: Routledge, 2000), 397–416.
77 Niranjana, *Siting translation*, 33.

takes a different tack. He documents how the Tagalog use 'mistranslation' as a strategy to resist Spanish hegemony.[78] Rafael's work differs from Niranjana's, even though both are interested in the subjectivity of the colonised, in that Rafael theorises that retranslation or mistranslation widely existed during the colonial period. The agency of the colonised to mistranslate may have puzzled the Spaniard priests, but it was logical to the Tagalog.

The study of early Thai translation of Western literature can gain from Rafael's conceptual framework. Even though Thailand was never directly colonised, the imposition of extraterritoriality by the 1855 Bowring Treaty compromised its sovereignty. Thus scholars have conceptualised Thailand as a semi-colonial state to try to make it fit into the conceptual framework of colonised Southeast Asia. Although the debate about how to situate Thailand in postcolonial studies is still unsettled, I would argue that even as a semi-colonial state or a crypto-colonial state (a term coined by Michael Herzfeld), the Thai had control over cultural production that served their own needs and not those of the hegemonic colonial powers. In this instance, I would also argue that translation was a way to cushion the impact of Western domination.

The policy urging translations was first announced by King Chulalongkorn in 1886 as a way to improve education and knowledge about the West.[79] The discourse of resistance was expressed as the necessity to keep abreast of the best achievement of *khwam than samai* (the latest achievement of human civilisation) regardless of where it originated. Asian humanistic culture was to be replaced by Western culture that emphasised rationality, science and industry. Beginning with King Mongkut, Thailand's leaders wanted to acquire the West's superior scientific and industrial achievements

---

78   Rafael, *Contracting colonialism.*
79   Suphanni, *History of the Thai novel*, 32. The sign of a shift from Chinese economic and cultural hegemony to an English/European hegemony is the suspension of tribute missions to China by King Mongkut in 1852 when Thailand began negotiations with the British about trade and legal authority that led up to the Bowring Treaty of 1855. See: B.J. Terwiel, *Thailand's political history* (Bangkok: Rivers Books, 2005), 145. Historians have concluded that the 1893 incident where French gunboat diplomacy forced Thailand to relinquish claims to territory on the west bank of the Mekong solidified Thailand's policy to emulate Western civilisation as a strategy to resist colonial conquest. See Patrick Jory, 'Problems in contemporary Thai nationalist historiography', *Kyoto review of Southeast Asia*, March 2003, accessed 24 April 2007: kyotoreview.org/issue-3-nations-and-stories/problems-in-contemporary-thai-nationalist-historiography-abstract/. It should be noted that soon after that crisis King Chulalongkorn sent two sons, Prince Vajiravudh and Prince Aphakorn, to study military and naval science in England. Others were soon to follow.

together with the cultural forms that supported those achievements. But the Thai would only select what was best and appropriate them through translation or adaptation.

Translation, interpretation and rewriting are processes that appropriate what is transformed as one's own. Thai translators do not always see themselves as technicians of language, but as artists, authors and composers. It is not unusual to see authors list themselves as such and not as mere translators. In fact, the first Thai author/translators exercised freewheeling agency by including their own stories and ideas that exceeded what was actually in the novels themselves.

Another way to theorise translation is to consider it as vernacularisation or localisation of knowledge—turning something foreign into Thai. The historian David Wyatt has made a strong argument for the emergence of what he calls the 'vernacular kingdoms', which invented their own writing systems in the late 13th century that facilitated the vernacularisation of idioms in art, literature, and music. This is why one can distinguish, for example, Buddha images that are Indian, Thai, Burmese or Khmer. The vernacularisation process in literature when applied to the novel, therefore, makes translated novels 'Thai'. Wyatt's colleague O.W. Wolters equates appropriation to localisation, whereby what is foreign becomes fractured, restated and drained of its original significance before being reconstituted with a new subjectivity.[80]

Translation is also a way to educate readers about other cultures. Many leading Thai intellectuals such as Phraya Anuman Ratchathon and Prince Wachirayan had *farang* patrons to help them with English and to understand Europe.[81] But for the rest of the middle class, translated

---

80 See Wolters, *History, culture, and region*, 55–7, 173–4, 182–8. David Wyatt's assertions were presented on numerous occasions in guest lectures in my 'Asian Studies 208: Introduction to Southeast Asia'. Appropriation, or to make something one's own, may explain why some of the early translators see themselves as authors and composers of new transformed literary works and therefore did not feel compelled to acknowledge the original manuscript or author. Plagiarism through translation is not seen as the bankruptcy of indigenous genius. Instead of being a prohibited behaviour, stealing knowledge through plagiarism is condoned and taken as clever or *keng*. Outwitting a better opponent is always *keng* in Thai culture. The practice of not crediting the work of previous scholars also occurs in retranslations. Later translations of Rider Haggard's *She* by Chaiwat [pseud.], *Sao song phan pi* (n.p.: 1943), found in the Chulalongkorn University Library, and Sotsai [pseud.], *Amata devi* (Bangkok: Praphansarn Press, 2004), never even mentioned that the first translation was made by Khru Liam. Note that Chaiwat also plagiarised Khru Liam's title.
81 Until recently, scholars believed that Phraya Anuman Rachathon's *Soraida: nangphya thalae sai* [*Zoraida: The desert queen*], published in 1915, was a translation of Rider Haggard's *Virgin of the sun*. Phraya Anuman translated many English novels—14 in all—with the help of his English

stories provided easy access to help them know the West and other cultures. Moreover, many translated works wrote into their compositions the equality or even the superiority of Thai culture over Western culture and practices.

For the Thai, translation was an appropriation of Western knowledge that helped to boost the Thai sense of self-assurance, cosmopolitanism and understanding of the benefits and pitfalls of modernity that would prepare them to deal with the encroaching West. Even though it was clear that the West was superior in many aspects, there was no need for the Thai to feel totally inferior. To emulate the West did not necessarily mean to submit to the West. 'Knowing the West' through translation could be an effective strategy to help prepare the Thai to resist Western hegemony.

Conclusion

Even this necessarily brief account should demonstrate that the current canon identifying *Lakhon haeng chiwit*, *Luk phuchai* and *Sattru khong jao lon* as the first authentic/real Thai novels obfuscates and elides the importance of other earlier novels. The intrusion of ideological sentiments into the formation of the canon prevents a better appreciation of cultural transmission and reception, especially during the period when the Thai had to cope with heightened pressure from the colonial powers. The labelling of those three novels as authentically Thai suggests that earlier novels were insufficiently authentic, too close to their Western models and, therefore, unworthy of consideration. Metaphorically, the 'bathwater' from which

---

supervisor in the Customs Department, Norman Maxwell. This misidentification was recently corrected by Runruthai Satchaphan in her book *Jak kao su mai wannasin thai mai sinsun* [*From old to new: Thai literature is not lost*] (Bangkok: Srinakharinwirot University Press, 2009), 151–86. She argues convincingly that the original novel was, in fact, William Le Queux's *Zoraida: The romance of the harem and the great Sahara* and that many Thai literary scholars have never really read the original novel for comparison. Over the years this novel has been republished with the error until Runruthai found a copy where Phraya Anuman indicated that it was a translation of Le Queux's novel. It is not unusual for the early Thai authors to publish translations without attribution, claiming that their translations were their original work. In 1913, for example, Phraya Anuman also published a novel *Amnat haeng khwam phayayam* [*The power of perseverance*] but failed to give the name of the original author or book title. The vernacularisation of Western literature through translation became an honourable pastime for the educated class, both for those who studied abroad, as well as for those who learned English at local schools such as Suan Kulab, Thepsirin and Assumption. These early writers translated and wrote original prose fiction out of duty as well as to seek fame. They did this work while holding down their regular government jobs. Writing did not become a serious profession until the founding of the Suphab Burut group by Kulab Saipradit in the late 1920s.

the three canonical novels sprang forth was unceremoniously thrown out, and with it, some 'babies'. I have discussed the importance of three of these babies. There must be more.

Khwam phayabat is the first proper novel to be experienced uniformly by the literate and increasingly urban Thai. The novel allowed the Thai to form a common imagination and knowledge about the West. Because the novel was read in the vernacular and not in an imperial language, it could not be seen as an imposition of a colonial value upon the Thai public. The West was filtered through a Thai lens that made Western culture accessible, familiar, and less threatening.

But translation is also a process of vernacularisation and localisation that appropriates another culture's knowledge by transforming it into one's own. Thus, Mae Wan's *Khwam phayabat* is more than just a translation of an English novel: it is an original Thai appropriation of the English novel that is representative of a genre of literature that educated the Thai public about the West. Whether accurate or not, these early translated novels taught the Thai about the alluring yet dangerous Other. The cumulative effect of acquired and appropriated information constituted foundational knowledge about Europe, and other foreign cultures, for the Thai.

Prior to the arrival of print capitalism, the Thai foundational knowledge about Indian and Chinese culture came from appropriated translations of two major epics—the *Ramayana* [*Ramakian*] for India and *The romance of the three kingdoms* [*Sam kok*] for China. In both cases, but especially with the *Ramayana*, the transmission of knowledge is based on limited circulation of texts (even though *Sam kok* was printed in 1865, its circulation was rather limited), oral and dramatic performances and representations on mural paintings. But with print capitalism that took root in Thailand at the end of the 19th century and its subsequent flourishing in the early 20th century, foundational knowledge about the West and other cultures was rapidly formed by the process of simultaneous reading of a multiplicity of uniform and mass-circulated short stories, newspapers and novels.

The inclusion of *Khwam phayabat* and perhaps other translated novels in school and university curriculums will give Thai literature studies new directions for teaching and research that will help clarify when, how and what Thais knew about the world beyond, and how novels contributed to the Thai cosmopolitan world view, its prejudices, its sense of equality and its confidence with regard to Others. These translated novels should also undergo close study within translation theory, contextual historicism and postcolonial critical studies.[82]

I have also made the case that *Khwam mai phayabat* is not merely a satire or simply a parody of Corelli's *Vendetta*. It is far more than that. Stephen Greenblatt, the leading proponent of the New Historicism, suggests that literature as culture acts as a constraint to enforce cultural boundaries through praise and blame.[83] As the first original Thai novel that was highly critical of the effects of urbanisation and modernisation, *Khwam mai phayabat* is a very early example of how the novel can help enforce cultural, gender and moral values that have come under attack by modernity.

Aside from the opening page that refers to the belief of Westerners that 'revenge is sweet', *Khwam mai phayabat* is indeed a very Thai novel. Its plot is Thai. Its setting is entirely in Thailand. Its characters are all Thai and recognisable. Its underlying moral message is also Thai. This novel also suggests historical and anthropological problematics that can be explained by a close reading and a reconstruction of Bangkok middle-class society of the 1910s. I agree with the anthropologist Herbert Phillips who points out that Thai writers can be 'the most sensitive, reflective, [and] articulate ... members of Thai society ... The writing of literature is integral to the social process, as both historical precipitant and product'. He argues further that literature in the vernacular can be considered a 'noetic expression of a social and cultural milieu', and that it is possible to treat 'literary works as embodiments of culture'. Writing in the vernacular is writing for fellow Thais. Therefore, the communication is intracultural and reflects 'the native point of view'.[84]

---

82   Parenthetically, the fact that many societies in Asia read translations of similar novels could be a subject of investigation: Would different cultural and intellectual traditions lead to different translations and explanations? Would simultaneous literacy of European novels across different Asian cultures and communities conjure up uniform or dissimilar images of the West? How different is each translation intraculturally and interculturally? How does colonial status complicate translation? An excellent study of this line of research is Doris Jedamski's pioneering work 'Popular literature and postcolonial subjectivities: Robinson Crusoe, the Count of Monte Cristo and Sherlock Holmes in colonial Indonesia', in *Clearing a space: Postcolonial readings of modern Indonesian literature*, ed. Keith Foulcher and Tony Day (Leiden: KITLV Press, 2002), 19–48.
83   Greenblatt, 'Culture', 226.
84   Herbert P. Phillips, *Modern Thai literature with an ethnographic interpretation* (Honolulu: University of Hawai'i Press, 1987), 3–4. Phillips said that he owes his ideas to Malinowski.

Nevertheless, *Khwam mai phayabat* is a novel ahead of its time. It failed in the marketplace because it was too drastic a departure from the romances, mystery adventures, and detective stories popular at that time. It contained too harsh a criticism of the very people it was supposed to appeal to—that is, the emerging modern urban middle class. Hidden behind the salacious description of sexual orgies was indeed a stunning criticism of Bangkok society. Thailand's first original Thai novel was perhaps too modern, too serious, and ultimately too Thai for an audience which did not want to deal with the reality of a morally corrupt Bangkok society.

Nang neramit, on the other hand, was written to satisfy to the Thai reading public's thirst to learn about the Other and faraway places. As pure fiction, *Nang neramit* is an important novel because it showcases the professionalism of a Thai author, writing not about the familiar, but about the unfamiliar in convincing ways. As the first full-blown novel written by a Thai author in the Thai language about foreign characters in a foreign land, it represents the prototype of local literary genius. Khru Liam should be considered the first professional Thai novelist capable of composing original stories that transcend the limitations of local culture and space. Because most of his life was devoted to writing, translating and publishing books, he has to be considered the first modern professional literary figure in Thailand.

Nang neramit is entertaining as well as didactic. The novel allows the reader to be transported into a foreign land, to see life and adventure through Thai eyes, to imagine faraway places, and to imagine the lives and the foibles of Englishmen, Egyptians, Arabs, Ethiopians and Africans. Although he appropriates a Western literary form, in *Nang neramit* Khru Liam reverses the usual Western gaze, which looks at Thailand as an exotic and strange place, to allow the Thai to gaze back at the West and other cultures as strange, exotic, immoral and even backward.

Can these three novels be considered authentically Thai? Again, in my opinion, a discussion of authenticity is irrelevant and distracting. These novels are Thai because their authors are Thai and their compositions are in the Thai vernacular. In her essay of otherness in Thai literature, Suvanna Kriengkraipetch remarked that it is difficult to define the Thai 'us', the essential ingredient for Thai authenticity. She concluded that it is much easier to write about others. For example, she points to Rama I's *Inao* that identifies the *khaek* (Javanese Muslim) as people who 'did not eat pork'.⁸⁵ However, 'eating pork' is not an exclusive Thai characteristic. We know who 'we' are without thinking about it. We also define ourselves by knowing who we are not. The three novels that I have analysed clearly define the Thai 'us' and the foreign 'other'. The vernacular nature of the novels and their Thai authors make them accessible to just 'us' Thais. To reiterate, novels written originally in the Thai vernacular by Thai authors are quintessentially Thai, no different from *kaeng khiew wan kai* (chicken green curry) pizza, which I consider to be a Thai dish.

Some may argue that Khru Liam is just an opportunist, a fake *farang*, and no better than a mimic. But unlike colonial subjects writing in the language of the Metropole to be shared with those educated in their master's language, Khru Liam's work is in the vernacular accessible to a large number of literate Thai. It would be difficult to accuse him of mimicking the hegemonic culture of the West. Even though he had studied in England and would occasionally dress as an odd Englishman in Bangkok, he was far from being a colonial subject mimicking his master. In the colonies, subjects with pretensions who mimicked the mannerisms of their masters were seen as 'almost, but not quite'. They were loathed by fellow natives and masters alike.⁸⁶

Thongchai Winichakul interprets Khru Liam's *Nang neramit* postscript as the semi-colonial subaltern's declaration of freedom and autonomy from Western hegemony. In that postscript, Khru Liam chides his Thai

---

85 Suvanna Kriengkraipetch, 'Characters in Thai literary works', in Manas chitakasem, *Thai literary traditions* (Bangkok: Chulalongkorn University Press, 1995), 135. Suvanna concluded that 'the concept of "the otherness" helps to understand and then to define ourselves as belonging to a particular group'. She agreed with a colleague who she quoted that being Thai was not a set of criteria, but a lifelong process (Kriengkraipetch, 'Characters', 145–6). Another famous assault on Thai identity is Sujit Wongthes, *Jek pon lao* [*Chinese mixed with Lao*] (Bangkok: Silapa Watthanatham, 1987), which suggested that modern Thai identity is a hybrid of Chinese and Laotian cultures. Recently, a friend told me that the Cambodians see the modern Thai as someone who 'looks Chinese, acts like a *farang*, and speaks Thai laced with Khmer'.
86 On the subject of mimicry, see Homi K. Bhabha, 'Of mimicry and man: The ambivalence of colonial discourse', in *The location of culture* (New York: Routledge, 1994). The pitfalls of mimicry and imitation are not new to the Thai. These concerns were voiced by King Vajiravudh (1910–1925) in his short article *Latthi ao yang* [*Imitation cult*], where he warned the Thai people about how to retain their own Thai culture in the face of encroaching Westernisation. He wrote that for the Thai to appear European was comparable to a dog learning to sit. The human owner may think that the dog was cute because it exhibited human qualities, but yet it was still a dog. Similarly, a Thai who emulated the Englishman may gain the empathy of the English but that only emphasised the superiority of Europeans. King Vajiravudh urged the Thai to appropriate only what was only needed to modernise Thailand and not to try to become an Englishman. See *Latthi ao yang*, n.d. in the *Cremation volume of Khanet Rueksaphailin*, Wat Somanatwiharn, 3 December 1975. I am indebted to Craig J. Reynolds for suggesting this reference.

readers that if they were looking for the original *farang* novel ostensibly written by a good *farang* novelist, they will not find him or her. Instead, they are left with only that novel and Khru Liam who is just as good, if not better than the *farang*. Thongchai and I agree that Thailand's semi-colonial status allowed the Thai more freedom to be among the earliest to express postcolonial sentiments and to exercise postcolonial resistance.[87]

In Khru Liam's case, his hybridity, that is, his outward appearance and his ability to mimic a *farang* or a *farang* author, could be accepted as 'clever'. The foreign-educated Thai, even those who shamelessly emulate the lifestyle of the *farang* today, are still accepted as a valued and privileged class. Returning *nakrian nok* (students educated abroad) continue to be the stars of Thai society. They are not considered 'hybrids', but 'bicultural'— Thais who are comfortable in both Thai and Western culture.

Postcolonial theorists who seek the precolonial condition tend to treat colonisation negatively and to view translation as an instrument of empire. Others like Rafael, who celebrate hybridity, tend to see translation as a 'highly supple and creative channel of mutual and self-transformation'.[88] In the Thai case, its semi-coloniality allowed for a lesser disruption and a less distinctive demarcation of precolonial, colonial and postcolonial conditions. The Thai elite was able to engage in a domestic project of translation (vernacularisation) that turned translation and imitation into anti-hegemonic instruments of self-affirmation, self-interpellation, and resistance against empire.

To conclude, the Thai literary engagement in translation, composition, and imitation of Western novels during the height of Western colonialism in Southeast Asia is a strategy for the semi-colonial subaltern Thai to speak or talk back against Western hegemony.[89] The three novels identified in

---

87   Thongchai Winichakul observed that if we were to employ a postcolonial lens to look at *Nang neramit*, then Khru Liam's tactic of engaging the West would be an elaborate dance of deception by a subaltern to declare postcolonial independence from Western domination. Remarks made by Thongchai Winichakul, Council of Thai Studies Conference, University of Wisconsin, Madison, 1 December 2007. Thailand's semi-coloniality was a subject of 'The Ambiguous Allure of the West' conference held at Cornell University, 5–7 November 2004. Peter Jackson's conference paper 'Semi-coloniality and duality in Siam's relations with the West', raised important questions about the place of Thailand and Thai studies in postcolonial studies; Rachel Harrison and Peter A. Jackson, eds, *The ambiguous allure of the West: Traces of the colonial in Thailand* (Hong Kong: Hong Kong University Press and Ithaca: Cornell Southeast Asia Program Publications, 2010).
88   Douglas Robinson, *Translation and empire* (Manchester: St Jerome Publishing, 1997), 84.
89   Gayatri Chakravorty Spivak, 'Can the subaltern speak?' in *Marxism and the interpretation of culture*, ed. Cary Nelson and Lawrence Grossberg (Urbana: University of Illinois Press, 1988), 271–313.

this essay, no less than the three canonical ones, have appropriated the *rupatham* of the Western literary form, and by inserting Thai *namatham* their authors have made their novels Thai. Mae Wan's *Khwam phayabat*, and Khru Liam's *Khwam mai phayabat* and *Nang neramit* should be included in the canon of Thai literature as exemplary examples of the translated or vernacularised novel, the overlooked original Thai novel, and the dismissed imitative novel. A full accounting of the early novels predating 1929 will help us better understand the importance of the novel in preparing Thailand for modernity and for resistance against the negative effects of Western culture. And, more importantly, unlike elsewhere in Southeast Asia where many indigenous novels are written in the imperial language, the Thai novel is written in the vernacular and consumed locally. The Thai resistance against bad Western cultural influence and hegemony is exercised without the full knowledge of the West because vernacular Thai novels are not generally accessible to Westerners.[90]

---

90 The first Anglicised Filipino novel, Zoilo M. Galang's *A child of sorrow* appeared in 1921. By 1966, production of Filipino English novels exceeded those written in India, Singapore and Malaya. See Abdul Majid Bin Babi Baksh, *The Filipino novel in English* (Quezon City: The University of the Philippines, 1970), 3. Anglicised novels were not exclusively consumed by the indigenous, but they were more or less open to the world, very much in the tradition of Jose Rizal's *Noli me tangere* and *El filibusterismo*, which were written in Spanish for fellow Filipino intellectuals but were also accessible to the Spanish authorities. It should also be noted that vernacular novels in Tagalog appeared soon after the defeat of Spain by the United States. These novels were written by journalists and typesetters who combined local literary forms with the novel introduced by Rizal. Resil Mojares believes that the defeat of a repressive colonial Spanish regime freed the Tagalog mentally to allow them to write novels in the vernacular. However, those novels found limited circulation because Tagalog was a language limited to speakers around Manila. It is more recently that Filipinos have embraced Tagalog as their national language. Resil B. Mojares, *Origins and rise of the Filipino novel: A generic study of the novel until 1940* (Quezon City: University of the Philippines Press, 1998) cited in Shirlita A. Espinosa, 'Ethnicity and kinship in Filipino centennial novels', *Kyoto review of Southeast Asia*, 8 (March 2008), no pagination.

2
Racing and the construction of Thai nationalism

Prince Chula Chakrabongse and Prince Birabongse Bhanudej were sent to England to study at Harrow and Eton in the 1920s. They lived as Thai princes among the English upper class and indulged in the pastimes of that class, such as athletics, flying and motor car racing. Bira became a successful race car driver on the White Mouse Racing Team, managed by Chula. He even won the Gold Star, awarded to the best 'British' race car driver, in three consecutive years: 1936, 1937 and 1938. His achievements were celebrated in Thailand as a sign of national greatness and of Thailand's parity with the West. Racing was, and still is, closely associated with the nation. Bira and Chula's story contributes to the study of the top-down construction of Thai nationalism. Thai nationalism is not about an armed struggle against colonial oppressors. It is about mastering Western civilisation in attempts to appear equal. It is a nationalism closely associated with the monarchy, members of the royal family, aristocrats and bureaucratic servants of the Crown.

On 9 January 1988, a very strange event took place in the heart of old Bangkok. Fourteen vintage race cars were transported from secure military compounds to the Royal Equestrian Plaza for display and later to race up and down the Ratchadamnoen—the Royal Boulevard. There was much excitement and mayhem, as security was quite lax and no one really knew what to make of the sight of such old cars. The drivers and mechanics were all Caucasians, and the lone female driver, who looked European, spoke perfect Thai. Stern-looking military policemen provided what security there was, along with transportation. Thai spectators lined the two sides of the boulevard; many also walked freely among the staging race cars. A week later, the cars would also race at the Pattaya International Race Circuit near the famous beach resort town of Pattaya. For the occasion, the race circuit was renamed the 'Bira International Race Circuit' to honour Thailand's only successful international race car driver.[1]

This 1988 event on Ratchadamnoen was a 're-enactment' of the Bangkok Grand Prix International Motor Race that was supposed to take place on 10 December 1939. Race car teams and drivers from Europe committed to participate in that race in Bangkok. Posters designed by Prince Birabongse Bhanudej (Phiraphongphanudet, 1914–85) were printed, and an elaborate Thai silver cup was made especially for the grand occasion. The Bangkok Grand Prix was the brainchild of Prince Chula Chakrabongse (Chulachakraphong, 1908–63) and Prince Birabongse.[2] The two Thai princes had been sent to England to study and to learn the ways of the West. They became bicultural and bilingual Thais, and were two of the original Westernised Oriental Gentlemen, or WOGs.[3] Unfortunately, the Bangkok Grand Prix never took place because the outbreak of the Second World War interrupted it.[4]

One of the activities in which the two princes indulged while in the United Kingdom was automotive racing. They fielded a Thai racing ream—the White Mouse Racing Team—beginning in 1935. This team

---

1   Sanphasiri Wiriyasiri, comp., *Jao dara thong phu phlik prawattisat* [*The golden star who changed history*] (Bangkok: Grand Prix International, 1988), 70. A videotaped recording of the event has been released under the title *Romulus returns to Siam* (Isle of Man: Duke Marketing, 2011). Automobile racing is still popular in Thailand today and several new racing circuits have been built. The most modern facility is now in Buriram, built by the politician Newin Chitchob.
2   This chapter refers to the two princes as Chula and Bira. The name that Bira used during his racing career was B. Bira. At times, he was also known as Prince Bira. Prince Chula authored many books, using several versions of his name. These included Prince Chula Chakrabongse, HRH Prince Chula of Siam, Phrajao worawongthoe phraongjao Chulachakrabongse and others. Citations to his works in this chapter reflect the different versions of his name under which the prince published.
3   Craig Reynolds and I once toyed with the idea that we should write about Thai Westernised Oriental Gentlemen (WOGs) because through them we might better understand Thai culture. The original term WOG may have been used in British India to refer to natives who were 'worthy oriental gentlemen', although Reynolds now tells me that this etymology and others similar are false. In postcolonial parlance, WOGs are despised by their own people for wanting to be like their colonial masters. Yet they are seen by their masters as mimics who are 'almost but not quite'. But, in the Thai case, the WOGs are Thai princes sent to study in Europe who became models of modernity and sophistication to be emulated. Even today, fully Westernised Thais are esteemed and not ridiculed. For a discussion of mimicry, see Homi K. (Homi K. Bhabha) Bhabha, *The location of culture* (London: Routledge, 1994), especially Chapter 4.
4   Twelve drivers had committed to race in the Bangkok Grand Prix. They were from France, Germany, Great Britain, Holland, Italy, Switzerland and Bira from Thailand: Prince Chula of Siam, *Blue and yellow: Being an account of two seasons of B. Bira, the racing motorist, 1939 and 1946* (London: G. T. Foulis, 1947), 92–3.

was most active in 1936, 1937 and 1938 until the Second World War interrupted its activities. After hostilities ended, Bira continued to race into the 1950s during the early years of Grand Prix Formula One events. He drove for several teams, but less successfully than in the prewar period. His name and exploits are chronicled in most books about the early days of automobile racing.[5]

This chapter introduces the two princes and their racing successes in Europe. It contextualises their experiences in the Thai public's perception of the West, of modernity and of nationalism. Unlike neighbouring countries such as Indonesia, the Philippines and Vietnam, each of which struggles against how Western colonialism defined nationalism, in Thailand, nationalism was based on an embrace and mastery of Western modernity and on harnessing that modernity to raise the nation to an equivalent level of civilisation.[6]

Thai nationalism is thus top-down nationalism, constructed by members of the royal, aristocratic and political elites with little input from below. The successes of the two princes in racing and the celebration of their exploits by the post-1932 civilian–military People's Party regime in Bangkok reinforced top-down nationalism. This nationalism is still manifest today in the close connection between the nation on the one hand, and the monarchy and the 'good and morally superior' aristocracy and bureaucrats who serve the Crown on the other. The people are thus consumers of Thai nationalism, rather than active participants in its construction. During the 1988 enactment of the race that never happened, the Thai government was also proud to point out that Siam or Thailand was the first Asian country to be involved in international motor racing. This affirmation of national pride and nationalism underlined the close association of Thai nationalism with the monarchy and the exploits of members of the royal family.

---

5   Peter Stevenson, *Driving forces: The Grand Prix racing world caught in the maelstrom of the Third Reich* (Cambridge, MA: Bentley, 2000), 187–93; Robert Grey Reynolds Jr, *Prince Bira* (Smashwords ebook, 2016); Bruce Jones, ed., *The ultimate encyclopedia of Formula One* (Osceola, WI: 1995), 133.
6   Scot Barmé, *Luang Wichit Wathakan and the creation of a Thai identity* (Singapore: Institute of Southeast Asian Studies, 1993); Saichon Sattayanurak, *Khwamplianplaeng nai kansang 'chat thai' lae 'khwampen thai' doi luang wichit watthakan* [Changes in Wichit Watthakan's construction of 'the Thai nation' and 'Thainess'] (Bangkok: Matichon, 2002); Walter Vella, *Chaiyo! King Vajiravudh and the development of Thai nationalism* (Honolulu: University of Hawai'i Press, 1978). See also Chapter 1 in this volume.

The Bangkok Grand Prix of 1939

The year 1988 was significant because it brought King Bhumibol Adulyadej's 60th birthday, the important and auspicious completion of his fifth 12-year cycle. General Prem Tinsulanonda, who served as prime minister as the year began, was a major promoter of the authority and influence of the Crown in helping to maintain political stability—especially as an institution to counterbalance the growing political power of elected civilian politicians.[7] Prem, and perhaps the king, believed that the military still had a role to play in Thai politics, and that the prime minister need not be elected. The Crown and senior military officers were distrustful of the new class of politicians, whose wealth built political parties that contested the power of the military–monarchy alliance put into place by the regime of Field Marshal Sarit Thanarat in the early 1960s.[8]

Appointed prime minister with the firm support of the palace, General Prem weathered coups led by young army officers in 1981 and 1985.[9] The coup in 1981 was especially significant because Prem was able to escape from Bangkok to the headquarters of Thailand's Second Army Region in Nakhon Ratchasima, accompanied by the royal family. It was from that city that the queen broadcast a message on radio supporting Prem. From that time until the present, Prem has been most loyal to the palace. After the elected Prime Minister Chatchai Chunhawan replaced him in mid-1988, the king appointed Prem to the Privy Council. Soon afterwards, he received the title Statesman (*ratthaburut*). Pridi Phanomyong (1900–83) was the only other Thai ever to have held this title.

To honour the king's 60th birthday in 1987, Prem was willing to expend enormous government resources. He also led the popular call to confer the title *maharat*, or The Great, on King Bhumibol. This title had only been used to refer to King Ramkamhaeng (r. 1279–98), King Taksin

---

7   Munlanithi ratthaburut (The Statesman Foundation), *Ratthaburut chue Prem [A statesman named Prem]* (Bangkok: Matichon, 1995).
8   Duncan McCargo, ed., *Reforming Thai politics* (Copenhagen: NIAS Press, 2002), 1–12. The standard text on the Sarit regime is Thak Chaloemtiarana, *Thailand: The politics of despotic paternalism* (Ithaca: Cornell Southeast Asia Program Publications, 2007; revised edition).
9   Chai-anan Samudavanija, *The Thai young Turks* (Singapore: Institute of Southeast Asian Studies, 1982); Suchit Bunbongkarn, *The military in Thai politics, 1981–1986* (Singapore: Institute of Southeast Asian Studies, 1987).

(r. 1767–82) and King Chulalongkorn (r. 1868–1910). King Bhumibol also enjoyed the title of *maharat jao haeng kankila* (Great King of Sport), a reference to the king's successes as a fierce competitor in sailing events.[10]

Before his untimely death in a London Underground station on 23 December 1985, Prince Bira had wanted to recreate the never-staged Bangkok Grand Prix to honour the king. He had discussed his idea with Sanphasiri Wiriyasiri, a well-known media personality.[11] Sanphasiri later established a museum commemorating Bira and his racing career at Bangkok's Chatuchak Park.[12] With Bira deceased, Sanphasiri suggested this event to General Chaowalit Yongchaiyut, the newly appointed army commander-in-chief.[13]

By 1987, General Chaowalit had begun to position himself to replace General Prem as a future national political leader. He was already army chief, and the unofficial head of the faction of generals known as the 'Democratic Soldiers' who had put together Prem's successful strategy to weaken the Communist Party of Thailand and bring disillusioned students back from the jungles.[14] Chaowalit also had family ties to the palace. This last fact became clearer to the public when the army decided to organise the Bangkok Grand Prix to honour King Bhumibol.

General Chaowalit promoted the event as a celebration of the king's prowess as a great sportsman. He also pointed out that both Prince Bira and Prince Chula were military men, having served as officers in the Palace Guard.[15] More importantly, their royal fathers—Field Marshal Prince Bhanurangsi and Field Marshal Prince Chakrabongse—had helped to build the modern Thai army. Prince Bhanurangsi was a younger full brother of King Chulalongkorn; Prince Chakrabongse was the favourite son of King Chulalongkorn, born to one of his major queens, Queen Soawabha.

---

10   Sanphasiri et al., *The golden star*, 37.
11   Sanphasiri was the main author of the commemorative volume *Jao dara thong phu phlik prawattisat* [*The golden star that changed history*] (1988).
12   The one time that I visited the museum, it was closed. Through the grimy glass windows I could see a shrine to honour Bira and some very dusty memorabilia. It was as if to say that all his achievements had been forgotten.
13   Sanphasiri et al., *The golden star*, 6.
14   Suchit, *The military in Thai politics*, Chapter 50.
15   Prince Bira was given a military appointment as first lieutenant in the Thai army after winning the Gold Star award for his racing (*Prachachat*, 17 November 1937).

General Chaowalit, a commoner, is nonetheless related to Prince Bira through Bira's commoner mother, whose family name was Yongchaiyut.[16] Therefore, with General Chaowalit's endorsement, the 14 race cars, their drivers and crew were able to bypass the usual bureaucratic red tape that would have blocked such an event.

The most special car was Prince Bira's 1935 ERA (English Racing Automobile) R2B race car that he campaigned with from 1935 to 1947. Momratchawong Narisa Chakrabongse, Prince Chula's only daughter, now owns this car, which is on display at the Toy and Model Museum in London. It was the sixth race car of only 17 that the ERA company produced before it folded in 1939 at the beginning of the Second World War. Bira named his first race car Romulus. He bought a sister—or, perhaps more appropriately, brother—car shortly after as a spare; it was called Remus. Romulus and Remus sported the Bira hyacinth blue colour on their bodies, while their chassis and wheels were painted yellow, symbolising the Thai royal house of Chakri.[17] These colours became known later as the Thai racing colours. During the early days of racing, each nation chose its 'racing colours'. The modern Thai red, white and blue flag was also painted on the hood and rear quarter of Bira's racing cars. A whimsical cartoon caricature of a white mouse standing on its hind legs also appeared on the cowling that protected the side mirror on the driver's left. The Thai team was known as White Mouse Racing, playing on Prince Chula's Thai nickname Nu, meaning 'mouse'. I am not certain whether 'white' was an ironic reference to his complexion, which was quite different from other Thai because Prince Chula's mother was Russian.[18]

A short passage from a 1964 book covering seven decades of Grand Prix motor racing gives testament to Bira's achievements.

---

16   A simplified chart of Chula and Bira's family tree appears in Princess Ceril Birabongse, *The prince and I: Life with the motor racing Prince of Siam* (Dorset: Veloce, 1992), 5.

17   At the start of his career, Bira raced under the auspices of the British Racing Drivers' Club. A few years later, Thailand became the first Asian member of the International Automobile Association, which sanctioned races in Europe. Because the colour blue was already claimed by France, Thailand chose blue and yellow instead. The blue colour was from a dress worn by a Danish girl whom Chula and Bira met at a restaurant. They asked her for a small piece of the dress and she obliged: Prince Chula of Thailand (Prince Chulachakrabongse), *Wheels at speed* (London: G.T. Foulis, 1946), 16.

18   Chula's mother was Ekaterina Ivanova Desnitsky. The story of his father and mother's relationship can be found in Eileen Hunter and Narisa Chakrabongse, *Katya and the Prince of Siam* (Bangkok: River Books, 1994). Another good source for Chula's life is Narisa Chakrabongse, *100 pi chunchakraphong 1908–2008* [*The centenary of Chulachakrabongse 1908–2008*] (Bangkok: River Books, 2008), which includes a foreword by his daughter Narisa.

The remarkable successes of the Chula-Bira equipe have been modestly chronicled by Prince Chula in his four books … and these together with Bira's own contribution, *Bits and Pieces*, give a very interesting and well-balanced account of racing during the years 1935–1946. Although Bira only started racing in 1935, he rapidly gained an international reputation, whether at the wheel of an ERA, Maserati, BMW, or Delahaye, winning many races during 1936–1939. In the three immediate post-war years the Chula-Bira equipe ran with limited success, and towards the end of 1948 the partnership was dissolved. In 1949, Bira drove a 1½ litre 4CLT Maserati for the Plate Stable in a great many events, being first in the Swedish Grand Prix, second at San Remao, Mar del Plata, Albi (France), Perpignana (Juan Manuel Fangio won first), and the Grand Prix of France, and third at Zandvoort and in the European Grand Prix. Bira was an extremely polished and tremendously fast driver, more than capable of holding his own with the best.[19]

In November 1987, Romulus arrived in Bangkok by Thai International air freight and was received with great respect and honour. The car was placed in a specially constructed pavilion, draped with auspicious garlands and ultimately blessed by the Supreme Patriarch of Thai Buddhism himself. The Thai automotive magazine *Grand Prix* celebrated the return of Romulus to Bangkok after a 50-year absence by proclaiming that the car 'represent[ed] the bravery and superiority of the whole Thai nation'.[20] Later sections of this chapter explore the symbolism of the car, Bira's achievements and their relationship with Thai nationalism.

Most of the drivers and owners of the cars flown to Bangkok for the January 1988 event were men from England, the United States and Australia. The only female driver was Narisa Chakrabongse, the owner of Romulus—Bira's most successful race car. Because her mother was English and her father was half-Thai and half-Russian, she was three-quarters European. However, she spoke impeccable Thai, much to the astonishment of the Thai spectators, as we can see in the video *Romulus returns to Siam*. The presence of *luk khrueng*—Thais of mixed heritage—is today not unusual, as they have found a niche in the Thai entertainment and modelling businesses. But it was unusual to come across an older *luk khrueng* in the late 1980s, especially one who appeared more European than Thai but spoke perfect Thai. Narisa's background meant that the only

---

19 George Monkhouse and Roland King-Farlow, *Grand Prix racing: Facts and figures, 1894–1963* (London: G.T. Foulis, 1964), 158.
20 'Rot khan ni khue tua thaen khwamyingyong khong khon thai thang chat' ['This car represents the greatness of the entire Thai nation'], *Grand Prix*, 17(6) (1987): 65–8.

'Thai' among the group of drivers was the lone female and that perhaps the only obvious outward sign that identified her as 'Thai' was her ability to speak the language.

Narisa pushed the boundaries of what it means to be Thai even further than her father had, with his own ambiguous identity. Prince Chula had inherited European looks from his mother. Had his mother been a Thai, he would have been in line for accession to the throne after the abdication of his uncle, King Prachathipok, in 1935. Prince Chula at times expressed his bitterness about not being fully Thai.[21] More European-looking than her father, Narisa epitomises the central argument of this chapter: Thai nationalism is an embrace of European or Western culture. It is grounded in the ability of the Thai elite to 'pass' as culturally European. That elite, and the Thais more broadly, are therefore equal to their Western counterparts. This is the nationalism that is passed on to the rest of the population, people outside the elite, for their consumption.

Of the 14 race cars used in the January 1988 event in Bangkok, five were cars that Bira had raced. Three of the cars made famous by Bira's exploits were ERA race cars. The most famous of the three were the first pair of ERA cars that Prince Chula had bought for Bira. Giving the cars names reflected the heritage of the owners, whose forebears had given royal war elephants, barges, coaches and automobiles elaborate names suited to the chariots of kings. The gods in Thai and Hindu mythology had mighty steeds with formidable names. Why not then give names to the modern chariots of kings and princes?

---

21   According to Bira's first wife, Ceril Heycock, Chula was unhappy that his mother remarried after his father's death. He allegedly remarked that his chances of becoming king were diminished now that his mother was married to an American; Ceril Birabongse, *The prince and I*, 20. The jury is still out on whether Chula wanted to be king. It is revealing, however, that his uncle, the future King Prachathipok, wrote a letter to Chula asking him never to think about this possibility. This letter was written in English, a fact that reinforces the notion of the ambiguous identity of the royals raised in this article. The following is a relevant quotation from that letter of 26 June 1929:

> You asked me whether you will be allowed to have any responsible post when you return. Of course you will. What I meant was that you must never think of occupying the throne. I doubt what are your ambitions, but I only wish to warn you about one ambition that you will have to put away forever for you and yours …

(Narisa, *100 pi chunchakraphong*, 66–7). The letter also reflects the growing tension between Chula and this uncle. In contrast, his other uncle, King Vajiravudh, doted on Chula. Vajiravudh's letters to Chula were always warm, in Thai, and ended with 'From your uncle who loves Nu [Chula's nickname].' Prachathipok did not like the fact that his elder brother, Chula's father, had married a foreigner. His letter of 29 June 1929 ended with, 'I wish you would address me as "Dear Uncle" as you used to'. Vajiravudh's letters to Chula appear in Narisa, *100 pi chunchakraphong*, 58–61.

Perhaps conscious or subconscious symbolism figured in the selection of the names Romulus and Remus for this pair of race cars, relating to the Thai princes' control or conquest of the best of Europe (Rome) in international competition. Romulus was the first successful race car driven by Bira. He used Remus sparingly and also as a source of spare parts for Romulus until it was sold to new owners, who continued to race it in vintage races.[22] It still sports the red, white and blue Thai flag on its left flank. The Bangkok Grand Prix of 1988 was the first time in decades that the two cars were reunited.

Another ERA car that saw some success in races was a later and more powerful model. The princes gave it the name 'Hanuman' after the mythical monkey warrior in the *Ramayana*. Bira won five races with this car during 1938–39. The car was hard to control, and Bira thought that it was *kere* (unruly). Hence its name, Hanuman. The anthropomorphised race car was said to have gone berserk (*phlaeng rit*) in July 1939 when it flew off the track, barely missed hitting a tree and landed in a bush.[23] Bira walked away unscathed and unperturbed. The European press reported this incident and expressed awe at how calm and serene Bira had been.[24] The car was later sold to the team mechanic who restored and raced it.

The fourth among Bira's and Chula's race cars that came to Thailand for the 1988 event was a Delage race car made in France. The famous English driver Richard Seaman, who went on to European Grand Prix fame, had raced this car. Seaman was hired by the Mercedes Benz racing team, which was subsidised by Hitler. But in 1936, the newcomer Prince Bira in fact outscored Seaman in the competition for the prestigious Road Racing Gold Star award of the British Racing Drivers' Club.[25] Subsequently, Chula bought Seaman's Delage and replaced its 1500cc eight-cylinder engine with a 2000cc six-cylinder engine made by ERA.

---

22 Sanphasiri, *The golden star*, 49.
23 Prince Birabongse of Thailand, *Bits and pieces: Being motor racing recollections of 'B. Bira'* (London: G.T. Foulis, 1942), 11–15. Bira treated his cars as if they had souls and not as inanimate objects. He remarked that this was why he was successful as a race car driver; he really understood and could communicate with his cars. In his 1942 book, Bira made line drawings of his race cars with faces and limbs and in poses in which they interacted with him as driver and friend.
24 On 23 August 1936, King Ananda Mahidol (Rama VIII), Prince Bhumibol Adulyadej, Princess Galyani Vadhana and the Princess Mother attended a race to see Bira perform. Unfortunately, Bira's car suffered mechanical problems while he was leading the race. A picture of the king at this race was published in Bangkok and widely circulated. Bira kept this picture in his wallet until his death. This picture of the three siblings with Bira and an accompanying account appear in Sanphasiri, *The golden star*, 24–5.
25 Prince Chula of Thailand, *Dick Seaman: Racing motorist* (London: G.T. Foulis, 1948), 100.

Bira and Chula had also once owned the fifth car entered in the 1988 race, the Italian Maserati race car that they had bought in 1936. Bira won two races in that car and placed second eight times. The car was sold soon after the end of the Second World War. By 1988, its owner was an Englishman living in the United States. He had bought the car for £350,000 just before the Bangkok Grand Prix so he could participate in it.[26] The car still sported the painted caricature of a smiling white mouse standing on its hind legs, the symbol of Chula's White Mouse Racing Team.

The remaining cars in the 1988 field were an MG K3 Magnet similar to the one that Bira had used to start his racing career, four Bugattis (Type 51), an Alfa Romeo P3 (monoposto) and a 1939 BMW 328.

On 9 January 1988, the 14 cars raced up and down Ratchadamnoen Boulevard as an exhibition for the public to witness. This theatrical display was reminiscent of the demonstration that Bira gave on 5 December 1937, when he was invited back to Bangkok to show off Romulus to the adoring Bangkok public.[27] Bira blasted up and down the Royal Boulevard to the delight of the spectators, who were lined thickly along the two sides of the road. Although Narisa re-enacted Bira's original display of speed, the two events proved quite different.

There seemed to be less interest and less bewilderment the second time around. Perhaps the only bewilderment was that the re-enactment lacked the patriotic, even nationalistic meaning intended in the original. The demonstration was anachronistic and seemed out of place—a handful of old race cars, roaring up and down Ratchadamnoen at speeds that most Bangkok cabbies could match. The drivers were also all *farang*, or Caucasian, including a Thai woman who looked *farang*. It was quite a leap to connect this fanfare to the celebration of the prowess of King Bhumibol, the 'Great King of Sports'.[28]

---

26 Sanphasiri, *The golden star*, 55.
27 Phrajao worawongsthoe phraongjao junjakraphong (Prince Chulachakrabongse), *Thai chana: rueang kankhaengkhan khong pho phira nakkhaprot Thai nai yurop* [*Thai victorious: The racing of B. Bira, a Thai race car driver in Europe*] (Bangkok: Thainitthi, 1973), 169–72.
28 The king's interest in fast cars was once again obvious when, on 18 December 2010, the Australian driver Mark Webber brought the winning Formula One Red Bull race car to Siriraj Hospital for the king to see. The Red Bull energy drink was invented in Thailand. Mark Webber also drove that race car up and down Ratchadamnoen Boulevard, just as Bira did in 1937 (*Bangkok post*, 18 December 2010). The appearance of the Formula One car was part of the celebrations for the king's 83rd birthday.

To top it off, the final garden reception for the participants in the 1988 event was a private affair held on the grounds of the British Embassy on Wireless Road. The statue of a seated Queen Victoria loomed over the guests, again somewhat anachronistically in 20th-century Bangkok. The scene suggested gentler times, a colonial era when the British were still lords and masters of the Orient, and when Thai royalty emulated the British and their pastimes in an attempt to appear *siwilai* (civilised) and *than samai* (modern).[29]

The royals, their toys and mastery of the modern

Maurizio Peleggi's provocative book, *Lords of things*, argued that the Thai royalty's acquisition of gadgets, flatware, art, technology and other objects was a way to project the self-image of an emerging modernising elite.[30] It was also a way for members of that royal elite to make a place for themselves among the other royals of the world. In a sense, the Thai royals wanted to appear the same as their counterparts in Europe. By demonstrating to the Thai people that they looked like modern, universal—read, European—royals, they were ipso facto the equals of the Europeans, the harbingers of modernity. This assumed equality was problematic because it was never clear if the European royalty accepted the Thai royalty as equals.[31]

---

29 *Siwilai* resonates with civilised, a Thai appropriation for what is considered high international culture; see Chapter 1, this volume, note 1. In the early 20th century, this meant British culture. The garden party at the end of the races recalled times for which there was considerable nostalgia. See Duke Marketing, *Romulus returns to Siam*.
30 Maurizio Peleggi, *Lords of things: The fashioning of the Siamese monarchy's modern image* (Honolulu: University of Hawai'i Press, 2002).
31 Having previously based its legitimacy on mythological Hindu gods, the late 19th and early 20th-century Thai monarchy had to deal with a modern ideal of kingship. The main models were no longer Asian but European. King Chulalongkorn's trips to Europe, visits with European monarchs, the acquisition of the trappings of European culture and the king's decision to send his sons to study in Europe demonstrated the shift in the way that the Thai monarchy viewed its own future. The king's sentiments may be glimpsed in *Phraratchaniphon rueang klai ban* [*Far from home*] (Bangkok: Sophonphatthana thanakan, 1923). Pictures of ruling monarchs that appear in European magazines or postcards would include the non-European monarchs of China, Japan and Siam. But in most instances, the major European monarchs appear in pictures larger than the others. This photographic depiction clearly hints that Chulalongkorn was accepted by other monarchs but perhaps not as an equal. See, for example, Nana Krailoek, *Bueanglang phrabatsomdet phrachulachomklao jaoyuhua sadet praphat yurop* [*Fact about King Chulalongkorn's visit to Europe*] (Bangkok: Sinlapawatthanatham, 2006), 18–19, 193.

Prince Chula was born in 1908, the son of Prince Chakrabongse, who was third in line to the throne. Prince Chakrabongse had been sent to Russia to study military science in response to a remark made by Czar Nicolas II to King Chulalongkorn, asking that the latter send a son to study in Russia.[32] After finishing military school, Prince Chakrabongse became an officer in the Russian army. He subsequently fell in love with a Russian woman, and they married without the king's consent. Had he asked for permission and had the king refused, Prince Chakrabongse would have had to obey his father's wishes. After returning to live in Thailand, the couple had a son, Chula Chakrabongse, who grew up under the watchful eyes of his grandmother, Queen Saowabha, two of whose sons would become Rama VI and Rama VII. Had Prince Chakrabongse lived longer, he might have been considered for the throne, with the possible objection that his wife was Russian.

Prince Chula's own account suggested that his grandfather, King Chulalongkorn, accepted him but that he was not among the king's favourite grandchildren.[33] Later in life, it was his uncle, King Vajiravudh, or Rama VI (r. 1910–25), who would be his patron. By the time of Prince Chula's birth, Bangkok had already become a nascent centre of modernity. King Chulalongkorn was determined to make Thailand modern, like the Western countries that he had visited and admired for their technological and military achievements. He believed that, if Thailand appeared to be modern like the West, the colonial powers would have fewer reasons to want to save Thailand from itself.[34]

Chulalongkorn's court became the centre of symbols of modernity. It adopted European couture, cutlery and dinnerware, furniture and art as decoration. English words soon inserted themselves into the speech patterns of the royals and educated elite. Consumption of all things Western, especially technological gadgets and machines, became symbols of modernity. And among these technological wonders was the motor car.

---

32   Royal Thai Embassy, Moscow, and Boon Rawd Trading International, *From your friend: 110 years of relations between Thailand and Russia* (Bangkok: Amarin Printing, 2007), 34–6; HRH Prince Chula (Prince Chulachakrabongse), *Brought up in England* (London: G.T. Foulis, 1943), 11.
33   Chulachakrabongse, *Brought up in England*, 18–20.
34   For a short account of the reforms instituted by King Mongkut and King Chulalongkorn, see David K. Wyatt, *Thailand: A short history* (New Haven: Yale University Press, 1982), especially Chapter 7.

The motor car was an especially powerful representation of modernity and power. Its complicated mechanical components, loud noise and immense power conveyed a sense of awe and excitement. While the majority of the Thai population still walked without shoes and rode horse- or water buffalo–drawn carts or buggies, the royals paraded up and down newly constructed avenues in Bangkok in their automobiles.[35] This parade of cars became 'spectacles of modernity' that were hard to ignore.[36]

After returning from his visit to Europe in 1897, Chulalongkorn was determined to transform Bangkok into a modern city. He built a new palace precinct, the Dusit Garden City, whose compound was crisscrossed with paved roads for the motor car—a model of the modern city. One of the earliest memories that Prince Chula had of his grandfather was a chance encounter in Dusit Palace. The king was trying out his new yellow electric car and stopped to talk to the young prince.[37] Soon after, the king gave Chula a red two-seater pedal car.

In addition to being driven along the roads in the Dusit Palace compound, these new motor cars needed to be displayed to the greater population. A new boulevard—named Ratchadamnoen, or the Royal Boulevard, and meant to imitate the grand boulevards of Europe—linked Dusit Palace and its surrounding aristocratic suburb to the Grand Palace. And as early as 1905, members of the royal family and aristocracy would parade up and down this boulevard as spectacles of modernity—a theatrical display of their consumption and mastery of Western technology. Commoners would line up on the two sides of the road to take in the sights, the signs and the symbolism of Thailand's entry into the modern world.[38]

---

35 Steve Van Beek, *Royal automobile stables of Siam* (Bangkok: Castrol Thailand, 1994), 19–31.
36 Marc Askew, *Bangkok: Place, practice and representation* (New York: Routledge, 2002), 35.
37 Chulachakrabongse, *Thai victorious*, 43–4. Chula disputes the popular belief that his grandfather, King Chulalongkorn, did not accept him fully. His grandmother and uncles doted on him. This was especially true of King Vajiravudh, who gave Chula his formal name and even elevated his title from Mom Chao to Phraongjao. The latter title was reserved for the children of a king's legitimate son, but, because Chula's mother was Russian, he had been demoted by one royal rank.
38 Askew asserts that King Chulalongkorn became the supreme consumer of modern artefacts, including the motor car. In a caption underneath a picture of automobiles driving down Ratchadamnoen in 1905, he identifies what is in the picture as 'spectacles of modernity'; Askew, *Bangkok*, 35. Members of the Bangkok elite would eventually own cars and would also drive up and down Ratchadamnoen Boulevard to show off their beautiful women. This modern culture of showing, borrowing the English word 'show' for use in Thai, is mentioned in the novel *Khwam mai phayabat*; see Chapter 1 in this volume.

Another road constructed for the motor car and the electric tram was Charoen Krung (modern city) Road, often referred to as New Road. This paved road connected the Western and Chinese business and residential communities to the Grand Palace and government ministries. In a sense, Charoen Krung Road was built for the Europeans and their motor cars and symbolised an acceptance of the superiority of Western technology. But Ratchadamnoen Boulevard allowed members of the Thai elite to demonstrate their mastery, control, consumption and perhaps victory over all things Western, too. The importance of the motor car to the Thai court is reflected in Queen Saowabha's remark that one of her great joys was 'to buy some twenty cars every year after the London Show, which she then gave to her sons, relatives and friends'.[39] When Prince Chula was nine years old, he was sent to study at the royal military college in Bangkok.[40] Prince Chula wrote that he was one of the few cadets who were driven to school.

Tragically, Queen Saowabha died on 20 October 1919, and, in June of the following year, Chula's father passed away during a trip to Singapore. Even while he was sick and dying in Singapore, his father told Prince Chula, then 12, to go take a drive around town to lessen his stress and anxiety. After the death of his father and grandmother, in February 1921, Chula was sent to study in England as a companion to his uncle Prince Prachathipok, the future Rama VII (r. 1925–35). He wrote that he was sad to have 'to part from Chom [his nurse], my home, my favourite car, my friends, then my uncle'.[41] Chula was only 13 years old, and his favourite possession was his miniature electric car.

Prince Bira was born on 15 July 1914, six years after Prince Chula.[42] But Bira was in fact Chula's uncle. His father, Prince Bhanurangsi, was a younger brother of King Chulalongkorn. Bira held the royal title

---

39   In 1917, Princess Phimramphai became the first Thai woman to drive solo around the streets of Bangkok in a two-seater car; Chulachakrabongse, *Brought up in England*, 69.
40   Among his classmates were Sarit Thanarat, the future military dictator (1958–63), and the famous writer of comedic fiction writer Po. Intharapalit, whose father taught Thai at the academy. Po. Intharapalit is famous for the wildly popular series of *Phon Nikon Kim Nguan* novels, which began in 1939 and continued for 30 years. Wichitwong Na Pomphet studies the significance of these novels in *Wiwatthanakan sangkhom thai kap hatsaniyai phon nikon kim nguan* [*The evolution of Thai society and the comedic novel Phon nikon kim nguan*], vols 1–2 (Bangkok: Saengdao, 2001–02).
41   Chulachakrabongse, *Brought up in England*, 75, 78. A picture of his first car appears on page 65 of this book.
42   Princess Ceril Birabongse in *The prince and I* writes about her life with Bira even after the two divorced. Of all of his wives, she remained his soulmate.

Phraongjao, as a son of a Jaofa. Although Prince Chula's father was also a Jaofa, his mother was a non-royal foreigner. Therefore, Chula's royal title was only Mom Chao. But after his uncle King Vajiravudh ascended the throne in 1910, Chula asked his uncle to promote him to the rank of Phraongjao. Chula was quite concerned about his status as a Thai prince.

In *Brought up in England*, Chula asserted that as the grandson of King Chulalongkorn and the nephew of the incumbent king, Rama VII, he was well received by the English court, which honoured and recognised the Thai sash that he wore.[43] He was proud that King George V invited him to breakfast on many occasions, and that when he attended public functions, such as horse races, protocol placed him very near to the English royal family. If this is true, then it is not difficult to imagine that these young Thai princes were accepted in England and Europe as 'royalty' first and perhaps 'Thai' second. As we shall later see, their portrayal as heroes returning to Thailand in 1937 reversed this perception; their Thainess was emphasised over their royal status.

Chula was a good student who went from Harrow to Cambridge to study history. When he was at university, he was assigned the task of looking after Bira, who followed him to England and began studies at Eton in 1927. At first, Bira was expected to study military science and thus to follow in the footsteps of his father. However, Bira loved art and preferred painting and sculpture to horses and guns. And, for a slightly built man, he had formidable athletic abilities and a daring character suited for racing cars and flying planes. At Eton, he was awarded school colours for several sports and even held the long jump record. Although he would be later known for his racing prowess, there is little awareness of his once having held the altitude record for sail planes. Bira was also a good sculptor. Many sculptures on display at the racing drivers' clubhouse were his work, although few realised it.

Following the 1932 revolution toppling the absolute monarchy in Thailand, Chula became Bira's guardian. After this change in the political situation in Thailand, instead of receiving a stipend from the king of £1,000 per annum, Chula was given his father's entire estate to manage.[44] His income thus jumped twentyfold, to £20,000 per annum. Further,

---
43 Chulachakrabongse, *Brought up in England*, 213.
44 Chulachakrabongse, *Brought up in England*, 176. Prince Chula's father had been dead for many years, but Rama VI and Rama VII had taken care of him with a yearly stipend and, after the latter abdicated in 1935, he gave Chula his father's estate to manage.

after abdicating in 1935, Rama VII was no longer able to support Bira financially. He thus asked Chula to take over that responsibility. The jump in his disposable income allowed Chula to live in style and to present Bira with an MG K3 sports car with a supercharger on the latter's 20th birthday. By this time, Bira had already tried his hand at amateur racing in a Riley sports car. The princes also had other cars and, during the holidays, Bira would act as Chula's chauffeur when they toured Europe.[45]

The small Riley sports car allowed Bira to try his hand at serious racing. The Riley was not very powerful, and its speeds were low. But driving it was a good introduction to racing. It is not difficult to go fast on the straights, as anyone with a lead foot can do that in a powerful car. The test of a gifted driver is how to negotiate tricky corners. Bira was talented in the corners, as the racing press was quick to notice and to write about.

In 1935, when Bira turned 21 years old, Chula bought him a proper race car, a 1500cc ERA that they named Romulus.[46] The car was a fully-fledged race car, capable of speeds up to 130 miles per hour. The princes also established the White Mouse Racing Team that same year. Chula became the team manager and financier. He was responsible for administration, paperwork, managing the mechanics, logistics and public relations.[47] In a sense, Bira, as the driver, mastered Western technology, while Chula mastered the art of managing a modern organisation. The two princes thus epitomised 'Thai' mastery of modernity. They would eventually engage the West on equal terms and win.

By his second year of racing, Bira was already hard to beat. Because Thailand was not a member of the sanctioning International Automobile Association, Bira had to find an established racing organisation to sponsor him. With the help of Chula's connections, Bira was licensed to race as a member of the British Race Car Drivers' Club. Because of this membership, he was eligible to compete for the overall annual prize—the Gold Star award for best driver. This award was very prestigious and it was considered the championship for sports car racing in Europe.

---

45 Chulachakrabongse, *Brought up in England*, 177. Chula and Bira had a large stable of cars that impressed friends and acquaintances. They lived large as Thai princes. A 1935 photograph shows Chula and Bira standing in front of some of their cars: Aston Martin, ERA, MG Magnette, Riley Imp, Rolls Royce, Bentley, Voisin, MG Magna, MG Midget, Ford; Chulachakrabongse, *Brought up in England*, 36.
46 Prince Chula of Siam (Prince Chulachakrabongse), *Road racing 1936: Being an account of one season of B. Bira, the racing motorist* (London: G.T. Foulis, 1937), 13.
47 Narisa, *100 pi chunchakraphong*, 68–79.

2. RACING AND THE CONSTRUCTION OF THAI NATIONALISM

To the astonishment of racing fans and the automotive press, Bira won several races in his class of light race cars. His most famous win was the race at Monaco in April 1936. Bira soon became the rising star among many famous race car drivers from Europe. The Monaco circuit was run on city streets, and the course two miles long. The race was 50 laps. In 1936, 22 cars were entered, with drivers from England, France, Greece, Italy, Switzerland, Germany and Australia, in addition to the lone Thai. Of the 22 cars, only 18 qualified for the race. Bira started from the third row. Before the age of radio communications, signals from the pits were written in chalk on black signboards. The White Mouse Team wrote their signals in Thai to confound competitors.[48] Miraculously, Bira won the race. As an added bonus, he was granted the privilege of driving the race course in the opening ceremony for the Grand Prix cars. Chula noted that the crowds cheered the Thai driver during that opening lap.[49]

Before and during the Monaco race, eight national flags were flown, representing the participating drivers' countries. The Thai red, white and blue flag[50] was among the eight. After the race was over, only the winner's flag was left flying. At the awards ceremony, the winning nation's anthem was played. In the case of Thailand, the song used was the royal anthem; racing and the princes were thus symbolically linked to the prowess and *barami* (karmic power) of the Thai monarchy.

Chula emphasised this point in a radio address during his visit to Bangkok in 1937. He told his listeners about the race in Monaco, and about his pride in witnessing the Thai flag flown after the race and hearing the royal anthem played. He asked his listeners to imagine how they would feel to see the *farang* take off their hats to pay respect to the Thai flag and to stand up for the anthem. He told the audience that few in Europe knew about Siam, as it was then called, but that Bira's racing success had brought fame to their country; the Thai was now equal to the *farang*.[51]

---

48 Ceril Birabongse, *The prince and I*, 22.
49 Prince Chula of Siam, *Road racing 1936*, 30–44.
50 For a history of the Thai flag, see Chanida Phromphayak Phueaksom, *Kanmueang nai prawattisat thongchat thai* [*Politics in the history of the Thai flag*] (Bangkok: Sinlapawatthanatham, 2003). The red, white and blue flag replaced the red flag with a white elephant in the middle in 1917. The new flag was designed by Rama VI to reflect the modern idea of the state. It was also easier to make. During one of Rama VI's trips he noticed that his subjects flew red or white flags without the elephant to greet him. As he thought that this looked like China's flag, he was prompted to redesign Thailand's flag.
51 *Prachachat*, 11 November 1937.

From all accounts, English and European drivers acknowledged Bira's special ability as a race car driver. The famous French Grand Prix driver Louis Chiron gave Bira encouragement before the Monaco race by predicting that he would win. That race was the only time that small sports racing cars ran the course. Prior to the actual race, Bira challenged the drivers to race his wind-up toy car around a miniature course set up in their hotel. All the famous race car drivers present, including Hans Stuck and Count Carlo Felice Trossi, tried their hand at it. Bira was only beaten by Count Trossi.[52]

International motor racing was and is still closely tied to the nation-state. From the beginning, race teams represented their countries in competition. In the 1930s, there was great rivalry between France and Germany. Determined to show the superiority of the Aryan race, Hitler poured money into race teams in order to defeat the British, the French and the Italians. By this time, race teams sponsored by car manufacturers were in fact national teams. Even today, the national anthem of the winning driver of a Formula One race is played at the awards ceremony. In fact, the national anthem of the winning car manufacturer is also played. And the national flags of the winners are flown at the ceremony, too.

It is doubtful that Thailand could have competed in such an expensive sport. Chula was aware of this. He wrote that national teams racing the large cars would spend 100,000 baht per season.[53] But there was another class of smaller machines that could be fielded for 10 per cent of that cost. It was in the latter class that Chula and Bira competed. Drivers in that class were still considered representatives of their countries and their people. Bira's victory at the Monaco Grand Prix was therefore indeed a win for Thailand, a source of pride for the Thai princes and the nation. It was the first time that the Thai flag was flown and the royal anthem played before spectators at a major international sporting event.

Bira's racing victories allowed him to edge out the famous race car driver Richard Seaman for the Gold Star award in 1936. At first, many observers thought that it was just beginner's luck, but Bira went on to win two more of these awards consecutively. As the White Mouse Team's publicist, Chula

---

52 Stevenson, *Driving forces*, 190–3. Bira soon had the courage to approach and to talk to the other famous drivers, including Tazio Nuvolari, Alfred Neubauer Manfred von Brauchitsch, Rene Dreyfus, Piero Taruffi, Count Trossi and Hans Stuck.
53 Phraongjao Chulachakrabongse (Prince Chulachakrabongse), *Dara thong: sarakhadi kankhaeng rot khong phraongjao phiraphong* [*Golden star: The story of Prince Bira's racing*] (Bangkok: Samnakphim Karawek, 1978), 11–27.

2. RACING AND THE CONSTRUCTION OF THAI NATIONALISM

was clever in translating 'Gold Star' as *Dara thong* and not *Dao thong*. Dara means the 'star' of a show or of a movie, rather than a star in the sky. This twist in meaning allowed the Thai public to view Bira as a star driver, and not as a winning race driver who won a medal that looked like a star. Thanks to Chula, Bira became a star and a celebrity in Thailand. News of his successes appeared in the Thai press, and the reading public became aware of Bira's exploits and his victories over world-class European drivers.

All in all, during the four years (1935–38) that Bira raced in Europe and Africa, he won 16 races, came in second 13 times and was third three times. And, among the drivers who brought fame to the ERA marque, Bira topped the field with 14 wins. The famous race car drivers Raymond Mays, Pat Fairfield, Richard Seaman and Art Dobson were no match, winning nine, seven, three and two races, respectively. The races that Bira won were held all over Europe—England, Germany, Monaco, France, Italy, Czechoslovakia, Switzerland, Scotland, Sweden and other countries. With each win, the Thai flag was left flying as the flag of the losers were lowered. Bira and Chula were very proud that the spectators and other famous drivers stood up to respectfully listen to the Thai royal anthem. Thailand was slowly becoming an Asian country familiar to the West.

Telling the Bira story

Chula documented Bira's successes, as well as his own, by writing four books in English and two books in Thai.[54] Bira wrote only one book.[55] But stories about their racing were also covered in Chula's *Brought up in England*, and in 1992 Bira's first wife, Ceril Birabongse, published

---

54 The books by Chula in English are *Wheels at speed* (London: G.T. Foulis, 1946), published privately in 1936; *Road racing 1936: Being an account of one season of B. Bira, the racing motorist* (London: G.T. Foulis, 1937); *Road star hat trick: Being an account of two seasons of 'B. Bira'; The racing motorist in 1937 and 1938* (London: G.T. Foulis, 1939; reprinted in 1944, 1945 and 1948); *Blue and yellow: Being an account of two seasons of B. Bira, the racing motorist, 1939 and 1946* (London: G.T. Foulis, 1947). The first of the Thai-language books is *Dara thong: sarakhadi kankhaeng rot khong phraongjao phiraphong* [*Golden star: The racing exploits of Prince Birabongse*] (Bangkok: Samnakphim Karawek, 1978). The preface of this book has a 1936 date and mentions *Wheels at speed*; the edition drawn on here was published in 1978. *Thai chana: rueang kankhaengkhan khong pho phira nakkhaprot Thai nai yurop* [*Thai victorious: The racing of B. Bira, a Thai race car driver in Europe*], published in 1941 or 1945, with a preface by Field Marshal Po. Phibunsongkhram, Thailand's prime minister at the time, written in 1941. In addition, Chula wrote about one of the princes' friends in *Dick Seaman: Racing motorist* (London: G.T. Foulis, 1948).
55 Birabongse, *Bits and pieces: Being motor racing recollections of 'B. Bira'* (London: G.T. Foulis, 1942).

The prince and I: Life with the motor racing Prince of Siam, documenting their life together. Ying Muet also wrote *The golden star prince*, which focused on Bira's love affairs.[56] And, most recently, *A historical remembrance of Prince Bira, the racer* was published.[57]

Chula's and Bira's English-language books were all published by G.T. Foulis Company in London. The authors confessed that they wrote the accounts of Bira's racing mostly to be shared with friends. However, the books also contained useful information about racing, such as the various classifications of race cars, the many tracks in use and the major personalities active in racing at that time. The books were quite straightforward narratives with few embellishments. They also chronicled in detail the lifestyle of the two princes: where they went, the kinds of entertainment and food they liked, where they vacationed, whom they knew, which European women they dated, and much more. Their lives are normalised as the lives of rich, aristocratic and privileged European young men. Perhaps unconsciously, the authors wanted to show that they were, as Thai, no different from the *farang*.

Chula's and Bira's books quoted accolades from the motoring press in praise of Bira's driving and cheerful personality. Many of his contemporaries were amused that Bira anthropomorphised his race cars. He drew pictures of them with faces and gave them personalities in his book. Even after accidents, such as when Hanuman went berserk and crashed, Bira drew a picture of the car in bandages and recuperating. Peter Stevenson writes:

> When he'd crash, coming as close to death as any of them, Bira would draw cartoons of his car in bandages, and vow to make it up to his 'friend' the race car, as soon as possible. A curious Eastern/Western mechanical-age animism?[58]

While Chula's books were like history texts, with abundant detail and carefully selected information, Bira's 1942 account of his own exploits was much more personal and touching. The writing was not as polished as Chula's, but it did have heart and feeling. His book was not introspective

---

56   Ying Muet (Momratchawong Malini Chakraphan), *Jaochai dara thong* [*The golden star prince*] (Bangkok: Matichon, 2003).
57   Sala Bunkhong, *Yon tamnan jaochai nakkhaeng praongjao phira* [*A historical remembrance of Prince Bira, the racer*] (Bangkok: Kaoraek, 2011). Bira was married six times, twice to Ceril Heycock. Ying Muet is the pen name of *Momratchawong* Malini Chakraphan. *A historical remembrance* treats current Formula One racing drivers with a nostalgic look at Bira's career in perspective.
58   Stevenson, *Driving Forces*, 189.

like Chula's books, but Bira showed that he let his senses and hunches guide him. Perhaps this unconscious consciousness made him a good artist and a good driver. While Chula's books had a purpose to them, Bira's book was more like putting a stream of thought on paper. Their personalities, different yet complementary, made them a perfect team.

The first Thai book about racing, *Dara thong* [*Golden star*], written by Prince Chula, was most likely published in 1937. The author's preface was written in October 1936. However, it has proved impossible to locate copies of the original edition; the only available edition is a 1978 reprint. *Dara thong* promoted Bira as the Golden Star and not as the winner of the Gold Star award. Just as Bira was able to anthropomorphise his racing machines, the Gold Star as an object in turn animated the man and made him a star, a celebrity.

The second Thai book, *Thai chana* [*Thai victorious*], indicated September 1945, directly after the end of the Second World War, as the date of publication. The 1941 date of Phibun's foreword suggests, however, that publication was delayed because of the war. The title of the book is suggestive: *Thai chana*, meaning Thai wins or Thai victorious, left out the obvious. Victorious over what and whom? Obviously, winning in itself is good, but, in this case, what is left out is mention of winning against the *farang*, against the West. In the early 1940s, the Phibun government was also promoting hyper-nationalism to help ensure that the Thai people would be ready to face unknown enemies because of the conflicts in Europe and Asia.[59] *Thai chana* could also mean that Thailand would win over whomever it had to fight.

Phibun's foreword linked Bira's success to the newly christened Thailand's nationalist agenda and noted that the two princes were iconic examples of good citizens who dedicated their lives and successes to the nation. Unlike the English-language books *Wheels at speed* and *Road racing 1936* on which *Thai chana* was based, the latter book did not cover the luxurious lifestyle of the two princes. There was perhaps a tacit understanding among members of the Thai public that, of course, the *jao nai* (royals and masters) or princes had the wealth, knowledge and ability to engage in this European sport. Their victories in this activity simply illustrated the greatness of the Thai people, albeit its ruling class.

---

59 Joseph J. Wright, *The balancing act: A history of modern Thailand* (Oakland: Pacific Rim Press, 1991), 94–115.

Prime Minister Phibun's foreword thanked Chula for donating the proceeds from sales of the book to support the Army Youth Corps (*yuwachon thahanbok*) and reminded the youth of the nation that Bira's exploits should be an example for them to emulate. The book was dedicated to the Thai youth, and in the frontispiece a statement was inserted touting the importance of the Thai flag. It noted that the hoisting of the flag after Bira's winning drive was important, not just because the driver was Thai, but at that moment the Thais and the Thai nation also won because both became known to people all over the world.

Hitler had Hans Stuck, who drove Auto Union and Mercedes Benz race cars; Phibun had Bira, Chula and the ERA. The comparison of course shows the difference. The Thai had to depend on British equipment. But, even though the Thais could not build the technology, they could borrow and master it for their own benefit. Far from being a sign of a colonial mentality, the privileging of Western culture and technology was proclaimed a clever policy of selective borrowing and co-optation. This argument only remained plausible as long as Thailand insisted that it had always been independent and had never been colonised.[60]

Racing and nationalism

Chula's writing suggests that he wanted to be remembered as a royalist who believed in democracy. Perhaps his upbringing in England convinced him that Thailand's absolute monarchy could not survive under the stresses and strains of modernity and the rise of the middle class. Chula appeared to be sympathetic to the democratic cause and admitted to warning Rama VII about a possible rebellion of the new civilian and military officials. He referred to the leaders of the People's Party who took power after toppling the absolute monarchy in 1932 as the Dee Ones, playing on the Thai word for good (*di*).[61] Although Chula was critical of some of the leaders for benefiting from the forced sale of the properties of princes, he praised some of its leaders, especially Pridi Phanomyong, for not participating in such abuses.

---

60 Perhaps this argument explains why Thai scholars resist admitting that Thailand was indeed semi-colonial and that the discipline of postcolonial studies is irrelevant to Thai studies. Attempts to grapple with this question appear in Rachel Harrison and Peter Jackson, eds, *The ambiguous allure of the West: Traces of the colonial in Thailand* (Hong Kong: Hong Kong University Press; Ithaca: Cornell Southeast Asia Program Publications, 2010).
61 Chulachakrabongse, *Brought up in England*, 164, 173–4.

Chula also distanced himself from some of the more conservative princes who were bitter after the 1932 revolution, such as Prince Chumphot Boriphat. In fact, he decided to give the People's Party a chance and went as far as expressing support for it. He even helped to promote the idea of the modern nation-state and the idea that the Thai people should be loyal to the state and do their best to promote the state. His support of the new military–civilian elite exacerbated the difficult relations between Chula and his uncle King Prachathipok.

Chula also supported the new government's cause financially. Soon after the 1932 revolution, the government floated a million-pound bond to help fund its expenditures. Chula bought £80,000 worth of the million-pound bond. In March 1933, on his 25th birthday, he donated another £25,000 to Thai charities.[62] With the beginning of hostilities in Europe that forebode impending war, he wrote to Phibun asking if he should return to serve in the army as a Thai patriot and to follow in the footsteps of his father. The government responded that it was no longer necessary for princes to serve in the military as a matter of duty. This news was welcome, particularly to Bira, who did not want to join the military. He had been worried because the Thai government had in fact given him a military commission as a reward for winning the Gold Star. Nonetheless, the two princes ended up serving in the British Home Guard during the war. Thailand had sided with Japan and was therefore an enemy of Great Britain. Chula's and Bira's wartime service and their close relations with the British government helped to soften somewhat the demands that the Allies made of Thailand after the Second World War.[63]

Although Bira passed the university entrance examinations and was accepted to Cambridge's Trinity College in 1934, he convinced Chula that he was more suited to be an artist and not a historian like Chula. So, instead of studying history, Bira elected to study art. To help fund Bira's studies and his racing career, Chula published a biography of Frederick the Great in Thai.[64] The book was dedicated to Bira, who was then turning 20. The income from that book enabled Chula to buy the MG K3 Special sports car as a birthday present for Bira. This gift placed Bira on the path towards becoming a race car driver. In characteristic and playful form, Bira promptly named his new car 'Fidget'.[65]

---

62 Chulachakrabongse, *Brought up in England*, 176.
63 Ceril Birabongse, *The prince and I*, 139–48.
64 Phrajao worawongthoe phraongjao Chulachakrabongse (Prince Chulachakrabongse), *Frederik maharat haeng pratsia* [*Frederick the Great of Prussia*] (Bangkok: Rongrian Changphim, 1935).
65 Chulachakrabongse, *Brought up in England*, 76.

Having forgone Trinity College, Bira chose to study at the Byam Shaw School of Art in London. His short period of enrolment had deep implications, for there he and Chula met Ceril Heycock and Elizabeth (Lisboa) Hunter. Bira would eventually marry Ceril, and Chula would marry Elizabeth.[66]

At first, the two were uneasy about dating English girlfriends because there were rumours that Rama VII planned to abdicate and that some military members of the People's Party were considering nominating Chula as king. However, his candidacy was hampered by the fact that his mother was neither Thai nor royalty, despite the fact that Chula was next in line because the other sons of Queen Saowabha did not leave any male heirs. In the end, the government decided that succession should go to heirs of the other main queen, Saowabha's full sister. Thus, succession to the Chakri throne went to Prince Ananda Mahidol, whose mother was a Thai commoner. In consolation, the government promoted Chula to the rank of captain in the Thai army and assigned him as aide-de-camp to the young king in 1935.

Further evidence of Chula's and Bira's close connection to the English court, aside from Chula's accounts of his breakfasts with King George V, was the fact that, when that king died in 1936, King Ananda chose Prince Chula to represent him at the funeral. Chula also represented the Thai king at the coronation of King George VI.[67] Before the coronation, Chula had already attended several other important events in Europe on behalf of King Ananda and, that same year, Bira was presented to the new King George for winning the Gold Star award for the best 'British' driver.

Bira's success in Europe was widely publicised in articles and news reports in the Bangkok newspapers. It coincided with Luang Wichitwatthakan's campaign of hyper-nationalism. The exploits of the princes buttressed the claim that the Thai were a proud, competitive, militant and successful race. The Thai race and the successful Thai race car driver seemed well suited for each other.

During this campaign of hyper-nationalism, past kings who 'served' the Thai nation by liberating them from Burmese domination or saving Thailand from colonialism were embraced as 'good royals'. Others were

---

66   Ceril Birabongse, *The prince and I*, 15–16.
67   Chulachakrabongse, *Brought up in England*, 191, 227.

2. RACING AND THE CONSTRUCTION OF THAI NATIONALISM

ignored or shunned. In this way, the People's Party did not abruptly rid itself or Thailand of the royals, but it chose rather to support those who could advance its political cause. Chula and Bira fit the mould of the new 'national' heroes, even though they were part of the ancien régime. The centuries-old value of respecting the *jao nai* was hard to discard, and the country's new leaders were smart in exploiting this feature of Thai social identity.

In November 1937, the two princes decided to return to Bangkok for a short visit.[68] Not least, Chula also wanted Bira to return to Thailand so that he could have some contact with the young women there. At that time, Bira had already decided to marry Ceril Heycock, but Chula asked him to hold off the engagement. Chula wanted to make sure that Bira would not regret the choice of marrying an Englishwoman. Chula himself was also dating an Englishwoman of course, but, because his own mother was Russian and he was thus more or less disqualified as a contender to the Thai throne, it would not matter whom he married. The other reason for the trip was to allow Bira to show Romulus to the Thai people. Bira would be allowed to drive at speed up and down Ratchadamnoen Boulevard, and to let his countrymen see the prowess of the race car and of its driver. By this time also, driving fast had become de rigueur for the rich young men of Bangkok.

Accompanying time trials also took place before Bira's demonstration drive. Interestingly, the Thai press complained that holding such races would just encourage more dangerous racing on the streets of Bangkok.[69] It appears that Bira's successes had fuelled the imagination of many young Thai men. There were 16 prizes for the winners of the time trials. The cups were sponsored by the regents; the ministers of defence, foreign affairs and interior; and the ambassadors of the United Kingdom, France, Japan and Germany. Even Phibun sponsored a trial. The prize sponsored by Prince Chula was for the fastest female driver; Thailand seems by this time to have had many female drivers who liked to race. There was even a class for drivers with less than five years of driving experience. The winner of that trial would receive the cup donated by the Chinese commercial attaché. The trials were divided into sports cars of different engine displacements, a class for saloons and the trial for women drivers. The cars that competed

---

68 Chulachakrabongse, *Dara thong*, Chapter 10.
69 Van Beek, *Royal automobile stables of Siam*, 19–20.

in the trials included various marques such as MGs, Singers, Austins, Renaults, Fords, Dodges and Chryslers. The fastest driver of all would receive the B. Bira Cup.[70]

Chula described his return to Thailand in some detail, first in a radio speech that he gave after his arrival in Bangkok and later in his books. Chula and Bira were accompanied on the trip by a Colonel Phum of the Russian army and by an English friend who had not been to Thailand before. Colonel Phum Sakhon had in fact been sent from Thailand to study military science in Russia with Prince Chakrabongse, Chula's father. After graduating from military college there, he requested an extension from the Thai government to further his studies, but his request was denied. He was furious and decided not to return to Thailand. He eventually joined the Russian army, rising to the rank of colonel. Because of his actions, he was stripped of his Thai citizenship. After the Russian Revolution, Phum fled to France as a refugee. Chula helped his father's old classmate regain his citizenship and brought him back to Thailand after decades of absence.[71] The group travelled by ship to Singapore and took the train north. From European suits, the two princes changed to Thai clothing after crossing the border, in both a symbolic and a physical change that saw them becoming Thai again. At each stop that the train made, local people displaying welcome banners greeted the travellers. Military and Boy Scout bands played nationalistic marches during those stops. People were well informed about the visit of the two heroes and their winning race car and thus turned out in large numbers to greet Chula and their idol Bira.[72]

Chula and Bira decided that for official functions during the visit they would appear in Thai military officers' uniforms; for semi-official business, they would wear Western suits; and, if they entertained visitors, they would wear Thai clothing appropriate for princes—*pha muang* (purple silk pants). These choices of what to wear reflected this period of change and the attempt of Thai to engage in cultural adaptation. It also represented the three domestic contenders for political power—the military in its uniforms, the civilian bureaucratic elite dressed in Western suits and the old nobility dressed in *pha muang*. Phraongjao Athitthipapha Aphakorn,

---

70 *Prachachat*, 25 November 1937.
71 Chulachakrabongse, *Thai victorious*, 146–8.
72 Chula and Bira had also been greeted as heroes by members of the Ceylon Automobile Association during their short stopover in that colony. This welcome reflected the degree to which Bira's success was treated as a major achievement for an Asian race car driver.

one of the regents who was also a cousin and a friend of the two men, was the first to welcome Chula and Bira back. However, it proved an uneasy moment for the princes, because many of the royals in exile did not trust or like Athit. They felt that he did not protect the interests of the Crown.

The two princes stayed at Prince Chakrabongse's palace at Tha Tian on the bank of the Chaophraya River. Romulus was also displayed there. The car drew at least 20,000 visitors to the palace. Even members of the cabinet, including Foreign Minister Pridi, and the Dowager Queen Sawangwatthana came to look at this symbol of Thai prowess and success. At the palace, the princes wore Thai garments to greet the guests, while Pridi and cabinet members came in Western suits or military uniforms.[73]

The Bangkok press reported the activities of the two princes as if they were movie stars. The newspaper *Prachachat* in particular ran daily features on and pictures of the activities of the two princes. It also published the text of their speeches. *Prachachat* was owned by Prince Wanwaithayakorn, a progressive royal who supported the People's Party. The paper also employed the famous novelist Kulab Saipradit as editor. In one of the featured articles, Kulab wrote a detailed history of Bira's racing exploits, based on Chula's English-language books. His article suggested that Chula's *Wheels at speed* was readily available on the Bangkok book market.

The Thai newspapers dubbed the two princes *nuea hom* (sweet-scented flesh), meaning that they were very desirable and eligible. They received invitations to movies, concerts, plays and dances. They were seen in the company of all the beautiful women of Bangkok. Just before a major ball to honour the princes, the Phahurat market ran out of Bira blue cloth because all the young women invited to the dance wanted to attend in gowns of that colour. Having grown up with privilege in England, the two princes did their best to show outward appreciation of Bangkok high society and its tastes, but privately they complained about their compatriots' lack of good taste and especially about the decline of classical Thai drama. They lamented that Luang Wichit's rewriting of history and the insertion of militaristic themes into the performances ruined Thai art forms. As Thai heroes, socialised by life in the palace and conditioned by newly acquired European tastes, they were critical of the emerging plebeian nationalistic art forms.

---

73 A photograph of Chula in traditional attire together with others in uniforms and Western suits appears in Chulachakrabongse, *Thai victorious*, 166.

While Chula was invited to give scholarly lectures at Chulalongkorn University and on national radio, Bira was spared these tasks. He did agree to one interview about car racing with the president of the Royal Automobile Society, later published in *Prachachat*.[74] Chula was billed as a scholar, an intellectual and the brains behind the success of the White Mouse Racing Team. Bira, on the other hand, was the one with the special talent, whose physical prowess, daring and reflexes matched the best that the world had to offer.

On 5 December 1937, Ratchadamnoen Boulevard was closed to traffic, and Bira fired up Romulus to race raucously up and down the road for two miles. Fifty thousand of his fellow citizens lined the two sides of the road while he roared up and down at 120 miles per hour. The crowd was impressed. A woman was quoted to say that at those breakneck speeds and with that control, no wonder the *farang* liked Bira.[75]

A week later, Romulus was on display at the annual fair celebrating Constitution Day on 10 December, thus linking the two princes to the emerging democratic form of government. Chula spoke on their behalf to indicate that he supported the new leadership as long as there was a balanced working relationship between the civilians and the military. He implied that the future of Thailand should not be in the hands of an absolute monarch. Because of his support of the new regime, many princes and royalists boycotted dinner parties organised by the government for the two. Nevertheless, Thai nationalism was still formed, supported and legitimised by two 'modern' princes.

To further the cause of Thai nationalism and to demonstrate to the world that Thailand was a modern and civilised nation, the government gladly supported the princes' proposal to stage the Bangkok Grand Prix, to be held in December 1939. At that time, Phibun was already the major force behind the government. Although he did not attend the public celebrations during the princes' visit for fear of another assassination attempt, he did have a private meeting with them. He was very supportive and appreciative of the princes' successes, and he even agreed to write a very complimentary foreword in Chula's Thai-language book about Bira's success.

---

74   *Prachachat*, 17 November 1937.
75   Chulachakrabongse, *Thai victorious*, 172.

Thai beauties were unable to dissuade Bira from marrying his English girlfriend. Soon after their visit to Bangkok, both Chula and Bira were able to obtain the king's permission, countersigned by Jaofa Narisara Nuwatthiwong, to marry their English girlfriends. The young King Ananda granted this permission, as Rama VIII had already abdicated. That abdication was fortuitous because Chula was not on good terms with his uncle, who accused Chula of collaborating with the People's Party.

The announcement of the weddings appeared in the Bangkok papers. It does not appear to have met with any controversy or public criticism. It seems that Thai princes and heroes were the equals of the Europeans; why should they not marry their women, too? In this instance, Thai men should also conquer and capture beautiful European woman—a reversal of the colonial-era white men's practice of taking native mistresses and wives.

Not only were Chula and Bira Westernised Oriental Gentlemen, but the two were also close to another important family with a similar background. Chula and Bira regularly visited Rama VIII and his younger brother the future Rama IX in Europe. The two brothers, King Ananda and Prince Bhumibol Adulyadej, teenagers at that time, enjoyed playing with miniature electric cars. They regularly asked Bira to take rides with them. Chula noted that the future kings of Thailand spoke Thai and French but could only read French. The two brothers also spoke only French with each other.[76] I can but pose several questions here. If the future kings of Thailand spoke French, does Thainess become ambiguous? Was the new Thai elite a hybrid of Thai and European? What, then, is the European Other when the West is embedded in Thainess?

Conclusion: Ambiguous other, Thai acceptance of the West and Thai nationalism

The re-enactment of the Bangkok Grand Prix in 1988 seemed incredibly anachronistic. Modern, Westernised and traffic-congested Bangkok was asked to make way for a re-enacted race that highlighted the prowess of a Thai race car driver who mastered *farang* technology and the *farang* game of automobile racing. But instead of Bira, Thailand was represented by M.R. Narisa, who is three-quarters *farang* and looks European.

---

76   Ceril Birabongse, *The prince and I*, 111. In fact, King Bhumibol (1927–2016) also loved fast cars in his youth. He was involved in an automobile accident in October 1948 and lost his right eye.

By the late 1980s, Thailand had already mastered *farang* technology and administration. The embrace of Western modernity had been relatively smooth and proved all-encompassing, and we have yet to fully assess its impact on Thailand's culture or its religion, language, literature, arts and basic values. One side effect of this process is that, among the people of Southeast Asia, the Thais have long seemed more at ease in dealing with the West and with the *farang*. In fact, colonial and postcolonial thinking is still problematic to most Thai scholars. How does this matter relate to the events of 1937–38, or to the Bangkok Grand Prix of 1939 that did not take place?

Bira and Chula's triumphant return to Thailand allowed members of the public to not just imagine heroes, but to see them in the flesh. They were able to witness firsthand the talents of a Thai driver and his manager—men who were able to manipulate and control (Western) technology, to compete with and to beat their Western counterparts. If the Bangkok Grand Prix had been held and Bira had won the race, the event would have reinforced feelings of national pride and national equality with the West. But would that victory have been a complete one?

Even though Thai kings tried their best to modernise the country and to appropriate Western technology and culture in order to protect Thailand from colonialism, and even though it is true that Thailand was never directly colonised, it was nevertheless forced to concede territory and sovereignty.[77] Therefore, the victory, the claim that Thailand was always independent and never colonised, is problematic. The royalist historical interpretation holds that the Thai were smart diplomats who knew the art of give and take. But it downplays what appears in hindsight to have been more give than take—loss of territory and the concession of extraterritorial rights. There is no real incident to which Thais can point and say that Thailand was victorious over the *farang*. At best, the argument for winning against *farang* colonial expansion is that Thailand ceded its Laotian and Cambodian tributaries to safeguard the core of Thai civilisation. Some scholars have cited the cleverness of the Thai by pointing out that Thailand gave up lands it no longer controlled, peripheral principalities on the Malay Peninsula and the eastern bank of the Mekong River. There is truth to this reading. Prior to the establishment of borders mostly

---

77 For a path-breaking study of these concessions and their impact on Thai national consciousness, see Shane Strate, *The lost territories: Thailand's history of national humiliation* (Honolulu: University of Hawai'i Press, 2015), doi.org/10.21313/hawaii/9780824838911.001.0001.

determined by Britain and France, peripheral principalities (*prathetsarat*) were semi-autonomous states that accepted Thailand's hegemony but not complete political control. The 'loss of territory' discourse was later formulated by Luang Wichit in the 1930s following the establishment of a Thai nation-state.[78]

I would argue that what Chula and Bira achieved on the racing circuits of Europe was really a first important win for Thailand. Bira actually won races against the best of the *farang* drivers. Because racing is so closely tied to national pride, as demonstrated by its rituals with the flags and anthems of the winners, Bira's victory was indeed a victory of Thailand over European countries. It should be noted that automobile racing is very much a European sport, and there were no teams or drivers from Asia until the Honda Motor Company decided to compete in Formula One in the 1960s.[79] Even to this day, no Asian has ever won a major international racing title. In this sense, Bira was unique.

If the events surrounding the visit of Chula and Bira to Thailand in 1937–38 were any indication, the common Thai construction of the West framed in a discourse of modernity was filtered and naturalised or moderated by the achievements of the two princes. The fact that Prince Chula was accepted into the inner circles of the British royalty, and that Bira was accepted as an equal by elite European race car drivers, allowed the Thai public to look at the West through a Thai filter, to see the West through the lenses of the princes. However, these lenses were also tinted. They were not common Thai lenses but, rather, princely lenses tinted by Chula's and Bira's European upbringing and tastes. The Thainess of the princes was probably as alien as the Otherness of the Europeans that their Thai brethren were straining to see.

The princes' acceptance by the European press and peers may have been due primarily to their royal and privileged status. It did not therefore necessarily translate into how the West would view the Thai people more generally. A more recent account of the successes of the two princes is less flattering:

> Sent from the tropical splendor and relaxed attitudes of the royal palace in Bangkok straight to the hallowed halls of Eton and then Cambridge, 'Bira', as he came to be known to his racing pals, saw life in the 1930's Europe as

---

78   Barmé, *Luang Wichit Wathakan*, 163–71.
79   Jones, *The ultimate encyclopedia of Formula One*, 83.

a culture shock rivaling a voyage to a nearby planet. Accompanying Bira had been his older cousin, Prince Chula Chakrabongse, his quieter, more restrained duenna in the curious West.

Bira quickly mastered life in England and went searching with boundless energies to ride every attraction this carnival, England, had to offer, in his own very earnest little-boy, Peter-Pan way. To Bira, the kind of endeavors we take as serious undertakings laced with drama, he saw only as another new world to explore, like a new kid's game.[80]

But even through this ambiguous filter, members of the Thai public were, with the help of state propaganda, made to feel that they were quite the equals of the West. The reverse gaze back at the West was in fact a double gaze—seeing the West by gazing at its own princely Other as a model and manifestation of modernity.[81] The Thai public was seeing the West without the West. This sort of nationalistic imagining fits well in the Thai case, in which nationalism has been imposed from the top—from the court and later from the leaders of the People's Party.

Thai nationalism is a nationalism of the elite and not a nationalism of the masses. This is why democracy is not easily implemented; the Crown and the royal aristocracy were never neutralised as 'subjects' of politics. Nevertheless, this elitist nationalism and the ability of the royals and elites to deal with the West on equal terms may have unwittingly allowed the common Thai person to be more at ease with the West and less resistant to the Western influence that was, in many quarters of Asia, viewed as domination and hegemony. If there were any lingering doubts, they were allayed by the princes.

In an interview during his visit in 1938, Chula was asked if the British still looked down on the Thai people. He responded by saying that the educated Englishmen did not look down on the Thai—that is, on him—but rather accepted him as an equal.[82] This was probably true of a Thai prince who had European features, whose uncle was the king of Thailand, whose wife was English, and who had access to the king of England.

---

80 Stevenson, *Driving forces*, 187.
81 I modify the concept 'postcolonial gaze' popularised by Edward Said, *Orientalism* (New York: Pantheon Books, 1978). Of course the concept of the gaze has been refined over time by Lacan, Foucault and Derrida. In the case of the Thais and their relationship to the West, the gaze involves not just the West and the common Thai. It was also mitigated and complicated by the relationship between the Thai 'Westernised Oriental Gentlemen' and their gaze on the West.
82 *Prachachat*, 10 December 1937.

2. RACING AND THE CONSTRUCTION OF THAI NATIONALISM

Both Chula and Bira were the ambiguous Thai Other—at once Thai and European. They, and many other members of the royalty, nobility and emerging bureaucratic elite, were the prototypical Westernised Oriental Gentlemen, truly bilingual and bicultural. It is this hybridity that makes them historically pivotal figures, cultural mediators and arbiters of Thai *siwilai* culture. The West that the Thai public of that period understood was mediated by this ambiguous Thai Other. Through these lenses, the 'West' appeared more familiar, less formidable and less threatening. But were they seeing the real West?

This chapter only deals with the formative years of a modern Thai nationalism and does not pretend fully to analyse the development of Thai nationalism in more recent decades. The main purpose of this account is to demonstrate how the regime that overthrew absolute monarchy continued to harness the achievements of members of the royal family to buttress the sense of nationhood that was emerging. The dilemma faced by the promoters of modern Thai nationalism was the issue of preserving the sanctity of the monarchy in light of humiliation at the hands of Western colonial powers.

Scholars have argued that Thailand became a semi-colonial state because it accepted extraterritoriality and compromised its sovereignty.[83] However, this view is valid from the standpoint of a modern nation-state. The Bowring Treaty of 1855 was not overly detrimental to the rulers of Thailand. It allowed them to engage in the new international economic regime in ways that helped to fill the coffers of the monarchy, the nobility and their Thai-Chinese allies. Even the loss of territories to France in 1893 did not diminish the central role of the monarchy in Thai nationalism. In that instance, the king and his ministers were depicted as clever in trading territories that Thailand did not fully control to protect the core. It is later, under the Phibun regime, when Thailand embraced the modern concept of a nation-state with clear boundaries and what Thongchai calls a Thai 'geo-body', that the discourse of national humiliation was constructed by Luang Wichit.[84] Phibun's irredentist foreign policy pushed

---

[83] A good summary of discussions on this topic may be found in Harrison and Jackson, *The ambiguous allure of the West*, especially chapters by Jackson, 'The ambiguities of semicolonial power in Thailand', 37–56, and Herzfeld, 'The conceptual allure of the West: Dilemmas and ambiguities of crypto-colonialism in Thailand', 173–86.
[84] Thongchai Winichakul, *Siam mapped: A history of the geo-body of a nation* (Honolulu: University of Hawai'i Press, 1994).

for the return of these 'lost territories' from France during the course of the Second World War. However, the blame for their loss was not put on the monarchy but on the evil French.[85]

As corollary to this construction of Thai royalist nationalism, the Thai people are required ipso facto to owe unending gratitude to their enlightened leaders—especially their kings, their kings' progeny and their loyal officials. The Thai public is constantly reminded in school books, media pronouncements and other subtle ways that it was the kings, other royals and the royal civil service that saved Thailand from colonial subjugation through a strategy of emulating and appropriating what they saw as adaptable and useful Western culture, administration, knowledge and technology. Even today, this nationalism is still in constant struggle with emergent democratic pressures from below. To members of the power elite, dominated by the military and civilian bureaucracies and their supporters, Thai national leadership should be in the hands of the educated, especially the foreign-educated, the wealthy cosmopolitan and globalised class, and military officers and civil servants whose moral authority is derived from their loyalty to the king. But, with the advent of popular or populist democracy in a Thai political system that allows the participation of the larger public, an inevitable clash of power references has occurred. The current political tension in Thai society today reflects the anxiety of uncertainty on the side of the royalist nationalists and the anticipated rise of a more inclusive democratic political system.[86]

Postscript

Although the collaboration between Chula and Bira ended in 1948, Bira continued to race until 1955. His ability as a world-class racing driver was well documented. He enjoyed many wins in the 1935–39 racing seasons. I have highlighted some of his victories in this chapter. It is difficult, however, to provide complete statistics on his races because records are scattered, though his early racing career was recorded and summarised in great detail in Chula's books.[87]

---

85 See Strate, *The lost territories*, 4–19, which details the construction of a nationalism that exploited the national humiliation represented by the 'loss' of territory to the French in 1893 while preserving the integrity of the monarchy.
86 Federico Ferrara, *The political development of modern Thailand* (Cambridge: Cambridge University Press, 2015).
87 In his first five years of racing, Bira competed in 68 races, winning 20 times, and coming in second 15 times and third five times; Prince Chula of Siam, *Road racing*, 87.

2. RACING AND THE CONSTRUCTION OF THAI NATIONALISM

Grand Prix racing began in Europe in the 1920s and flourished in the 1930s. In 1946, after the end of the Second World War, the Fédération Internationale de l'Automobile instituted general rules for international racing, the precursor to today's Formula One racing. In 1950, a World Drivers' Championship was established. Bira became the first race car driver from Asia to compete in Formula One. He raced for several marques, such as the Maserati, Gordini and Connaught teams. After his retirement from racing, Bira tried his hand in several enterprises, such as making prescription racing goggles and starting an air transportation company. Because of his bad eyesight, he endeavoured to make racing goggles for those who needed prescriptions (his own racing goggles had prescription lenses). Bira's corrective lenses allowed him to 'see' the West, but, if his fellow Thais had used those lenses, the West might appear out of focus. After giving up racing, Bira took up competitive sailing. He represented Thailand at the Melbourne (1956), Rome (1960), Tokyo (1964) and Munich (1972) Olympic Games. Bira died from a heart attack on 23 December 1985 at the Barons Court tube station in London. He was 71 years old.

3
Adventures of a dangerous Thai woman: *Huang rak haew luk* (1949)

Luang Wichit Wathakan's bestselling novel, *Huang rak haew luk* [*Sea of love, chasm of death*], addresses three major themes: modernity, nationalism and gender.[1] Prior to the novel's publication in 1949, Luang Wichit was well-known both as the architect of modern Thai nationalism and, perhaps equally important, as the dramatist who popularised militant feminism. In his plays (1936–40), upper-class Thai women took up arms to fight alongside their men in wars of liberation.[2] Luang Wichit even made these women instigators of uprisings against foreign enemies

---

1   Luang Wichit Wathakan, *Huang rak haew luk* [*Sea of love, chasm of death*] (Bangkok: Sangsan Press, 1999). In the foreword of the first edition (Phloenchit Press, 1949), written on 7 February 1949, Luang Wichit writes:

> I compare a *haew luk* or deep chasm to the *huang rak* or sea of love because everyone is ready to jump into the sea of love even though it is dangerous. Water flows clear in the sea but one can die if one drinks it. Likewise, love entices us to taste and to drink from it. But in fact, to indulge in the sea of love is no different from descending into a deep chasm where a hasty fall will prove deadly. One should descend carefully because once in the chasm and danger rears its head, it is too late to climb out.

The novel was originally published in 26 instalments totalling 3,229 pages. The reprint cited here comes in four volumes and uses finer print, totalling 1,461 pages. The entire novel was written in less than five months. The first printing sold an average of 15,026 copies per instalment, which translates to about 390,000 books sold. The author boasts that there is insufficient space in the National Library to shelve the number of books sold. Luang Wichit also claims in the preface of the second edition that the novel was mentioned in parliamentary speeches, university debates, exhibitions, etc. He claims that because of the novel's popularity the public must surely accept the novel's leading character, Praphimphan, as the exemplar of the modern Thai woman.

2   See Scot Barmé, *Luang Wichit Wathakan and the creation of a Thai identity* (Singapore: Institute of Southeast Asian Studies, 1993), especially pages 119–31.

111

who had subjugated the Thai. With *Huang rak haew luk*, however, Luang Wichit went beyond the notion of nationalistic militant feminism to break new ground: common and lower-class women offer a new, exciting and international model of the modern militant Thai woman.

But before examining this important novel, it is useful to review briefly Luang Wichit's long career as a government official, diplomat, educator and writer. Born as Kimliang Watthanaparuda to a poor family in Uthaithani Province in 1898, Luang Wichit received a Buddhist education as a novice but was only briefly a monk.[3] He exhibited early promise as a writer and thinker as a student at Wat Mahathat in Bangkok when he topped the nation in the fifth level Parian Pali examinations. Luang Wichit taught himself English and French, a feat that alarmed his superiors because monks were prohibited from learning foreign languages for fear that they would be exposed to insidious foreign ideas. After spending only two months as a monk, he left to join the Ministry of Foreign Affairs in 1918. Two years later, he won, through examination, a post to the Thai legation in France. There he continued his law and political science studies but he was transferred to London before he was able to finish them. During his six years in Europe, Luang Wichit became friendly with Pridi and Luang Phibun, the two leaders of the People's Party that overthrew the absolute monarchy in 1932. He also married a French woman with whom he had two children, a fact that is not widely circulated.[4] Prior to 1932, Luang Wichit carefully navigated a career in the bureaucracy and was somewhat neutral and apolitical. He did not join the People's Party but later became the ideological architect for nation-building, especially in the Phibun

---

3   For a detailed biography, see Luang Wichit's cremation volume, *Khana Ratthamontri, Wichitwathakan Anusorn*, 16 September 1962. When asked about his own racial background, Luang Wichit denied that he was part Chinese. He insisted that his Chinese first name was a popular convention at the time. This may be plausible because I know of several relatives whose names began with the Chinese 'Kim', which means 'gold'. They, too, deny any ties with the Chinese. Of course, another explanation is that the pressure to be accepted as Thai was so intense that most local-born ethnic Chinese, or those who have lived for generations in Thailand, do not want to identify themselves with the Chinese. More recently, of course, ethnic Chinese who are called '*jek*' insist that they are not really Chinese '*jin*' but a new hybrid of Thai and Chinese that is really 'Thai'. See Chapter 5 in this volume for further discussion. Is it plausible that Luang Wichit's fixation with race and pure blood lines reflect his own insecurities?
4   Luang Wichit married his French teacher with whom he had two children. They were divorced in 1933. This little-known fact may explain his gender bias when it came to the consideration of Thai conversion. Women can become Thai when married to a Thai man, but a foreign male can never become Thai; Barmé, *Luang Wichit Wathakan*, 43.

and Sarit governments. He took his role as teacher and nation-builder seriously: all of his writing, including his plays and his novels, is overtly didactic.[5]

Although he was fascinated by modern ideas, Luang Wichit was able to promote the construction of the modern Thai state by exploiting its past. In spite of accusations that he took many liberties when writing Thai history, it is undeniable that Luang Wichit Wathakan left a lasting imprint on how Thais view their past and how that view has influenced their self-understanding. Luang Wichit was the ideologue behind the post-1932 nationalism campaign under the Phibun regime. He wrote academic texts, essays, speeches, plays, songs and official state proclamations that established new values for Thai society. Luang Wichit's imaginative mind helped to promote a belief in the primacy of the state, the immutability of the Thai race, the necessity of militarism and the worship of historical personalities as national heroes and heroines. He was one of the first to insist that the word 'Thai' means 'to be free' or 'independent', and made sure that Thai heroes and heroines were only those who gave up their lives for the nation.

Luang Wichit was, however, selective in his choice of examples of the heroic deeds of past kings and the royals—the good royals such as Ramkhamhaeng and Naresuan who fought against foreign enemies to protect Thai independence. He believed that Sukhothai embodied the essence of 'Thai', an essence that became diluted and then polluted during the Ayuthaya period when the kings adopted Khmer forms of architecture and rituals. His didactic plays relied on national crises during the wars between Ayuthaya and Burma as settings. Because of his fascination with international politics, he also used his plays not just to promote

---

5 Luang Wichit's first books focused on world history, biographies of great men, Thai history, and on self-improvement. He authored 49 books that can be classified under these categories. Later, during the height of the nation-building campaign in the early 1930s, he turned to writing semi-historical plays, which were successful in providing a 'foundational' knowledge of popular history for his Thai audience. All in all, he penned about 24 plays. Luang Wichit also lectured on law and history at both Chulalongkorn and Thammasat universities. He prided himself as an intellectual and academic, and published no less than 24 volumes of his lecture notes. Incredibly, Luang Wichit also found the time to write 84 short stories and novels. Most of his novels focused on how people can struggle against all odds and win. One of his later novels, *Sang chiwit* [*Building a life*], which was published posthumously in 1971, chronicled the struggle of a peasant girl against the injustices of society. In that novel, Luang Wichit addresses the controversial issue of class exploitation and the urban–rural divide.

nationalism, but to highlight other causes as well.[6] He deviated from the example of Prince Damrong, the acknowledged father of Thai history, when he reinterpreted Thai history to include heroic deeds of the common folk. Perhaps most importantly, Luang Wichit concluded that common Thai men *and women* played important roles in protecting the nation.

As a playwright, Luang Wichit wrote 10 plays between 1936 and 1940. His efforts coincided with the intense promotion of Thai nationalism. What Wichit did was to emulate Rama VI's attempt to use performance and theatre to establish a more cultured citizenry.[7] As a concept, culture or *watthanatham* had been only introduced into the Thai discourse on modernity or *khwam than samai* in the 1930s. This discourse was also central to the fascist ideas of state and racial supremacy that were rampant in Europe. The refinement of culture was important to the Thai leadership. To escape the fate of its neighbours, the Thai should be seen by Western powers as a 'civilised/modern' people.[8] Wichit's early

---

6   Of his 24 major plays, the most influential were the nine that he wrote from 1936 to 1940. *Lueat suphan* [*The blood of Suphan*] (1936) promoted Japan's policy of Pan-Asianism; *Ratchamanu* (1937) asserted that the Thai and the Khmer were the same people to support irredentist claims; *Jaoying Saen Wi* (1938) claimed that the Thai and Shan in Burma should unite supported Pan-Thai claims. The play also reflected his fascination with Nazi Germany's policy of creating a new political entity based on race; *Phrajao Krungthon* [*The king of Thonburi*] (1937) claimed that the Thai and Chinese were brothers. He wrote another 10 plays between 1947 and 1949 in an attempt to make a living. He even formed his own theatre company in 1947 to perform the 10 plays that he wrote after being forced out of government service after returning to Thailand from Japan, where he had served as the Thai ambassador during the war. He was accused of war crimes and tried in court but was acquitted. Luang Wichit wrote four last plays, known as the *Anuphab* series, lauding the prowess of Thai leaders. These last plays were written at the request of Phibun in his last-ditch attempt to revitalise his political leadership (1954–57). His successor, Sarit Thanarat, reaped the benefits of Luang Wichit's last works as a playwright. For more detail see Pisanu Sunthraraks, 'Luang Wichit Wathakan: Hegemony and literature', PhD thesis, University of Wisconsin-Madison, 1986; Charnvit Kasetsiri, 'Latthi chatniyom latthi thahan [Nationalism and militarism]', in *Chomphon P. kap kanmueang thai samai mai* [*Field Marshal Phibun and modern Thai politics*], ed. Charnvit Kasetsiri et al., (Bangkok: Thammasat University Press, 1999), especially 389–92; Jiraporn Wiriyasakpan, 'Nationalism and the transformation of aesthetic concepts: Theatre in Thailand during the Phibun period', PhD thesis, Cornell University, 1992. Jiraporn outlines Luang Wichit's role in redefining Thai performances according to Western categories.
7   See Thamora Fishel, 'Romances of the sixth reign: Gender, sexuality, and Siamese nationalism', in *Genders and sexualities in modern Thailand*, ed. Peter A. Jackson and Nerida M. Cook (Chiangmai: Silkworm Books, 1999), 154–67. Fishel demonstrates that the use of plays to promote modern ideas and nationalism can be traced to Rama VI. She also makes a very good point about how nationalistic ideas are promoted through 'performance'.
8   See 'Dialogue between Nai Mun Chuchart and Nai Khong Rakthai broadcast over the radio between 1941–1942', in Thak Chaloemtiarana, ed., *Thai Politics, 1932–1947: Extracts and documents*, volume 1 (Bangkok: Social Science Association of Thailand, 1978), 270–3. The rationale put forth to the listening public is that colonial powers are interested in a civilising mission. Therefore, to escape colonialism, the Thai should become civilised in the eyes of the West. To be civilised is to be modern, and the West represents both. Interestingly, one device that Luang Wichit used to show that Thai

writings focused on 'great men', mostly Europeans, and how they became prominent as a way to demonstrate to his Thai readers how they could improve themselves: a civilised nation (*prathet siwilai*) could not be great unless its peoples were civilised. Nevertheless, the discourse here is not whether the Thai should emulate the West, but that certain achievements in science, technology, and culture, even though Western in form, are in fact indicators of modernity and high culture.

Luang Wichit's first play was called *Luk ratthathammanun* [*Children of the constitution*]. The play was a box office disaster.[9] Sensing, perhaps, that his audience was not ready for theatre based solely on modern, abstract themes, he wrote his first semi-historical drama, *Lueat suphan* [*The blood of Suphan*]. The play *Lueat suphan* boldly pairs a Burmese military officer with a local Thai woman as unlikely lovers. Tragically, both are killed during the Burmese occupation of Ayuthaya. The heroic deeds of Duangchan, the play's heroine, also acknowledge the martial spirit of all Thai women. In the play, Duangchan in fact instigates the uprising against the Burmese invaders. Luang Wichit's second play became an instant hit. Ticket sales allowed him to build a theatre and to buy sets and musical equipment. Recognising the importance of culture, Luang Wichit had accepted the directorship of the newly created department of culture. He also founded the School for Performing Arts. It taught the usual subjects but included music and theatre on top of regular schoolwork. Conveniently, students from the school performed Luang Wichit's plays.[10]

---

women were the equal of others was the promotion of a national beauty pageant. The first Miss Siam contest was held in 1936 as part of the Constitution Day Celebrations. Contestants came from all over the kingdom, representing their provinces. Provincial beauty queens discard their traditional *chongkrabaen*-style dress for the modern *phasin* at the national competition. Thai beauty queens became the model of the sophisticated modern Thai woman. See Suphatra Kohkitsuksakun, *Tamnan kanprakuat nangsao thai* [*History of the Thai beauty pageant*] (Bangkok: Samnakphim Dokbia, 1993).

9   During this period, other writers also wrote stories about valour and how citizens made sacrifices to protect the new state that was defined by its constitution. For example, Kulab Saipradit wrote a short story about a recently married young man who died trying to protect the new state from the Boworadet royalist forces that tried to re-establish the authority of the Crown in 1933. Si Burapha, *Lakon ratthathammanun* [*Farewell dear constitution*] (Bangkok: Withawat Press, 1979). This short story was first published in *Thoet ratthathammanun 2476* [*Honour the 1933 constitution*].

10 Wichitra Rangsiyanon, *Riang thoy roy chiwit wichitwathakan* [*The life of Wichitwathakan*] (Bangkok: Sangsan Books, 2000), especially Chapters 3 and 4. This book, written by his daughter, gives an inside look at Luang Wichit's life and work habits. In particular, she describes the struggle her father had to go through to find funds to build Thailand's first national theatre. His first musical play was staged in what could be described as a tent. Its success brought badly needed revenues that helped build a proper theatre. Luang Wichit was convinced that Rama VI was right to think that culture would change the Thai people. To find competent actors and musicians, he founded the School for Performing Arts.

Luang Wichit was also instrumental in influencing Thai historiography: female historical figures became accepted as national heroines. An obvious example is the somewhat controversial credit given to Thao Suranari.[11] He also wrote numerous nationalistic songs played over the radio, even though he did not know much about music. His plays and songs gave special emphasis to the heroism of common people, especially women, and the public readily embraced their ideas as historical truths.

Between 1939 and 1942, at the height of the nationalistic campaign, Luang Wichit chaired a committee that drafted the famous State Convention proclamations known as *Ratthaniyom*.[12] These proclamations changed the country's name from 'Siam', which was based on Chinese, to the more modern 'Thailand'; forced the public to salute the flag at eight o'clock every morning; to dress properly; to eat and exercise properly; and generally to behave as civilised people. The *Ratthaniyom* focused on ways to make Thailand a 'modern' state, one that must galvanise its citizens for war and colonial resistance. The *Ratthaniyom* campaign was reinforced by Luang Wichit's plays emphasising the ideal characteristics necessary to build the modern nation. Many of these characteristics—daringness and bravery, compassion, love of honour, love of duty, self-control, and perseverance—were, in fact, borrowed from Inazo Nitobe's *Bushido*, the Japanese code of the warrior.[13]

---

11 Thao Suranari was the wife of the deputy governor of Khorat at the time of the Jao Anuwong rebellion in 1827. She was credited with helping to defeat the Laotian forces at the battle of Thung Samrit. Laotian historiography questions the accuracy of the story. For more on this subject see Charles Keyes, 'National heroine or local spirit?' paper presented to the 6th Annual Conference on Thai Studies, 14–17 October 1996. Also, Thak Chaloemtiarana, 'Towards a more inclusive national narrative', in *Luem khotngao ko phao phaendin* [*Forget the past, torch the earth*], ed. Kanchanee La-ongsi and Thanet Aphornsuwan (Bangkok: Matichon Press, 2000), 76–82. Chetana Nagavajara argues that in order to promote gender equality in democratic Thailand, women's historical status was re-examined. Some scholars contend that Thai women were quite powerful and held high status during the Sukhothai period, where historical evidence shows that the Queen was required to follow the King out to battle. In something of a parody of this ancient practice, Phibun's wife also took to dressing up in a military uniform and was in fact granted a commission. And, during the 1940s when the National Culture Council was established, an active Woman's Department was also created. See Chetana Nagavajara, *Comparative literature from a Thai perspective* (Bangkok: Chulalongkorn University Press, 1996), 185–7.
12 For English translations of the *Ratthaniyom* documents, see Thak, *Thai politics*, 245–54.
13 Barmé, *Luang Wichit Watthakan*, 87.

When the popularity of his plays declined in the late 1940s, Luang Wichit turned to writing novels as a way to reach the public.[14] After becoming established as a novelist with *Morasum haeng chiwit* [*A stormy life*], he wrote his epic novel *Huang rak haew luk*.[15] Here he projects his view of Thai women to a higher level. From being actors on the national and regional stage, Thai women are given new roles as important *international actors*. In this novel, Luang Wichit also blurs the lines of gender by showing how a Thai woman can be like a man and yet retain her femininity. As in his plays glorifying an imagined past, *Huang rak haew luk* allowed the Thai to imagine new categories of roles that they could dream about fulfilling some day.

Such possibilities are suggested by what Benedict Anderson has identified as 'unbounded seriality'. Parochial and insular thinking could be replaced by new understanding of possible roles to play in real life that are open to the world and universal in application. For example, through exposure to modern print and performance media, people can begin to imagine that it is possible to assume new roles such as a Hollywood or local movie star, a national hero, a national heroine, a gun runner, a guerrilla fighter, a queen, or even a sophisticated international adventuress.[16]

---

14   Wichitra tells us that after Hollywood movies became popular and displaced live drama performances after the end of the Second World War, her father turned to writing novels instead. For a brief history of the Thai cinema, see Dome Sukwong and Sawasdi Suwannapak, *A century of Thai cinema*, trans. David Smyth (London: Thames & Hudson Ltd, 2001). So why did Luang Wichit finish his writing career as a 'lowly' novelist? In the Thai book market, novels are sometimes referred to as *nangsue an len* (a book to read for fun), meaning that they are not serious creative literary works. Although his daughter Wichitra tells us that Luang Wichit was able to make more money from his novels than from his salary as a cabinet minister, her father did not write novels just to make money. More importantly, he told her that people should not look down on this lowly form of writing. In fact, novelists remain famous for eternity, unlike academic authors whose texts must undergo constant revisions to remain useful. New texts also make older texts obsolete. But writers such as Shakespeare and Molière remain current and are still taught in schools. Luang Wichit believed that the novel is a very potent form of teaching because people are influenced without realising it. He went on to cite how history has been changed by the use of novels and plays that affected people's thinking and actions. Luang Wichit was convinced that literature is a powerful weapon for social engineering. Wichitra, *The life of Wichitwathakan*, 40–1.
15   It should be noted that even though Luang Wichit was most proud of *Huang rak haew luk* because it covered all of his favourite themes, recent scholars have picked his less lengthy novels as the best of his work. For example, the committee that wrote *Nangsue di 100 lem* [*One hundred good books*] (Bangkok: Samnakngan Kongthun Sanapsanun Kanwichai, 1999) did not select Luang Wichit's most famous novel, *Huang rak haew luk*, nor was he cited for his popular plays. Instead, they picked *Sang chiwit*, a later and much shorter novel. In Pratheep Muannil, *100 nak praphan thai* [*One hundred Thai writers*] (Bangkok: Suweeriyasan, 1999), Luang Wichit is cited for his voluminous production. Pratheep acknowledges that *Huang rak haew luk* was one of Luang Wichit's most popular novels.
16   Benedict Anderson, *The spectre of comparisons*, (London: Verso Press, 1998), Chapter 1.

Not surprisingly, Luang Wichit's model of the modern Thai woman differs radically from previous role models. Traditionally, the possibilities for a Thai woman could be said to derive from traditional literary models: Sita in the Indian epic, the *Ramayana* (*Ramakian*), Nang Wanthong in *Khun chang khun phaen*, or Queen Jamathewi in *Jamathewiwong*. Surely, the idea of a traditional Thai woman as *pha phap wai* or a 'neatly folded piece of cloth', presumably to be unfolded by whoever becomes her husband, must come from aristocratic ideas based on Hindu Buddhist beliefs embodied, for example, by Sita, Rama's consort in the Thai *Ramakian*. Scot Barmé has also argued that modern model of the Thai woman is found in the proto-feminist discourse around the mystical figure Nang Noppamas, a fictional character dating back to 13th-century Sukhothai. This *yot ying* or supreme woman, he concludes:

> was said to have possessed a rare combination of qualities: an agreeable disposition, a lustrous golden complexion (to which her name refers), and above all a keen intelligence and an outstanding ability as both a scholar and poet.[17]

And, again according to Barmé, in 1905, Thianwan, a controversial Thai thinker, became the first Thai intellectual to dare to write about the role of women in modern Thailand.[18] Thianwan argued that women should

---

17 Scot Barmé, 'Proto-feminist discourse in early twentieth century Siam', in Jackson and Cook, *Genders and sexualities*, 140–2.
18 Scot Barmé, 'Proto-feminist discourse', 140–2. Luang Wichit also acknowledges a sense of gratitude for the bravery of Thianwan to speak his mind. He wrote a short preface in 1951 for a book about Thianwan by Sangob Suriyin: *Thianwan* (Bangkok: Ruansan Press, 2000). This version is the third edition of a book published in 1951. In Scot Barmé's book, *Woman, man, Bangkok* (Oxford: Rowman and Littlefield, 2002), the national debate regarding the social position of Thai women during the 1920s and beyond was discussed in great detail. Keeping this background in mind, Luang Wichit's literary production, especially his focus on women engaged in dangerous activities, must have been tempered by his exposure to the various exciting new 'models' of Thai feminism that were being publicly tested. For example, several years before Luang Wichit wrote his nationalistic plays and novels celebrating Thai feminism, a startling short story entitled *Jon jori* [*The female bandit leader*] appeared in the weekly *Suphap nari* [*Genteel lady*] in 1931. The story portrays a young Thai woman as a notorious gang leader who planned and staged daring robberies. A picture of this masked female bandit (looking like the Lone Ranger) riding a horse and chasing a speeding car appears on page 200 of Barmé's book. Barmé asserts that this early story is an attempt to challenge the traditional model of the Thai female and to replace it with character that negates feminism as the weaker sex. During this same period, the magazine also serialised historical accounts of the exploits of Queen Suriyothai, who died in elephant combat trying to save her husband in a war between Ayutthaya and Burma in the 16th century. Interestingly, the exploits of Queen Suriyothai has been made into a multi-million dollar movie in 2001, funded by the Thai royal court. The movie took great liberties with historical accuracy and clearly conveyed the message that Thai women, albeit the aristocracy—both good and bad—played a pivotal role in statecraft and the many deadly struggles for political power. The film had its gala showing in the United States in October 2002 with the Thai Queen in attendance.

be allowed to get an education equal to men, and that they should be allowed to work and contribute to the economic wellbeing of the country. He concludes that the modern Thai woman is one who is educated, graceful, civilised, progressive and Western in orientation. Unfortunately, this view is incomplete.

Although space will not permit any discussion of the relevance of traditional and classic literature in a debate on gender, it may be most helpful to say that the construction of the modern Thai female identity is a contestation and amalgamation of several ideal types and 'possibilities' suggested in popular plays, religious beliefs, traditional practices, lived experiences and works of fiction. Due to its popularity, Luang Wichit's epic *Huang rak haew luk* figures prominently among the mid-20th-century literary works that focus on gender issues. And, although more studies will have to be conducted to fully assess its impact, there can be no doubt that this novel played a major role in helping construct a new and more modern model of Thai feminism.[19]

Observers of Thai society have marvelled at how the Thai female is such a multi-faceted being. She is described as the de facto head of the family, a businesswoman, a sweet, caring mother and wife (whose public demeanour downplays her sexuality), a day labourer, a beauty queen, a whore, a masseuse, a murderer, a nun, etc. In a recent study, the contemporary public image of Thai women has been essentialised to represent two opposite models that Rachel Harrison has called the 'Madonna and the Whore': whether a woman is good or bad depends on her relationship to the family as an institution.[20] One problem, of course,

---

19 As gender is a cultural construct, understanding literature can be one avenue that can give us a window into that culture. Literature not only reflects and expresses features of culture, but it can also contest old values and propose new ones. See Thelma Kintanar, 'Notes on tradition and the construction of gender in Southeast Asian literary texts', in *Texts and contexts: Interactions between literature and culture in Southeast Asia*, ed. Luisa J. Mallari-Hall (Quezon City: Department of English and Comparative Literature, University of the Philippines, 1999), 17. Gender is defined partly by social relations—the Asian female gender is traditionally represented as wives, lovers, mothers, cooks, etc. Women are expected to be gentle, nurturing, faithful, pragmatic and not necessarily romantic.

20 Rachel Harrison, 'The Madonna and the Whore: Self/Other tensions in the characterization of the prostitute by Thai female authors', in Jackson and Cook, *Genders and sexualities*, 168–90. To be fair, Harrison was focusing mainly on sexuality and sexual mores of Thai women. Most current research and writing is focused on traditional feminine roles as it relates to the family, the role of women in the economy, and/or the commodification of the female body in the sex trade. Much of the literature on the last topic explains feminism and sex in economic terms. For example, Virada Somsawasdi and Sally Theobald, eds, *Women, gender relations and development in Thai society* (Chaingmai: Women's Studies Center, Chaingmai University, 1997); Ryan Bishop and Lillian Robinson, *Night market* (New York: Routledge, 1998); Andrea Whittaker, *Intimate knowledge* (St Leonards: Allen & Unwin, 2000);

with dividing things into two is that it slights the undistributed middle. In this case, a glance at Thai tabloids will reveal yet another possibility, one we may call the 'dangerous woman'.

Thai newspapers consistently exploit those who have lost their lives through love. Many of the headlines and front-page pictures show murder scenes where the victim is a male lover who has been shot. Other times, the reading public is treated to a picture of two lovers, dead by gunshot wounds, laying naked or semi-naked in bed. Another famous story that has been circulating among Thai males for several decades is the report of a woman who cut off her philandering husband's genitals and fed them to her ducks. The story is still discussed with much nervous humour among young men, but there is also a warning side to that story. Thai women do in fact commit such acts, but theirs seem not to be merely crimes of passion, but crimes calculated to punish. Therefore, not only are Thai women represented as the mysterious exotic beauty found on tourism posters, or as sexual objects advertised in sex tour brochures in Europe and Japan, they are also represented in the popular press as dangerous lovers.

The evidence is clear that Luang Wichit deliberately set out to create this new role for Thai women. In his preface to the second printing, Luang Wichit asserts that the novel's heroine Praphimphan represents the new Thai woman: her imaginary life of love, lust and murder provides lessons to the reading public about how women can overcome their adversaries.[21] Indeed, the very structure of the novel divides neatly into three parts, each defined by Praphimphan's age and the location of the plot. The first part is devoted to Praphimphan's early adult life in Thailand, and her studying and vacationing in Europe. The middle is devoted to Praphimphan's returning to Thailand, but with a twist: she remains on the periphery on the Malay border and, after committing still more crime, goes into exile

---

Jeremy Seabrook, *Travels in the skin trade* (London: Pluto Press, 1996); Cleo Odzer, *Patpong sisters* (New York: Arcade Publishing, 1994); *Kankha ying* [*Trade in women*] (Report of the Thai Women's Foundation, 1997); Suleeman Wongsuphab, *Nang ngam tu krajok* [*The beauty behind the glass case*] (Bangkok: Khlet Thai Press, 1987). More research is still needed on the effects of the media, popular culture, music and popular literature on our understandings of what is feminine.

21   Wichitra tells us that the wives of soldiers stationed at the military camp in Prachinburi routinely ambushed the weekly shipments of the individual volumes that came by rail. To make sure that they would not miss an instalment, they would hijack the books before they reached the book stores. Wichitra, *The life of Wichitwathakan*, 39. Luang Wichit also tells his readers in the preface of the second edition that he has heard from his many students now stationed as district officers throughout Thailand that *Huang rak haew luk* was read by people of all walks of life, from the governor down to the literate farmer.

to Africa and Arabia. The last part concerns her recovery from insanity, her homecoming and her death. Each of these three parts, moreover, has its own distinctive themes. What follows is a necessarily brief summary of the way Luang Wichit has interwoven these themes with the three narrative stages of Praphimphan's life.

I

The story of Praphimphan's early adult life prepares her for a future of international adventure and militant feminism. As the dutiful daughter of a retired, minor government employee whose wealth is dwindling fast, Praphimphan first leads a traditional life. She soon shows her independence, however, by secretly learning how to shoot her father's pistol and then, wanting to revenge a prank played on her father, by challenging Thongthet, the son of a local notable, to a duel. He does not accept, but does fall in love with this daring woman. Throughout the novel, men fall for her female charms and her physical beauty. And, amidst these feminine characteristics, Praphimphan also exhibits masculine identification marks—she likes to shoot, to challenge her tormentors to duels; she enjoys drinking coffee (not done by Thai women at that time); and is unforgiving of those who have wronged her. She can be a nurturing woman with her friends, but a vengeful executioner of her enemies.

Refusing Thongthet's suit, she then moves away from home and takes a job in a factory. Like her becoming a legal aide later, this is a new opportunity for her generation of women. After Thongthet again dupes her father, he visits her to ask her to marry him. Pretending to fall for him, Praphimphan lures him into her bedroom and shoots him three times. She then convinces the police that he tried to rape her. In a Hobbesian twist, the weaker sex can kill the stronger when the man is blinded by love or lust.

Once more working as a housekeeper, Praphimphan must look after a family friend, Manote, who is recovering his health. While studying herbal medicine with Dr Gautier, a French doctor in Vietnam, Manote had fallen in love with Waenfa, the lovely daughter of another French doctor and his Laotian wife. Unfortunately for their love affair, Waenfa had ingested so much poison during her father's medical experiments that she could not be his wife. When Manote kisses her anyway, he promptly falls into a coma. Here, Luang Wichit has created a female figure that is in all senses 'poisonous'. The story of Manote and Waenfa describes the tension between love and passion, beauty and poison, modern and traditional medicine, and even Thailand and colonialism. Underlining this theme of the novel, Dr Gautier warns Manote about women:

> All women are poisonous … They only differ in the kinds of poison they possess. Some are so poisonous that they kill us; some make us bankrupt; others make us their love slaves who can never be redeemed. Don't forget that the sea of love is the deep chasm of death. If you slip and fall you will not survive.[22]

One can equally argue that Waenfa is an expression of a longstanding misogynistic view of women as polluting and negating man's inner strength. The Buddhist legend of Queen Jamathewi, written in 1570, telling the story of the founding of Lamphun in the 11th century is a good case in point. Queen Jamathewi promised to marry a powerful suitor if he succeeded in throwing his spear from a mountain top into her city. In one version of the story, the Queen tricked her suitor into wearing a hat she had given him smeared with her menstrual blood. The unclean blood drained the prince's power and his spear fell short of its target. Menstrual blood is seen as unclean and debilitating by Thai men, even in modern Thailand.

Praphimphan promptly extends this theme by telling Manote that she is more dangerous than the poisonous Waenfa because she was willing to kill—and, indeed, she already had killed a man. It would be easy to kill someone she loves if that person betrays her love, she warns him:

> Because I have never loved, love is sacred to me and must be worshipped. Before I admit to loving someone, I must think and rethink carefully. If I utter my love, I want that person to know that this is a grave matter. And the person whose love I accept will be courting danger.[23]

In a concession to tradition, however, Luang Wichit has their respective parents forbid their marriage and arrange a marriage for each of them. Defiantly, the two lovers vow to keep loving each other despite their spouses: status and 'face', while still dominant in modern, democratic Thailand, can be ignored and subverted. However, Manote would become

---

22 Luang Wichit, *Huang rak haew luk*, 123.
23 Luang Wichit, *Huang rak haew luk*, 145.

Praphimphan's second victim. After luring him into her bedroom while her husband was away, she shoots him for not upholding his end of their bargain.[24]

In a reverie later in the novel, we learn that just before Praphimphan decides to move with her father to live in the southern part of Thailand, a backwater, she disguises herself, lures her husband into a dark alley and executes him with her pistol. By the age of 22, Praphimphan has become a dangerous woman: of the four men who have loved her, she has killed three. She even confesses humorously to her lawyer, Atthapphit, one of the four men who is in love with her, that she has learned to be economical and not use more than two shots to kill her latest victim. She had emptied her gun when she shot her lover, Manote.

Instead of staying in the south of Thailand, her father tells her that he has received a large sum of money from Thaimchan and is taking Praphimphan to Europe to continue her studies.[25] In Singapore, Praphimphan encounters a 19-year-old Thai woman, Waewta, who asks to become her servant. Telling Praphimphan her life story, Waewta reveals that she is a poor villager who made a living selling seaweed, and that she, too, has been involved in a murder. Waewta is thus a younger version of Praphimphan. Together, they go off to explore Europe as a pair of kindred souls.[26]

---

24 The novel actually begins with a meeting between Praphimphan's husband and her attorney, Atthapphit. The latter is defending her in a case of manslaughter. Praphimphan at first denied that she had indeed planned to murder her lover, Manote. And, in a twist of logic, Praphimphan says that her real husband was in fact Manote and her relationship with her legal husband was an adulterous affair. But even after Atthapphit finds evidence that his client was indeed guilty, instead of pulling out of the case, he continues and wins her acquittal. Instead of condemning her, Atthapphit praises Praphimphan for being true to her love, a 'one hearted woman' (*phuying jai diaw*), and falls in love with her.
25 In another twist of morality, Praphimphan's financial benefactor is Thiamchan, a woman who was having an affair with Atthapphit. Thiamchan poisoned Atthapphit's wife and tried to pin the crime on Praphimphan. Perhaps recognising another kindred soul in the ruthless Thiamchan, who murdered for love, Praphimphan destroys evidence that would have incriminated Thiamchan. In fact, she wishes Thiamchan and Atthapphit well as she leaves Bangkok, intent upon living a life in the countryside.
26 Waewta was a village girl who, for dubious reasons, strangled the sick father of her future husband, Khwan. She wanted to help him inherit his father's fortunes, which would have gone to his stepmother. In the beginning, she had no interest in Khwan and only agreed to marry him many years later after returning from Europe, and at the insistence of Praphimphan. In a way, the murder was senseless at the time.

The two women go off to study in Europe, something that had been nearly exclusively the prerogative of Thai men. That tradition continues, for their male friend Songwut accompanies them, but their journey clearly represents modern female emancipation. What this emancipation consists of is rather less clear, however: Luang Wichit is vague about their course of study. It is almost as though the Thai women are in Europe to learn English and to see the world. The experience was a kind of 'finishing school' for them.

Songwut's role is also representative: he shows that the Thai are the equal of Europeans. Far from being unmistakably Thai, he is assumed to be a Persian prince! He is tall, smart, plays tennis well and is a superb dancer. Most importantly, he is a good speaker of English. He even has a brief affair with an older woman, a wayward Countess.

Perhaps because this 'prince' is so *sympathique*, the Countess unburdens herself on the nature of women, suggesting that pronouncements about gender are universal and not just Thai or European. The Countess makes a series of observations about the nature of women and their relationship to men, especially husbands. She says emphatically that women are by nature verbal beings who need to have a good and sympathetic listener. Women do not want to be alone but want to be loved and appreciated. At one point she says:

> Women do not want anything more than to be considered human beings. Women do not want equal rights to men. All they ask is to be allowed to have a life and the right to think for themselves.[27]

She laments the fact that women are treated like pets and that men think that all they have to do is to provide women with a nice house, with food, money and clothing. Women are expected to act like song birds in a gilded cage and never to escape into the wider world to enjoy themselves. But most women end up sacrificing their bodies out of duty to their husbands, which is no different than being raped. Men should not be so cruel. Husbands and wives should be friends and equal partners, and it is the duty of husbands to listen to what their wives have to say. If not, wives would seek friendship elsewhere. It is important to listen to women who are, by nature, worriers. Men think logically in terms of cause and effect, but women act on instinct without concern for consequences. Women

---

27   Luang Wichit, *Huang rak haew luk*, 563.

are not rational beings but emotional ones. However, it is most important for men to forgive women for what appears to be irrational.[28] Traditional (if not, perhaps, universal) as these assertions are, they have almost nothing to do with the way Praphimphan acts in this novel. They instead serve as a muted counterpoint, implicitly contrasting the traditionally passive role of Thai women with the far more compelling actions of Praphimphan.

This first part of the novel ends with a transition that frees Songwut from his sworn obligation to Praphimphan. After failing to win Praphimphan, Songwut falls in love with a half-German Gypsy, Salome, who is soon given a new Thai name, Khomkham ('Sharp and witty'). In short order, she finds a Thai-language text in Rome and learns the language. Luang Wichit's Thai readers, of course, had no idea that this is preposterous; they presumably believed that Thailand must be an important country and that foreigners would want to study Thai. By this device, Luang Wichit raised Thai to the level of French, Spanish, German and English. By learning the language of her new lover, Khomkham leaves behind her identity of Salome and becomes Thai. Believing that her husband still loved Praphimphan, she runs away, becomes sick and dies. Her 'death'— by leaping into a gorge in the mountains—and 'resurrection'—once she knows that Songwut loves her, she comes back to life—is symbolic: she dies a Gypsy and is reborn a Thai.[29] Later, she even teaches her son Thai, a point the more telling because there is no real need to do so: she has left her Thai husband and has been reunited with her German father and they are living in South Africa. A woman can become Thai, but, as we shall notice later, a man cannot.

---

28   The Countess had an affair with her husband's younger brother, which led to their divorce. During that divorce, she fell prey to her employer's sexual advances. But, together with the employer's wife, the two plotted his murder, which was ruled a suicide. In spite of her indiscretion and complicity in a murder, the Countess pleads innocent. She acted the way she did because she was a woman who needed attention from her husband. This is not the only instance in the novel where a woman is allowed to have affairs just like men. However, the main differences are that they want to be forgiven if caught and, if their lovers cross them, then they will be killed. The Countess also flirted with Songwut and there is a suggestion that the two had a brief affair. According to Rachel Harrison, it seems that falling in love with European countesses is a common theme found among Thai *hua nork* (foreign and outward-looking) young men. A similar theme also appears in one of the earliest Thai novels, namely, M.C. Akatdamkoeng Raphiphat's *Lakhon haeng chiwit* [*Circus of life*], first published in 1929 (author's correspondence with Rachel Harrison, 26 July 2002).
29   In fact, what her husband witnessed was a mirage. She had already 'died' but her spirit was still out roaming about. When her husband found her, he only met her spiritual body or *kayathip* that ran up the mountain to commit suicide by jumping into the 'chasm of death' (*haew luk*).

II

The middle of the novel concerns Praphimphan's returning to Thailand to live in a village near the Malay border and, after she commits still more crimes, her going into exile to Africa and Arabia. While living in the south in Waewta's village and learning to become a writer, her father tries to make her marry her first cousin, Chuwong, who had recently divorced. Instead of doing so, Praphimphan befriends his ex-wife, Phuangrak, and they become good friends. Their friendship confirms the idea of female solidarity, especially among Thai women. When Phuangrak asks her if she can tell Praphimphan her life story when they first met, for example, Praphimphan answers:

> Thais do not have to stand on ceremony like the *farang* Westerners, we are friends belonging to the same race and same nation [*phuen ruam chat ruam prathet*]. Also as friends of the same gender [*phuen ruam phet*], we can easily get to know each other.[30]

This particular episode confirms Luang Wichit's intention of creating gender solidarity among Thai women, and that this new solidarity should liberate women from the traditional self-identity that is tied to the family and to the male; now she can, as a separate entity, bond with other females.

Being liberated, however, does not mean that the traditional concern for the family is altered. As Songwut had earlier reconciled the estranged Countess and Count, so here Praphimphan reconciles Phuangrak with her divorced husband. Luang Wichit still believed that the family is important and should be kept together, even in the face of the new tensions created by modernity.[31]

---

30   Luang Wichit, *Huang rak haew luk*, 777.
31   Phuangrak and Chuwong's divorce was the result of a senseless disagreement about how to treat a servant who had helped Chuwong when he was younger. Phuangrak wanted the maid to be more respectful and subservient, but her husband did not agree. It is not that he felt some obligation to show gratefulness, but he believes that if 'democratic' Thailand was to survive, equality and dignity should be accorded to all citizens. Because if not, there was the danger of class warfare. Chuwong explains to his wife that:

> revolutions and mass unrest where poor people take over the mansions of the rich and kill their owners resulted from minor incidents such as this ... All classes of people should be friends.

There is still some confusion about how to treat lower status people in the new democratic Thailand.

Set off against this reconciliation is the adultery of Waewta, married now to Khwan, the local farmer whose father she murdered before setting off to study in Europe. Despite being warned by Praphimphan, Waewta begins an affair with Sirisin, a friend of Songwut's who has just returned from Europe, where he had received a doctorate in economics. Six days later, Sirisin is dead, killed by the jealous husband. Reprimanding Khwan for spying on his wife (but not, incidentally, for murdering her lover), Praphimphan reunites Khwan and Waewta, persuading them to promise that they will remain faithful to each other. This is the third time in the novel that a family is kept together or brought back together.

Unfortunately, the police correctly suspect that Praphimphan has murdered Khwan's chauffeur, his accomplice in the murder of Sirisin, so Praphimphan must flee Thailand yet again. Sailing solo east towards the Nicobar Islands, she encounters a storm. Lashing herself to the mast as the storms engulfs her small sailboat, she loses consciousness.

When she comes to, she finds herself in a large ship owned and captained by a nationalist, Supharat, a Mon-Malay gun runner from Tavoy, once claimed by Thailand. He told her he had seen her in Europe but was unable to introduce himself: he felt that, as a British colonial subject, he would be shunned by Asians who came from independent countries.[32] Praphimphan, of course, promptly replies that this distinction means nothing to her. Fellow Asians and nationalists are natural friends to the Thai whose country has never been colonised.

When they go ashore in Tavoy after the weapons are unloaded, Praphimphan and Supharat are quickly spotted by the police. Rather than surrender, they fire back as they make their escape by boat. This action resonates with Luang Wichit's earlier plays in which Thai women take up the sword to fight against foreign oppressors. Here, of course, swords are replaced by pistols, a modern weapon. Although Supharat is a 'good' nationalist, he is not Thai, a factor that weighs with Praphimphan when he too falls in love with her. In contrast to Khomkham, a woman who became 'Thai' because she learned to speak Thai and her son spoke Thai, the best that Supharat can be is someone who can *act* like a Thai. As a man, he cannot become Thai.[33]

---

32 Luang Wichit, *Huang rak haew luk*, 914.
33 Luang Wichit's concept of race is defined as the 'blood' of a people, as demonstrated by the title of his most famous play *Lueat suphan* [*The blood of Suphan*]. It is the concept of a common blood line that binds people together. He seems to conflate race, ethnicity and nationality. In this

Praphimphan and Supharat make good their escape, landing in Africa, where they are greeted by Songwut and Khomkham, now reunited.[34] After Supharat departs for Lorenzo Marguez, Praphimphan meets a good friend of Songwut, an Arab named Muni (a word similar to the Thai for 'sage' or 'monk'). He, too, is a nationalist fighting the authorities. After the (predictable) running gun battle, Praphimphan and Muni escape to a hidden valley, where they take control of the tiny kingdom of Senabad. The new queen of this kingdom is none other than Waenfa, the poisonous woman (in a wonderful moment, Waenfa's worthiness is revealed during the coronation ceremony when a poisonous snake bites her, and it dies). Praphimphan, the poisonous woman by choice, and Waenfa, the poisonous woman by nature, soon become good friends.

Praphimphan is in her element in this part of the novel: she not only is still the dangerous pistolera but the power behind the throne. The monarchy is indeed benevolent. The new rulers proceed to find ways to systematically exploit the valley's natural resources, such as gold and diamonds. New houses and roads are built for the people. To help with the mining and the extraction of gold and diamond, Praphimphan brings in Songwut, Khomkham and her father, who is an expert on diamond mines. They are soon joined by Supharat. Praphimphan also learns that her protégé Waewta had divorced her jealous husband Khwan. She, too, shows up in Senabad. In effect, Praphimphan has her whole 'gang' with her for this adventure. Waewta shows up with a writer by the name of Niphon. Niphon was educated in France and England. He had heard of Praphimphan and wanted to write about her adventures. No sooner has he met her than he, too, falls under her spell.

In this section, Luang Wichit's imagination takes flight. He writes about how a new dynasty is formed—rituals, myths and violence. It is not clear whether he is a royalist or a democrat. Although Luang Wichit has just created a new state from scratch, this state is a monarchy in which everyone

---

instance, he privileges the male who, upon marrying women with 'foreign blood', can make them Thai. This conversion appears throughout the novel, both symbolically and in real life. Luang Wichit reinforces this idea by making Praphimphan reject the offers of love from foreigners because they can never become Thai. But she readily accepts other women such as Khomkham, a German-Gypsy, and Waenfa, a French-Laotian as Thai. See footnote 4.

34 Luang Wichit uses a description of Africa and African culture to correct previous racist sentiments against the African popularised during the height of the nationalism campaign. 'Negroes' were posed as the uncivilised 'Other'. The author appears to have over-corrected his misguided prejudices by concluding that certain roof forms of Thai royal architecture are not Indian but really African in origin. Luang Wichit, *Huang rak haew luk*, 972–3.

speaks to the queen in the Thai sacred royal language. But Waewta is not even Thai; she is half Lao and half French. Nevertheless, this section also shows Luang Wichit's progressive thinking: a woman can be queen, which thereby questions whether gender should be an issue in Thai palatine law governing succession to the throne. The author also justifies exploitation by the state and its new rulers. He suggests that no new dynasty or regime can function if it does not engage in some sort of plunder that would fill the coffers of the new regime; he also suggests the ruler should also keep some of the new-found wealth. Money is needed for government or for the consolidation of a new leadership.

Such pragmatism seems to have been carried out by Thai political leaders like Police General Phao Sriyanon and Field Marshal Sarit Thanarat in the mid-1950s. The former traded in opium, while his rival skimmed money from the Lottery Bureau.[35] Luang Wichit also writes about different forms of succession in this section—usurpation of the throne through force, coup d'état by a military group, and the assumption of political leadership through the invocation of god's will. Each new dynasty must amass as much wealth as possible not just for itself, but so that its friends and family will also be rich so that they can help the people. In the mythical kingdom of Senabad, Waewta was at first reluctant to do this, but Praphimphan insisted that it was fine because, unlike other dynasties, the new ruler did not make the people slaves, and thus what they were doing was for the good of the people. Such ideas reflect the paternalism so common in many of Luang Wichit's political writings.

Luang Wichit also includes international politics in the novel. Implausible as it may seem, Praphimphan and Muni travel to Geneva to a meeting of the League of Nations to lobby for recognition of the small kingdom and its new queen. This attempt, of course, fails because, with only 300 people, their principality was much smaller than others such as Luxembourg, Monaco or Liechtenstein. More importantly, the proposed kingdom is located in the territory of a major colonial power. To make his readers think that Thailand was an important international player, Luang Wichit gives the Thai ambassador more international clout than is plausible. But the story highlights the author's fascination with diplomacy and Thailand's role in international politics.

---

35 Legitimising the use of force, Luang Wichit describes how Praphimphan personally trained a small army not only to protect the small kingdom, but to kill her political rivals. For the struggle between Phao and Sarit, see Thak Chaloemtiarana, *Thailand: The politics of despotic paternalism* (Ithaca: Cornell Southeast Asia Program Publications, 2007; revised edition), Chapter 2.

Muni eventually convinces Praphimphan to love him, but she cannot agree to marry him: he is not Thai, and, as a male, he could never become Thai. Only the male blood line is important to the determination of race. The female can be Thai because she will give birth to children who are Thai through the blood of their father (*jus sanguini*). Always the dangerous woman, Praphimphan unintentionally kills Muni while she is asleep: dreaming she was being assaulted by Thongthet, the first man she shot, she takes out her pistol and shoots him in the chest, only to awaken and find that she has shot Muni instead.

This deadly accident is soon followed by the apparition of her father's spirit, a sign to her that he has died, and Praphimphan suffers a nervous breakdown.

III

When Praphimphan returns to consciousness, it is four years later, and she is in Austria. She, too, has been reborn: during her sleep, none other than Dr Freud has administered a drug to her; she tells him all, and she wakes up cured from her mental agony. Interestingly, her behaviour does not alter: a nurse who has been cruel to her is found dead in a bathtub, and the circumstances strongly suggest that Praphimphan drowned her. She is also still eager to help others in illegal and even immoral acts that mete out justice to those who have wronged her or those close to her.[36]

She finally decides to marry, but her choice falls not on a virile male like Supharat or Muni but on a struggling writer, Niphon. The pen may well be mightier than the sword, but Niphon's proposal is not even romantic: he wants to be a great writer and make the world recognise the beauty of Thai literature, and since every man must have a good woman behind him, he asks her to be this woman. A good union, he says, would be the union of two good friends.

Characteristically, Praphimphan responds to Niphon's letter by asking practical questions, as well. She wonders why he would want to marry a middle-aged woman who is 33 years old, a woman who has been with

---

36   Praphimphan helps her landlord beat up an old Jew who raped his (the landlord's) daughter. The badly crippled old man suffered for many years before succumbing to his injuries.

two men, whose name is on the lips of tens and hundreds of thousands of people, and someone who has once lost her mind. She warns Niphon that at 33, it may be difficult for her to give him children, and that perhaps her insanity could be passed on to their children.

Again, in an inversion of conventional right and wrong, the author makes Niphon praise Praphimphan for setting a good example for other women, for representing the model woman. Niphon tells Praphimphan that:

> on face value, your life may appear to be difficult and soiled as you say. But if we were to examine it closely, having had two husbands is not that unusual for women. And after your divorce these past ten years, you have preserved your dignity and have not strayed. The other things that you did, even though they were evil, were acts that were to seek justice for yourself and for others. Your life is a life of struggle worthy of praise. Praphimphan is a name that is on the lips of tens and hundreds of thousands of people. But they do not speak of your name in negative ways. They see Praphimphan as the model woman. Heaven has created you to become a model for all women, an example of how women should face life.[37]

Luang Wichit's aim to present a radical model of the modern Thai woman could scarcely be more explicit.

After their wedding, Praphimphan allows Niphon to embrace her. She even turns her cheek to let him kiss her and allows him to kiss her passionately on the lips. She feels the 'venom of love' (*phit rak*) enter her body and thinks about the venom of death that coursed through Waenfa's veins. Love can be so sweet and so deadly. In the end, succumbing to the occasion, she implores Niphon:

> kiss me, make love to me. Your kiss will erase the fact that I have been kissed before. Embrace me tightly so I can forget past embraces. Caress me all over so I can cleanse my body of past blemishes. What remains is my pure self that belongs only to you.[38]

---

37 Luang Wichit, *Huang rak haew luk*, 1271.
38 Luang Wichit, *Huang rak haew luk*, 1285.

What Freud could not do, the writer-lover-husband Niphon can: she is now purified, cleansed by transcendent love.[39]

But, in almost karmic retribution, her husband comes down with incurable tuberculosis and, tragically, their daughter is born deaf. Niphon hangs himself out of grief. Praphimphan soon sinks into another depression. She laments that the life of a girl or woman is represented by the dismissive saying *di mueankan* or 'that's alright'—an acknowledgement that is really a sign of resignation or acceptance of one's fate. The birth of a deaf daughter was only *di mueankan*. This remark was what Rama VI said on his death bed when he was shown his only child. His only words after learning that he had sired a daughter was *di mueankan*. Such is the fate of traditional girls and of women.

In an effort to find the blossom of the *toey* plant to cure her daughter's deafness, Praphimphan and Waenfa embark on a *Thelma and Louise* adventure. The two women proceed to paddle a small canoe down the Danube in an expedition to search for the elusive plant.[40] There, some men also prospecting for medicinal plants make the mistake of trying to scare them away. Praphimphan promptly shoots two of them in the leg, after which the men tell her where the plant can be found. Their adventurous trip is exhilarating, liberating and empowering.

When the two women reach Hungary, immigration officers ask about their nationality. Waewta endears herself to Praphimphan when she tells the officers that she is 'Thai' and not 'Laotian'. This assertion reflects the author's Pan-Thai aspirations that emerged prior to the Second World War. It also emphasises the author's jingoism: being Thai is better than

---

39   Luang Wichit arranges to clean the blood on Praphimphan's hands through two devices. The first is through ritual cleansing or *sadok khro*. During the gun battle with the police in one of her adventures, Praphimphan receives a superficial wound in her side. In her mind, this is a good thing because she had shot other people but had never known what it felt like to be shot. After this ritual cleansing, she believes that her luck will become better. The second cleansing involves transcendence through love when she submits to Niphon.

40   *Thelma and Louise* refers to the Hollywood film starring Susan Sarandon and Geena Davis that established the female bonding film genre. The *toey* plant grows along the banks of a river, pond or lake: it is used as flavouring for dessert. The Thai variety does not flower and propagates through a root system. A popular Thai proverb about unfulfilled love compares the hopelessness of pursuit with attempts to make the *toey* plant blossom. The comparison here is that of Praphimphan's unfulfilled love life now epitomised by its flawed progeny—her deaf daughter. However, redemption would come in the form of a European variety of the plant. Once again, modern civilisation is represented by Western science and medicine. But the emphasis is not really on the superiority of the white man, but on their science and technology that could be mastered by the Thai—in this case, Waenfa, the Laotian-French woman who identifies herself as Thai.

being Laotian, an inferior people and nation. It is also interesting that the author asserts that Hungarians consider themselves Asian—pushing the scope of Pan-Asianism rather dramatically. Luang Wichit describes how happy the immigration officers were to meet the two Thai women who were fellow 'Asians'.

After discovering the herb and curing her daughter's deafness, Praphimphan decides to return to Thailand to make peace with her enemies and to cremate her father—very Buddhist motivations. She cremates her father, but she fails to placate the nephew of her godparents and his greedy wife. They betray her to the authorities who come to arrest her for the murder of Khwan's chauffeur. Instead of giving up, or allowing Khwan to take the blame for the murder, Praphimphan becomes once more the dangerous woman: she sneaks out of her hideout and murders her two tormentors. In the ensuing gun battle, she is taken out in the style of Bonnie and Clyde, Khwan dead at her side.

So, in the end, Praphimphan cannot escape punishment from the law and dies a violent death. But before the final shootout, it is still unclear whether she will surrender or resist. Her fate is finally sealed when she becomes wounded. Praphimphan reacts in an uncharacteristically non-feminine way. She calls out to Khwan, probably loud enough for the police to hear, that, as a wounded *sua* (literally 'tiger', but in this usage it refers to men who are hardened bandits or outlaws), (s)he must fight to the death. Two questions are raised here: 'Why must a woman be militant and dangerous in modern society?' and 'why is she breaking the law often and with impunity?'

Given the framework of Thai nationalism and its wars of liberation, Luang Wichit was able to justify the militant feminism that was incorporated into his nationalistic dramas. In those plays, he portrayed Thai women as wives whose loyalty extended beyond domesticity to serving their husbands in war by fighting alongside them. A popular reference to Thai women as the rear legs to the man's front legs of the elephant evokes images of elephants in war time, and the secondary role of women. Nevertheless, Thai historiography, and especially that of Luang Wichit, makes 'space' for women in the national narrative. But in *Huang rak haew luk*, the martial characteristic of Thai women takes on a different trajectory. Leaving Thailand, both voluntarily and involuntarily, symbolises a separation from the state, a liberation of women from traditional roles. Praphimphan, like other Thai heroines before her, fights alongside freedom fighters but, in this case, without explicitly defining that fight in the framework of Thai nationalism. The modern Thai woman has become a free agent who can fight for her own causes.

Luang Wichit also seems to suggest that, in entering the modern society, women have to be vigilant in protecting themselves, even if it meant breaking the law. In the novel, Praphimphan and the other women (and here the author includes Western women to emphasise the universality of their cause) take the law into their own hands to punish predatory men, men who have humiliated them, and men who have not honoured their words. It is as if to say modern society lacks the mechanisms to protect women after the erosion of traditional norms of gender relations that afforded more respect to women as idealised mothers, sisters and wives.

The author's disdain or distrust of the legal system pervades this novel. From the first episode to the last, Luang Wichit depicts the law in a bad light. The story begins with the revelation that Atthapphit had concealed incriminating evidence that would have convicted Praphimphan for murder. The novel also describes how Songwut, also another lawyer, used blackmail against his own client to help his father-in-law win back a diamond mine in South Africa. In another example, Praphimphan advises her landlord not to trust the law and lawyers but that they should mete out their own punishment for the man who had raped the landlord's daughter. And finally, on her last trip to Thailand, Praphimphan accidentally bumps into the district officer, now a provincial governor, who, many years ago, had led the police to apprehend her for killing Khwan's driver. Instead of informing the police, the governor carries on a friendly chat with Praphimphan and even light-heartedly asks her not to commit murder again. As a man, he, too, admires the dangerous woman. But the law does not make room for personal admiration or judgements of morality. This negative opinion of the legal system is most likely the result of Luang Wichit's own experience with the legal system. Perhaps he was still smarting from what, to him, must have been an unjust trial for war crimes. His only mistake was that he had picked the wrong side to win the Second World War.

Therefore, instead of treating Praphimphan like a dangerous criminal finally brought to justice, Luang Wichit uses her eulogy to valorise her as a woman of the people, a woman who was compassionate but was dealt a bad hand. Recalling Niphon's characterisation of Praphimphan as the model woman, Atthapphit's eulogy embeds within the novel itself the unbounded seriality of the dangerous woman:

Praphimphan belongs to you. She served you and the public by being the exemplar of a person who struggled with life. Her fight began when she took her first step and she fought until her last breath. Praphimphan is not a mean-spirited woman. In fact, she is a person with a good heart who is always ready to make sacrifices for her friends. She is loyal and grateful to those who helped her, but she is vengeful when she is crossed. She stood for justice and would not harm anyone who did not strike at her first. Even though the curtain that falls on the drama of her life is black, the color of mourning and grief, her shining name will remain forever on the lips of tens of thousands of people. And if one were to write about her life, it would take thousands of pages to do it justice.[41]

Of course, Luang Wichit has indeed taken over 1,000 pages to do her life justice. Praphimphan is the model of the modern Thai female who, while assenting to the traditional view of the female as one that must be protected and forgiven by the male, is also ready to punish those who are unkind to her or who do not keep their promises of love. She values the family, male fidelity, female friendship, and bravery. She is a leader, a world traveller, a freedom fighter, a founder of a nation, a soldier, an obedient daughter, a passionate lover, a wife, a loyal friend, a patron, a feminist and an executioner. Interweaving the themes of modernity, femininity, violence and nationalism on an international scale, Luang Wichit Wathakan glorifies in *Huang rak haew luk* a new role for the modern Thai woman. Neither good nor bad, Madonna nor whore, hers is a role of nearly boundless possibilities: the dangerous woman.

---

41   Luang Wichit, *Huang rak haew luk*, 1461.

4
A civilized woman: M.L. Boonlua Debhayasuwan[1]

Long-time admirers of Susan Fulop Kepner's translations and introductions to modern Thai literature waited a decade and a half for *A civilized woman: M.L. Boonlua Debhayasuwan and the Thai twentieth century*.[2] Most of us have read and used Dr Kepner's translations of Botan's *Letters from Thailand*, Kampoon Boontawee's *A child of the northeast*, and the anthology about women in *The lioness in bloom*.[3] These books, together with several others, helped to introduce modern Thai prose fiction to non-Thai readers and to students in Western universities.[4] We had heard of,

---

1   An earlier version of this essay appeared in *New mandala* on 22 November 2013, accessed 3 March 2017, www.newmandala.org/book-review/review-of-a-civilized-woman-tlc-nmrev-lxiv/.
2   Susan Fulop Kepner, *A civilized woman: M.L. Boonlua Debhayasuwan and the Thai twentieth century* (Chiangmai: Silkworm Books, 2013). An alternative spelling of Boonlua's name is M.L. Bunluea Thepphayasuwan, a transliterated spelling that appears in some databases.
3   Susan Fulop Kepner, trans., *Letters from Thailand* (Bangkok: Editions Duang Kamol, 1982); Susan Fulop Kepner, trans., *A child of the northeast* (Bangkok: Editions Duang Kamol, 1994); Susan Fulop Kepner, ed. and trans., *The lioness in bloom: Modern Thai fiction about women* (Berkeley and Los Angeles: University of California Press, 1996).
4   There are not many Thai prose fiction works (short stories and novels) available in English, but there are some notable examples: Prajuab Thirabutana, *Little things* (Sydney: Wm. Collins Ltd, 1971); Lao Khamhowm [Khamsing Srinawk], *The politician and other stories* (Kuala Lumpur: Oxford University Press, 1973); Tulachandra [pseud.], trans., *Kukrit Pramoj's four reigns* (Bangkok: Editions Duang Kamol, 1981); Gehan Wijeyewardene, trans., *Khammaaan Khonkhai's The teacher of Mad Dog Swamp* (St Lucia: University of Queensland Press, 1982); Benedict R. O'G. Anderson and Ruchira Mendiones, eds and trans., *In the mirror: Literature and politics in Siam in the American era* (Bangkok: Editions Duang Kamol, 1985); David Smyth, trans., *K. Surangkhanang's The prostitute* (Kuala Lumpur: Oxford University Press, 1994); David Smyth, trans., *Siburapha's Behind the picture and other stories* (Chiangmai: Silkworm Books, 2000). There is also a collection of translations of novels done by Marcel Barang, *The 20 best novels of Thailand* (Bangkok: Thai Modern Classics, 1994).

if not read, her 1998 dissertation written under the guidance of Herbert Phillips at Berkeley, and we wondered when we would have the chance to read a book version of that dissertation.[5] The wait is now over, and Kepner has not disappointed us.

Dr Kepner's book is a biography of one of Thailand's best-known teachers of literary criticism, a pioneer who wrote university texts, and an accomplished novelist. As a novelist, her works were often judged as wanting when compared to her more famous sister Dok Mai Sot, the pen name of M.L. Buppha.[6] *A civilized woman* chronicles Boonlua's early upbringing as the youngest of 32 children of a senior aristocrat and minor noble; her education in Catholic convent schools in Bangkok and Penang; her university education at Chulalongkorn University and the University of Minnesota; her career as a teacher, educator and civil servant; her bouts of illness; her late marriage; her life after retirement; and her career as a writer and novelist.[7] My comments here on Dr Kepner's book will focus on three topics. First, I will discuss the fading world of the Thai nobility after 1932, and especially how elite upper-class *phu di* women, exemplified by Boonlua, adjusted to political changes. Second, I will highlight Boonlua's difficult time working in and dealing with the Thai bureaucracy. Finally, I will examine Boonlua's views about use and abuse of Thai literature.

The biography

To start, it is rare that scholarly biographies are written about modern Thai personalities in the English language. There have been books on Thai monarchs and political leaders, but none on academics or professors. Dr Kepner is the first to write a serious biography of a modern literary scholar. I must confess that I did not think readily of Boonlua as a famous national figure, or a major author of modern fiction. Most of us knew her as the author of textbooks on Thai literary criticism. Her texts on how to read modern literature in a systematic and analytical way are still used

---

5   The choice of Phillips as dissertation adviser was logical, because he had written about modern Thai literature and had interviewed M.L. Boonlua. See Herbert P. Phillips, *Modern Thai literature with an ethnographic interpretation* (Honolulu: University of Hawai'i Press, 1987).
6   Dok Mai Sot is best remembered for her 1929 novel, *Sattru khong jao lon* [*Her enemy*].
7   For an insightful comment on the book see Chris Baker's review in *Bangkok post*, 4 November 2013.

in universities.⁸ To many of us, Boonlua's novels were not so successful as those of her better-known sister M.L. Buppha, whose pen name was 'Dok Mai Sot'.

Boonlua admitted that, at first, she did not want to write novels because her elder sister was already famous, and she did not want to be known as the 'other sister' who also wrote. This sentiment, tinged with some resentment, may explain why Boonlua chose a different career path as an educator and literary critic. In the end, she even became well-known as an expert on Dok Mai Sot. Boonlua refrained from writing novels until late into her career, when she was close to retirement from government service in 1970, and her sister had passed away.⁹ But this biography is not just about literature or Boonlua's contribution to how Thai literature is taught. It is also about how a woman from the ruling class adjusted to life after the fall of absolute monarchy.

A civilized woman relies quite a bit on Boonlua's autobiography, *Successes and failures*, published to mark her 60th birthday in 1971.¹⁰ According to Sulak Sivaraksa, this autobiography is considered one of the best Thai autobiographies because it does not focus just on the achievements of the writer, but it also highlighted her failures and disappointments. Boonlua's autobiography was reprinted and presented as a gift to those attending her cremation in 1984. This volume was accompanied by a sister volume *Bun bamphen* [*Religious observations for Boon*]—playing on 'Boon', which refers to Boonlua and *bun* as Buddhist merit—in which her friends, husband and students wrote eulogies to celebrate her life.¹¹ Dr Kepner used these two editions as the backbone for her book. Cremation volumes tend to be hagiographic accounts of the deceased, but, in Boonlua's case, the frank assessments of her own successes and failures in the autobiography leached into the eulogies of the second volume where the theme of successes and failures (and disappointments) were again addressed.

---

8   See M.L. Bunluea Thepphayasuwan, *Nae naeo thang bunluea wicha wannakadi* [*How to study literature*] (Bangkok: Bundit Kan Phim, 1975); *Waen wannakam* [*Insights into literature*] (Bangkok: Samnak Phim Aan Thai, 1986); *Hua liao khong wannakhadi thai* [*Turning points in Thai literature*] (Bangkok: Thai Watthana Phanich, 1973).
9   Dok Mai Sot died in 1963. See her brief biography in Pratheep Muannil, *100 nakpraphan thai* [*100 Thai authors*] (Bangkok: Chomromdek Publishing House, 1999), 150–2. Boonlua's first novel *Saphai maem* was published in 1962, and her other novels were published after her sister's death.
10 M.L. Bunluea Thepphayasuwan, *Khwam samret lae khwam lom laeo* [*Successes and failures*] (Bangkok: Social Science Association of Thailand, 1971).
11 *Anusorn ngan phraratchathan phloengsop mom luang bunluea thepphayasuwan na wat makutkasatriyaram* [*Cremation volume on the occasion of the royally sponsored cremation of M.L. Bunluea Thepphayasuwan*], 7 June 1984.

Boonlua's autobiography, *Successes and failures*, told a very personal story, but it lacked specific details, helpful markers and historical context. Her friends, family and those who were familiar with Thai history and culture might know what and about whom Boonlua was writing but, to outsiders, the autobiography could be puzzling and unclear. Dr Kepner's intervention provided much needed details—names, substance and context—to the autobiography by connecting Boonlua's life (1911–1982) to Thai history and including explanations about Thai behaviour and culture when necessary. In fact, *A civilized woman* tells us more about Boonlua than her own autobiography.

Because Boonlua's autobiography was written when she turned 60 in 1971, it predated the appearance of her better-known novels, especially *The land of women*, published in 1972.[12] She had already published several novels, such as *Western daughter-in-law* in 1962 and *Thutiyawiset* (the name of a royal decoration conferred to wives of prominent officials) in 1968, but most of her writing was not as successful as her sister's.[13] It should be noted here that in her autobiography Boonlua did not say much about her publications except to note that editors had changed the titles of her manuscripts without asking her permission. Similar to other remarks she made in the autobiography, she mentioned these episodes without telling us how she felt. Besides embellishing Boonlua's autobiography with references to historical events, Dr Kepner's book also extends Boonlua's autobiography by another decade to include a chapter on Boonlua's major novels, and another chapter on her engagement with Thailand's second culture war of the early 1970s, when radical university students and young literary critics questioned the relevance of classical Thai literature.

Both Boonlua's autobiography and Dr Kepner's book begin with Boonlua's early life, especially her interactions with the two major male figures—her father and Prince Narit—both of whom helped shape her adult character. Her father was Mom Ratchawong Lan Kunchon, the keeper of the king's elephants and manager of the royal dance troupe. The Kunchon family traced their lineage to the Second Reign. Although all descendants of kings are related, in status-conscious Thai society, even the nobles have rank distinctions that, to the outside world, may appear confusing and

---

12   M.L. Bunluea Thepphayasuwan, *Suratnari* [*The land of women*] (Bangkok: Phrae Phittaya, 1972).
13   M.L. Bunluea Thepphayasuwan, *Saphai maem* [*Western daughter-in-law*] (Bangkok: Phrae Phittaya, 1962); *Thutiyawiset* (Bangkok: Phrae Phittaya, 1968).

4. A CIVILIZED WOMAN

even byzantine. The rank order of Thai royalty is a descending one by generation. That is, by the third generation, the great-grandchild of a king holding the title Mom Ratchawong would no longer be considered a prince or princess. Boonlua, with the title Mom Luang, is the last to claim a title, but she is not considered royalty.

Boonlua's pride in her birthright included the fact that, not only was her father a Mom Ratachawong, he also held the royally conferred rank of Jaophraya, the top rank for the nobility (*khunnang*). In many places in the biography, it is clear that Boonlua's identity as the daughter of a Jaophraya was very important to her. To Boonlua, class and upbringing (*oprom*) determined who could be considered a cultured, upper-class person (*phu di*). Other people were common, uncouth folks referred to in Thai as *phrai*. At one point, an acquaintance retorted that Boonlua was always sickly because she was *phu di*, but the *phrai* were robust and did not get sick easily. Boonlua always complained of having *lom phit*, the common term for hives. But, after consulting medical doctors, Dr Kepner writes that Boonlua actually suffered from shingles.

Boonlua credited her father and another high-ranking prince for encouraging her, even as a child, not to take anything at face value and that she should not be afraid to question or to speak her mind. She wrote in her autobiography that her character was influenced by her close association with men. For example, Boonlua said that her father and his friend, a prince she called *Somdet*, encouraged her to be outspoken, analytical and iconoclastic whenever possible. When she asked her father what he thought about the story of Moses parting the Red Sea that she had learned from convent sisters, her father asked her to think about what kind of god would kill innocent people. Boonlua, in later life, would practice what her father taught her by not being afraid to speak up and to look at all questions from many angles.

Interestingly, Boonlua never named the high-ranking prince who was her early mentor. As a matter of fact, Boonlua seemed reluctant to name names and mentions very few people by name in her autobiography. This is a conundrum. Given how prideful she was about her rank, one would think that she would be dropping names, as most Thai elite who wrote autobiographies tended to do. But those who were close to her knew the identity of that high-ranking prince who lived nearby. In Dr Kepner's book, we learn that the prince referred to loosely as *Somdet* was in fact Prince Narisara Nuvatiwongse, known as Prince Narit. His title of Somdet

Jaofa conferred on him the rank of a son of a king born of a royal mother. However, when Prince Narit was born, his rank was only Phraongjao (a grade lower than Jaofa) but his half-brother, King Chulalongkorn, elevated him to that higher rank. Prince Narit was known as a man of letters and a progressive thinker. The complexity of noble ranks and conferral of special titles can easily lead to misidentification.[14]

Although officially no longer considered a princess, Boonlua was proud of her heritage and continued to consider herself a member of the nobility. In her autobiography, she said that her older siblings were told by her father to call him *Somdet sadet pho* or 'royal father', and the younger ones to call him *sadet puu* or 'royal grandfather', allowing this group of Mom Luang, who were four ranks below Prince Narit, to remember and to imagine themselves still connected to the ruling House of Chakkri. Another interesting fact about Boonlua's male-centric world was her own explanation of why her father, who bedded most of the female dancers in his charge, never designated a major wife. She believed that it was her father's way of maintaining equality among all of his children and to prevent the children of the major wife having higher status than the children of other wives. In a sense, this thinking was different from what was traditional practice. Even in the royal court, children of the king by a queen held a higher rank than children born of non-royal mothers.

Under absolute rule, the monarch had to rely on his children and close relatives to conduct the affairs of state. In such a system, it is not surprising that Rama I sired 42 offspring, Rama II 73, Rama III had 51, Rama IV, despite his advanced age when he became king, had 84 children, and Rama V sired 97 children. Although not all of the royal offspring survived to adulthood, of those who did, many became important players who helped guide Thailand towards *siwilai,* making Thailand a civilised nation.[15] The system of polygyny and the practice of having many children

---

14   For example, Prince Wan Waithayakorn is identified in Kepner's biography as the son of King Chulalongkorn. In fact, Prince Wan held a bureaucratic title similar to his father and the two could easily be mistaken for each other. Prince Wan's father, Krommameun Narathip Praphanphong, was Chulalongkorn's half-brother. His son, Prince Wan, born as Mom Jao, was later elevated to Phraong Jao and conferred the title of Krommanuen Narathip Phong Praphan. He is known as the creator of many modern Thai neologisms and as a prince who was friendly with the leaders of the People's Party that overthrew absolute monarchy. He served as ambassador to the USA and was president of the UN General Assembly and Minister of Foreign Affairs.

15   For a discussion of *siwilai,* see Thongchai Winichakul, 'The quest for *siwilai*: A geographical discourse of civilizational thinking in the late nineteenth- and early twentieth-century Siam', *Journal of Asian studies,* 59(3) (August 2000): 528–54.

also extended beyond the king to include other princes down the line. In Boonlua's case, her father had 40-odd wives and 32 children, Boonlua being the youngest, born when her father was 59 years old.

This system of rule, which relied on royal relatives, began to unravel after Rama VI (r. 1910–25), and those who followed him adopted the European *siwilai* practice of monogamy. Rama VI had a daughter just before he died; Rama VII had no children, nor did Rama VIII. The number of high princes and princesses declined precipitously during the lifetime of Boonlua, who was born soon after Rama VI became king. The world of the nobles dominating national administration would end in 1932, when military officers and progressive civilians seized power from the king and his relatives. At that time, the number of princes, princesses, Mom Ratchawong and Mom Luang was quite considerable. But the end of absolute monarchy created a dilemma for the backlog of royal personalities up and down the hierarchy about their place in the new order. They would need to find ways to contribute to the new Thailand.

Chris Baker writes:

> The Thai aristocracy faced a crisis after 1932. They lost privileges and they lost purpose. Many of them spiralled downwards, clinging to past privilege and flirting with reactionary politics while gradually selling off their remaining property. A few embraced change with only a modicum of grudge, building on the cultural capital they had inherited from the old order to become prominent educators and artists.[16]

Although I am in total agreement with this astute observation, I should add that this adjustment was much harder for women of the *phu di* class, whose role was no longer just as mothers and wives who took care of aristocratic and noble men. In the new order they had to find meaningful jobs.

Loss of privilege and the plight of upper-class women

Both Boonlua and her more famous sister Buppha did not marry until late into their 40s. Marriage for women of the *phu di* class was not easy when they were required to marry men of the same or preferably higher

---

16   *Bangkok post*, 4 November 2013.

status. As elite social circles shrank in size, upper-class women had few choices for spouses. This may perhaps explain why both sisters married late, and to men who, prior to 1932, would have been considered below their station. Democratic sentiments helped elevate former *phrai*, or commoners, to higher status, thus allowing Buppha and Boonlua to marry. Sukit Nimmanhemin, who married Buppha, and Chom Debhayasuwan, who married Boonlua, were, in fact, upper class by the 1960s. The former eventually became an ambassador, and the latter was a medical doctor, but it took many years before they would be acceptable to the families of the old *phu di* elite. The plight of ageing upper-class women was the subject of Kulap Saipradit's famous novel *Khang lang phap* [*Behind the painting*].[17] In Kulap's novel, the heroine, Mom Ratchawong Kirati, a fading beauty who held the same rank as Boonlua's father, decided that it was best to maintain her upper-class position by marrying Jaokhun, a form of address reserved for a person of the Phraya and Jaophraya rank. Jaokhun was an older man, but his rank, the same rank as Boonlua's father, made him a suitable husband. Kirati eventually fell in love with a young university student when she and her husband took a business trip to Japan. The story was about tragic love and the sad plight of privileged women from the old regime. Staying home as an unmarried aristocratic woman was no longer an option in modernising Thailand.

Although Boonlua never said that the 1932 event gave her an opportunity to enter Chulalongkorn University, Dr Kepner connected the two events to allow us to consider the benefits or the side effects of the overthrow of absolute monarchy. Boonlua was one of the first women allowed to enrol in Chulalongkorn University. Her degrees from the Faculty of Arts and the Faculty of Education led to careers in teaching English and Thai literature, and working for the Ministry of Education as head of the Education Inspection unit. Partly because writing as a profession was already the vocation of her sister, Boonlua chose to become a teacher instead. A teacher or professor in those days meant that one was also a member of the civil service.

In the mind of Boonlua and perhaps the elite women of her day, becoming a civil servant was an affront to their social class, a veritable demotion in status. Boonlua wrote in her autobiography:

---

17 Si Burapha [pseud.], *Khang lang phap* [*Behind the painting*] (Bangkok: Phadung Suksa, 1960). This novel was serialised in *Prachachat* newspaper from December 1937 to January 1938. It appeared in one published volume in 1938. I have been unable to find pertinent information on that edition.

The daughter of a government official was considered to have the same privileges and status as her father. As for the son, he had to start working to earn his own rank and privileges. *But as the daughter of a jao phraya, I had lowered my rank to work as a teacher.* If I had simply stayed at home, I would have kept the high rank that was mine by birth.[18]

This pride in her heritage may explain several things: her resentment of the new bureaucracy where officials failed to recognise her sacrifice and the noble way she went about doing a job that was beneath her station. It would also explain why she had few friends from her Chulalongkorn days. In fact, some classmates, who did not want to be identified in the book, said that she was quite stuck up and condescending. Boonlua would be furious if she was not addressed as Mom Luang during her Chula days.

In the end, she had to find work to help support her maternal grandmother, nieces and nephews. But her attitude about the place of women under the old regime and how underappreciated she was as a civil servant would cause her to be dismissed from several positions during her career. It was her pride as a Mom Luang, a daughter of a Jaophraya, and an educated woman with degrees from Chulalongkorn University and the University of Minnesota that made her struggle as a civil servant. She singled out her lack of success as a civil servant as one of her major failures.

The Thai bureaucracy

Boonlua's autobiography and biography chronicled her disdain for the civil service. She lamented that the Thai system was idiosyncratic, mixing old values with new ones, something that she could not explain to foreigners. Boonlua appeared fixated on how she was unjustly classified as a third-grade civil servant while leading a group of teachers who were a grade above her in one instance, and how her position as a first-grade civil servant disqualified her for a job that was a special grade classification. As someone whose life was predicated on social status, civil service ranks could be degrading. She lamented that the ability to perform a job was secondary to the rank one held or the degree one had. Status was still valued more highly than meritocratic achievement.

---

18 Kepner, *A civilized woman*, 207 (emphasis added).

As Mom Luang, daughter of an aristocrat, and a *phu di,* Boonlua could be outspoken and confrontational, a troublesome combination in an organisation that frowned upon such behaviour. She attributed her actions to her upbringing as a precocious child encouraged by her father and *Somdet* to speak her mind and to be critical. Boonlua also blamed her training in dance drama (*lakhon*), her mother's métier, for speaking out. She said that, as an artist, she would get carried away by her role. As a teacher, head of the education inspection unit, professor, dean, etc. she could not help but speak her mind if it would benefit those under her charge, even if it meant causing discomfort for her superiors. In fact, she appeared to be in her element when representing Thailand at international conferences where her English-speaking abilities and forwardness were valued qualities. She was an articulate and eloquent speaker in English. Boonlua seemed to get along better with international colleagues than with Thai ones.

In her cremation volume where, traditionally, no one speaks ill of the dead, her former boss, close relative and former Minister of Education Mom Luang Pin Malakul, praised her for her contributions to Thai education, but he also pointed out how unfit she was as a bureaucrat. He said that the reason Boonlua had to change jobs often was because she was a lady with 'high cultural values' (*mi watthanatham sung*). I think that Pin was referring to Boonlua's *phu di* upbringing, her high standards of integrity and her penchant for speaking out. Her struggle with and disdain for the Thai bureaucracy ended when she resigned a year before mandatory retirement age. The following year, when she turned 60, she wrote down her struggles and failures as a civil servant in her autobiography, *Successes and failures.*

Pin's remark about 'high cultural values' is perhaps a better description of Boonlua, and it refines the label referring to her as a civilised (*siwilai*) woman. The discourse on *siwilai* began during the reign of Rama IV, it flourished during the fifth and sixth reigns, and it culminated in Phibun's ultra-nationalism of the 1930s and early 1940s. How to make Thailand *siwilai* was a strategy for the Thai to escape colonisation. It was based on the assumption that if the Thai appeared to the colonial powers to be civilised, then Thailand would not become a target of the white man's civilising noblesse oblige.

4. A CIVILIZED WOMAN

The process of *siwilai* included the incorporation of Western, mostly defined by British, ways. Not only should Thailand appear modern materially, but its upper class and leaders should also master Western knowledge, customs and logic. Because Boonlua's family was related to the nobility and the male members were also high officials who embraced this strategy, she was ipso facto reared to become *siwilai*, receiving the benefits of a modern and Westernised education. She was also raised to be analytical and outspoken. I think that, in Boonlua's mind, she was a civilised woman by birth and upbringing. In Dr Kepner's biography, M.L. Pin's remarks were also cited. Interestingly, Dr Kepner translated *watthanatham sung* as civilised, and not 'of high culture'. We should note then that Dr Kepner's own term 'a civilized woman' to describe Boonlua conflates two Thai concepts: *siwilai* and *watthanatham sung*. The two terms are different, but together they describe the enigma that is Boonlua. She was brought up to be *siwilai*, but her high ideals and pride on being *phu di* holding on to high culture and standards (*watthanatham soong*) defined how she lived.

Although Dr Kepner skilfully narrates Boonlua's life as embedded in and interacting with significant episodes in Thai history, the biography is not a history text. For general readers, the book can provide a credible and accessible introduction to aspects of Thai history. My own enjoyment in reading this biography came from comparing it with Kukrit Pramoj's *Si phaendin* [*Four reigns*], a novel about political change in Thailand from Rama V to the death of Rama VIII.[19] Both Kukrit's novel and Boonlua's biography observed the unfolding of Thai history through the eyes of aristocratic women. Phloi in *Four reigns* was a romantic, and more of a passive observer of what was changing around her. She longed for the lifestyle of the fading *chaowang* (palace people), centred on the royal court and palace. Serialised in 1953, Kukrit's novel was a nostalgic look at the past that elicited warm feelings for the monarchy and disappointment at the loss of upper-class refinement and civility. The novel was not a general depiction of how all Thai people felt about kingship, the nobles and aristocrats, as Dr Kepner suggests.

The abdication of Rama VII in 1935, followed a decade later by the sudden death of Rama VIII in 1946, threatened the future and relevance of the monarchy in Thailand. Royalists like Kukrit carefully planned

---

19   Kukrit Pramoj, *Si phaendin* [*Four reigns*] (Bangkok: Samnak phim chaiyarit, 1953–54).

campaigns to revive the monarchy and to make it central once again in Thai life. The publication of *Four reigns* can be seen as part of that effort. But what I find interesting in Dr Kepner's biography of Boonlua, another version of *Four reigns*, is that, unlike Phloi, the passive heroine of Kukrit's novel, Boonlua was a real person who had also lived under four reigns (Rama VI to Rama IX). She was not a romantic, passive observer but actively participated in the historical events unfolding around her. More importantly, Dr Kepner's version of *Four reigns* chronicles the difficulties of what the old elite, in this case a woman, faced in coping with the catastrophic historical disruption of their lives and social status. *A civilized woman* is indeed more credible than Kukrit's novel because it is both raw as well as non-fiction (rather than real).

The use and abuse of literature

I conclude this chapter with what I consider to be an original and significant contribution of Dr Kepner's *A civilized woman*. As someone interested in rehabilitating, excavating, and reinterpreting lesser-known or lost novels, I am intrigued by Dr Kepner's introduction of Boonlua's five major novels to us. I must admit that I am among those who have overlooked Boonlua's contribution as a novelist. I know and think of her as a respected educator and a pioneer who wrote widely accepted texts on how to teach and to study Thai literature. Before writing this essay, I took an inventory of the directories that list prominent Thai authors and their works that I have in my own library and discovered that none included Boonlua in their list of famous Thai authors. The one place I found her name mentioned was in *A suggested list of the best 100 books that Thai people should read*. Boonlua was cited for her article on literary criticism that she wrote in 1971 to honour the life of Prince Wan Waithayakorn on his 80th birthday.[20] Had she lived, she would have been pleased that in *A suggested list of the best 100 books*, she had achieved the same recognition as her sister Dok Mai Sot.

Prior to Boonlua's intervention, Thai literature taught in secondary schools and universities was divided into classical literature (*wannakhadi*) and contemporary literature (*wannakam*). 'Classical literature' enjoyed

---

20 Withayakorn Chiengkul, Thawip Woradilok and Chonthira Sattayawatthana, eds, *Saranukrom nenam nangsue di 100 lem thi khon thai khuan an* [*A suggested list of the best 100 books that Thai people should read*] (Bangkok: Samnakgnan Kongthun Ssanapsanun Kanwijai, 1999), 640–50.

a higher status than 'contemporary literature'. This rather elitist view became the subject of debate during the brief open democratic period from the 14 October 1973 event to the 6 October 1976 massacre of students at Thammasat University. Before she was asked to debate the utility of classical literature, Boonlua had tried for many years to close the divide between classical literature and modern prose fiction. She wrote texts advocating a unified curriculum that included oral texts, performance (especially drama or *lakhon*), classical texts and contemporary prose fiction.[21] She also tried to implement such a curriculum at her last official post as Dean of the Faculty of Arts at the new campus of the Fine Arts University in Nakhon Pathom. She failed in this endeavour.

Although trained in the classics from the time she was a young child, she also understood why the younger generation of students and scholars viewed classical Thai literature obliquely as something created by and for the ruling class. Unless one knew a lot about Hindu and Buddhist mythology and words derived from Sanskrit, one could never have full access to understanding classical literature. This fact automatically disqualifies the majority of all Thai readers, except those who have studied literature at university. It is interesting to note that towards the end of her life Boonlua devoted her energies to modern prose fiction: reading, criticising and writing novels. Unlike classical literature, which was animated by courtly life and ritual, specialised knowledge of religion, and the sonority of language, modern literature's dynamism is derived from a spirit of immediacy and narrative realism. Prose fiction that appeared in Thailand at the turn of the 20th century was readily embraced as the modern form of entertainment that anyone literate in the Thai language could appreciate and enjoy. In Boonlua's case, she wanted her novels to be more than mere entertainment.

'The uses of fiction', Chapter 8 in *A civilized woman*, gives us a window into Boonlua's importance as a novelist. It should prompt literary scholars to pay closer attention to Boonlua's novels. With a familiarity gained from using Boonlua's novels in her class, Dr Kepner shared her thoughts about them in this fascinating chapter. Of the five novels, Dr Kepner focused her analysis on the two major ones, namely, *Thutiyawiset* (a royal decoration

---

21 The elevation of *wannakhadi* over *wannakam* was put in place by Prince Damrong Rajanubhab. Boonlua was originally trained to follow this tradition. She changed her mind, however, after she began teaching. See her articles in *Waen wannakam* [*Insights into literature*] (Bangkok: Samnak Phim An Thai, 1986). See also Kepner, *A civilized woman*, Chapter 10.

conferred on the wives of high ranking officials), and *The land of women*. *Thutiyawiset* was fashioned after the lives of Marshal Phibun and his wife Thanphuying La-iad. The novel begins in the 1920s and progresses to the coup of 1932 and beyond. Essentially it is about ambition, greed, how power corrupts and the important role that women played in post-1932 Thailand. This theme of ethical, strong and smart women appears often in Boonlua's novels. In a sense, it must reflect her own sentiments about her role in modern Thai society and the worth of women in all fields of endeavour, including leadership at the national level.

Boonlua's nascent feminist ideals may explain the writing of what I consider to be her best and most innovative novel, *The land of women*, published in 1972. It was finished soon after her retirement from the civil service. We should recall that Boonlua felt underappreciated and misunderstood by her superiors, perhaps because she was *phu di* and female. Interestingly, she selected the male voice to narrate her novel.

The land of women tells a story about the encounter of shipwrecked travellers with a country ruled by women. The inhabitants were Thai, as were two of the leading male characters whose ship sank in a storm. In the land of Surat, women were the rulers and heads of households. Women in Surat were in control because they were strong mentally, morally and even physically. Women in that country could have many male 'wives' and many children by them. For entertainment, they even had no qualms about going out at night to find men to have sex with. Unlike in Thailand where out-of-wedlock births are socially unacceptable (leading to abortions and deaths of both mother and foetus), in Surat, all children, including illegitimate ones, were loved.

When the novel appeared, readers found it difficult to understand and to appreciate. Readers did not find the novel entertaining and regarded the inversion of gender roles strange and unnatural. Boonlua also created new Thai Surat words that confused the Thai visitors in the novel, as well as her Thai readers. Moreover, the novel was not very entertaining because it constantly distracted and provoked readers to think about the larger social and political implications and purposes of the novel itself. For example, in Surat, some of the young men were sent to study abroad, the same practice instituted by King Chulalongkorn, but when they returned home with new ideas, the women leaders would ignore them. This is similar to how the Thai kings ignored the advice of returning students from Europe that Thailand should make major political reforms if the monarchy was to survive.[22]

In the novel, the Thai visitors noticed that the marginalised Surat men were also agitating for equal rights. Men were held suspect because at one point in Surat history, the queen's male consort sold out the country to the British and, for several years, Surat was a colony of Great Britain. Although the inversion of gender roles that stood standing convention on its head was puzzling at first glance, upon critical examination, Boonlua's novel was clearly a commentary on Thai society dominated by men. Boonlua herself said that her novels were more like social documentaries or, in the case of *Suratnari*, a critique of contemporary Thai society.

Boonlua is just as enigmatic as her novel *The land of women*. Although she accepted and, in fact, celebrated her status as a woman, albeit an outspoken one, she was unhappy with the male-dominated bureaucracy that she experienced. Remembering her father's unconventional interpretation of the Christian God, Moses, and the parting of the Red Sea, I am sure that *Suratnari* was inspired by those sensibilities. Surat women could have many men as wives, and keep all their children, but, in the final analysis, their lives were still different from male-dominated Thailand. We have seen how the kings and male nobles procreated hundreds of offspring to maintain their grip on power. But, for Surat women, this would not be possible because, during her fertile years, a single woman may have perhaps 20 children at most. And, unlike the real Thailand, female leaders who bore children risked their lives. Books that list the offspring of Thai kings tell of how many died before birth or soon after, but we know less about the survival rates of their mothers. Boonlua's own mother died when she was three.[23] In male-centric Thailand, fathers doted on their children who carry their blood line into the future, but Boonlua may have noticed that her own father failed to show his 40-odd wives the respect they were due.

---

22 See Tamara Loos, *Bones around my neck: The life and exile of a Prince Provocateur* (Ithaca: Cornell University Press, 2016), doi.org/10.7591/9781501706172. Prince Prisdang was Siam's first minister to Europe. His downfall came after he drafted a proposal to the king in 1885 outlining a program of reform that would have made Thailand a constitutional monarchy. Needless to say, he soon found himself exiled and punished.
23 Kalaya Kuetrakul's *Ratchakul Siam* [*Siam's royal families*] (Bangkok: Samnak Phim Gypsy, 2008), for example, lists the names of the offspring of Rama I to Rama V and their front palace princes, sometimes called deputy kings. The lists provide birth and death dates and the identity of the mothers, but only the names of the mothers are listed with no additional information.

Boonlua is not the first Thai author to use fantasy and feminist ideas to intrigue her readers. As discussed in Chapter 1, one of the earliest Thai novels is Khru Liam's *Sao song phan pi* [*The two-thousand-year-old maiden*], a translation of Rider Haggard's *She*, in which a country in Africa is ruled by a sorceress with magical powers.[24] One may also recall Luang Wichit's *Huang rak haew luk* [*Sea of love, chasm of death*], discussed in the previous chapter, whose main character is a woman who escaped prosecution for murder by leading a band of followers to Africa. In that adventure story, one of her entourage, also a woman, founded a country (queendom?) in Africa. The idea of fantasy and a place ruled by women were not new in Thai literature, but *Suratnari* is unusual in that the reversal of gender convention is almost total.

Boonlua's *siwilai* and her *watthanatham sung* may have led her to propose this audacious inversion of gender roles, but, in the end, her upper-class *phu di* upbringing prevented her from considering social egalitarianism as the ideal for Thai society. She admired Field Marshal Sarit Thanarat, the military dictator from 1957 to 1963, who encouraged the young King Bhumibol to play a larger role in national affairs, enabling him to be regarded as the symbol of the Thai nation abroad, as well as at home. Sarit also extended the promotion of *siwilai* to include the concept of *phatthana* (development) as the next strategy for Thailand's progress and modernisation.[25] Perhaps Boonlua did not mind his dictatorship, which may have reminded her of how Thailand was ruled under absolute monarchy. Reflecting her support of development as a policy for national advancement, Boonlua argued in *Suratnari* that the common people should remain happy as long as there was food, running water, schools, electricity, roads and other amenities—benefits of *phatthana* proclaimed in banners, radio and television slogans during the Sarit era. In short, Boonlua's notion of Thai society was still a conservative and static one—the upper class should dominate state affairs while the common folks should remain docile and happy.

I am sure that even after reading Dr Kepner's excellent analysis of this novel, many of us would be eager to read, reread and reacquaint ourselves with Boonlua's novels. We should read *Suratnari* through a new lens

---

24   Nok Nori [pseud.], *Sao song phan pi* [*The two-thousand-year-old maiden*] (Bangkok: Dokya, 1990). Nok Nori was the pseudonym of Khru Liam. The translation was done in 1913, according to information in Rachel V. Harrison, *Disturbing conventions: Decentering Thai literary cultures* (London: Rowman and Littlefield, 2014), 252. See also the discussion in Chapter 1, this volume.

25   See Thak Chaloemtiarana, *Thailand: The politics of despotic paternalism* (Ithaca: Cornell Southeast Asia Program Publications, 2007; revised edition), 135–6, 167–75.

now that we have a better understanding of the author's character and background. However, we will not be the first because Dr Kepner also tells us that Thai literary scholars have already begun to reassess the significance of Boonlua's novels and to do their best to unearth the meanings and messages hidden in them.

Finally, I want to address how Boonlua responded to the challenge that Thai classical literature should be banned from schools and universities. When addressing a rather hostile audience at Thammasat University in 1974, Boonlua quieted the audience with her unconventional but sincere analysis of classical Thai literature, mooting the accusation that these works are nothing but instruments of the ruling class produced and circulated to legitimise its political power. She surprised her young listeners by telling them that they should not believe the conventional wisdom that the *Ramakian*, the Thai version of the *Ramayana*, written soon after the founding of Bangkok, which was intended to celebrate the life of the royals and to support the legitimacy of the new Chakkri dynasty. She said that the royals in that story were weak:

> As for Prince Rama, oh dear, he can't seem to do anything right, can he? … The ruling class is good for nothing at all in the *Ramakian* … Prince Rama himself is consumed with jealousy and he has a shocking inferiority complex … As for the ruling class portrayed in *Khun Chang Khun Phaen*, can anyone who reads it say that it shows good rule? I say, we're awfully lucky not to have such a king ourselves … In the *Ramakian*, Siva has power but not always the wisdom to use it properly … Why don't we use this story to teach students about the *responsibility* that ought to accompany power?[26]

Once again, the *siwilai* Boonlua and the *watthanatham sung* Boonlua allowed the enigmatic Boonlua to look unconventionally and critically at literature, even foundational works such as the *Ramakian* and *Khun chang khun phaen*, and to speak her mind with confidence and conviction. Thus, even in the rapidly evolving Thailand of the 1970s, Boonlua, with her conservative and elitist sentiments, remained relevant, because she was able to articulate and to connect the conservative past to the contentious present in civil yet unconventional ways. In the end, she was grudgingly accepted by the radical students for what she was: *sakdina seri niyom*, a liberal aristocrat, and perhaps another name for a civilised woman.

---

26 Kepner, *A civilized woman*, 297, 299 (emphasis in the original).

5
Are we them? The Chinese in 20th-century Thai literature and history[1]

When I first arrived on the campus of the University of the Philippines in 1962, I was struck by the unexpected question that cropped up regularly in class and in conversations with my Filipino friends. They would ask, 'Who are the Filipinos?' My Thai friends and I felt rather smug about knowing who we 'Thai' were and somewhat sorry for the Filipinos. To the Thai students, Filipinos had ambiguous identities—they had Spanish/Mexican names; spoke English with a peculiar accent; served a cuisine that was a mix of Spanish, native Filipino, Chinese and American dishes; and spoke different tongues even though there was one 'national' language. Classes in the university were in English, and students used English to speak to each other.

Those of us from Thailand knew that we were 'Thai' because we all spoke the same language, practised the same religion and loved the same king. When King Bhumibol visited Manila in 1963, all of us went to pay our respects and show our loyalty to the monarchy by having group pictures taken with the king and the queen.

---

1   This essay had its genesis in my role as a panel discussant, 'Bringing literature into the study of twentieth-century Thai history', organised by Michael Montesano at the annual conference of the Association of Asian Studies in 2010. The discussion aimed to offer ideas on how literature, especially fiction, can complement historical sources to produce new perspectives.

In hindsight, it did not occur to me that we had 'Thai' classmates who spoke Thai with a heavy Chinese accent. Even though they had Thai names, they still called each other by their Chinese names on occasion. The fact that my best friend in college was a second-generation Sino-Thai who still spoke Thai with a Chinese accent did not make me think of him as non-Thai. It did not seem important for me to dwell on the truth that my own father was perhaps half or a quarter Chinese, or that my mother had both a Thai and a Chinese name. None of these facts ever made me feel that I was not 100 per cent Thai, even though my father's great-grandfather was Chinese, and his mother's ancestors came from a line of Hokkien Chinese shipbuilders. But after four generations of living in Thailand, my father, aunts and uncles had complete amnesia as far as their ancestral race was concerned. My mother conveniently explained that many in Chanthaburi province had Chinese names as well as Thai names. She said that because the Chinese in her home province were rich and successful, Thai families gave Chinese names to their children so they could become prosperous like the Chinese. I will never know whether this is true or not, but should it matter? I suspect that after several generations of becoming Thai, my own family had fallen prey to self-denial and self-lobotomy about its past, and had subconsciously severed all ties with and discarded all memories of its Chineseness.[2]

---

2   Besides their Thai names, my mother and her three sisters also had Chinese names—Kim An, Kim U, Kim Eng and Kim Yiam. A famous Thai who also had a Chinese name (Kim Liang) is Luang Wichit Wathakan, the ideologue of modern Thai nationalism. Luang Wichit also denied his Chinese roots: see Chapter 3 this volume. The classic study of the Chinese in Thailand is G. William Skinner, *Chinese society in Thailand: An analytical history* (Ithaca: Cornell University Press, 1957). Also see especially Chapter 3 in Akira Suehiro, *Capital accumulation in Thailand 1855–1985* (Chiangmai: Silkworm Books, 1989). An innovative study of the Chinese in Thailand is Nidhi Eoseewong, *Pen and sail: Literature and history in early Bangkok*, ed. Chris Baker and Ben Anderson (Chiangmai: Silkworm Books, 2005), 57–114. Nidhi, who admits that he is *jek*, says:

> *Jek* is a Thai word meaning those with Chinese heritage in Thailand ... To consider oneself *jek* only means that one acknowledges birthplace and certain practices and traditions that are related to the culture of the people of China, but it is not to say that they are imitations of Chinese culture ... *Jek* customs and tastes are a stable culture in Thai society.

(Quoted in Phimpraphai Bisalputra, *Samphao sayam: Tamnan jek Bangkok* [*Siamese junk: History of the Bangkok Chinese*] (Bangkok: Nanmee Books, 2001), n.p.). In the foreword of the same book, Sulak Siwarak, one of Thailand's best-known public intellectuals, writes:

> From the start, I am always agreeable to calling myself *jek* because ancestors from both my father and my mother's sides were from mainland China ... But the word *jek* is no longer a word preferred by the offspring of the Chinese even though *jek* is not derogatory but a word that people use to call the overseas Chinese in Thailand (n.p.)

The largest influx of the Chinese to Thailand took place from 1918 to 1931, when Chinese labourers were needed for modernisation projects in Bangkok. The behaviour of the lower-class Chinese coolies contrasted with the Thai norm of proper behaviour. The culture clash between what the Thai considered

In this chapter, I use Thailand to designate both the historical Siam and the current Thailand. Prior to 1939, the country was usually referred to as Siam. The name change was the result of Premier Phibunsongkhram's extreme nationalism. The name reverted briefly to Siam at the end of the Second World War. I also use 'Sino-Thai' loosely to describe the Thai with Chinese ancestry. Sino-Thai is a slippery concept because there is no clear definition of when an individual is no longer considered Sino-Thai following generations of intermarriage with the local population. In the past, first- and second-generation Chinese have been essentialised as *jin sayam* or *jek*—neutral descriptive designations of the Chinese in Thai. Over time, the Sino-Thai rejected *jek* because it had acquired derogatory and pejorative connotations. More common today is for a Thai to admit that he or she *mi chuesai jin*, or has Chinese blood, which is different from the previous designation of *luk jek* (children of the *jek*) or *luk jin* (children of the Chinese), suggesting a second- or third-generation Sino-Thai.

Texts, literature and the study of 20th-century Thai history and culture

In the mirror, edited by Anderson and Mendiones, used short stories to illuminate the history and politics of the late 1960s and early 1970s in Thailand; and, to the surprise and delight of the late Anderson, a third of the chapters in his festschrift, *Southeast Asia over three generations*, focus on the importance of fiction in Southeast Asian studies.[3] Four chapters in that volume are specifically about how literature informs historical and political knowledge. In 1982, Nidhi Eoseewong examined classical Thai literature to substantiate the rise of the bourgeoisie in Bangkok.[4]

---

refined etiquette and the unrefined behaviour of Chinese labourers from rural China resulted in an unflattering essentialisation of Chinese behaviour as *jek soom saam*, meaning the 'uncouth/blundering Chinese'. See Krit Sombatsiri, *Jek sakdina* [*Chinese nobility*] (Bangkok: Kaeoprakai, 1986). The most recent exploration of the *jek* topic is Jeffery Sng and Phimpraphai Bisalputra, *A history of the Thai-Chinese* (Singapore and Bangkok: Editions Didier Millet, 2015).

3   Benedict Anderson and Ruchira Mendiones, *In the mirror: Literature and politics in Siam in the American era* (Bangkok: Duang Kamol, 1985); James T. Siegel and Audrey R. Kahin, eds, *Southeast Asia over three generations: Essays presented to Benedict R. O'G. Anderson* (Ithaca: Cornell Southeast Asia Program Publications, 2003); see also Suvanna Kriengkraipetch and Larry E. Smith, *Value conflicts in Thai society: Agonies of change seen in short stories* (Bangkok: Social Research Council, Chulalongkorn University, 1992).

4   The English version of Nidhi's 1982 essay 'Bourgeois culture and early Bangkok literature' appeared in 2005 in Nidhi, *Pen and sail*.

The intersection between fiction and history is not new. Umberto Eco writes in *The name of the rose* that there are three ways to narrate the past: the romance, using the past as scenery, pretext or fairytale; the cloak-and-dagger mystery, using real and recognisable pasts and characters; and the historical novel, which creates characters and situations that make historical events and complicated ideas easier to understand.[5] Herbert Butterfield explains in *The historical novel* that literary authors could describe in human terms the historical period in which they live, and their writings could be mined for historical facts. Butterfield goes on to say:

> It is not exactly that history and fiction should dovetail into one another to produce a coherent whole … but it is rather that in the historical novel, history and fiction can enrich and amplify one another, and interpenetrate. They can grow into one another, each making the other more powerful. And they can make a special kind of appeal to the reader.[6]

More recently, Oliver Wolters' last book manuscript, available online at the Cornell University Library, experiments with Bakhtin's 'polyphony of dialogic exchange', which proposes the intertextuality of exchanges between literature and history. Wolters constructed fictitious conversations among groups of Vietnamese elites in the 14th to 16th centuries to show what the Tran dynasty meant to the various groups within those elites. He also wanted to show how the Le dynasty planned to erase those meanings in subsequent generations. Wolters' novel-history is an attempt to illustrate that the Buddhist Tran dynasty was more Southeast Asian than the Confucian Le dynasty, suggesting that Vietnam is intrinsically more Southeast Asian than Sinic. Perhaps the historian can become the amateur novelist in much the same way that the novelist can also become the amateur historian. Of course, the intersection or the blurring of boundaries between history and literature was proposed by Hayden White, who pointed out that historians skew their analysis by using literary tropes to emplot their narratives: romance, tragedy, comedy and satire.[7]

Linking literature to its contextual site, Stephen Greenblatt's New Historicism advocates the centrality of historical texts to provide deeper meaning to literary criticism and vice versa. To Greenblatt, literature as

---

5   Umberto Eco, *The name of the rose*, trans. William Weaver (San Diego: Harcourt Brace Jovanovich, 1983).
6   Herbert Butterfield, *The historical novel: An essay* (Cambridge: Cambridge University Press, 1924), 7.
7   Hayden White, *Metahistory: The historical imagination in nineteenth-century Europe* (Baltimore: Johns Hopkins University Press, 1973).

culture acts as constraints that enforce cultural boundaries through praise and blame. To do this, authors express their beliefs, values and criticisms of the society in which they write. Debunking elitist views, Greenblatt also suggests that we look more seriously and systematically at obscure or minor texts left behind by ordinary people to fully understand history and literature.[8]

In a similar vein, the anthropologist Herbert Phillips used literature to study culture. He argued that Thai writers can be 'the most sensitive, reflective, articulate … members of Thai society … The writing of literature is integral to the social process, as both historical precipitant and product'. To Phillips, vernacular literature could be considered a 'noetic expression of a social and cultural milieu', and it is possible to treat 'literary works as embodiments of culture'. He argues further that because Thai writers write for fellow Thai, the communication is 'intracultural and reflects the native point of view, making literature a valuable corpus of knowledge for anthropological inquiry'.[9]

This chapter will use literary texts and other selected texts to illuminate how the Chinese in Thai society are viewed and how they saw themselves over the last 100 years. By assessing textual evidence, I will explore the evolving nuances of demonisation, rejection, acceptance, assimilation and accommodation of the Sino-Thai in the Thai cultural imaginary. I argue that texts can be good sources to reflect social and cultural values when they are readily consumed and embraced by the general public. Large sales figures, multiple editions and persistence over time indicate acceptance or acquiescence of the portrayals of society, and the representation of characters within those texts.

The problematic Chinese: The Other Within

Although the Chinese had been living in Ayutthaya/Siam/Thailand for centuries without much controversy or severe discrimination, they were suddenly identified as being non-Thai by King Vajiravudh when he

---

8   Stephen Greenblatt, 'Culture' in *Critical terms for literary study*, ed. Frank Lentricchia and Thomas McLaughlin (Chicago: University of Chicago Press, 1995), 226.
9   Herbert Phillips, *Modern Thai literature with an ethnographic interpretation* (Honolulu: University of Hawai'i Press, 1987), 3–4.

penned *Jews of the Orient* in 1914.¹⁰ That short essay, published both in Thai and English, made clear that the Thai and Chinese were separate 'races' and that the Chinese, very much like the Jews in Europe, exploited the country where they resided to amass wealth, yet remained separate, aloof and ungrateful—never to become good citizens. In that article, the king demonised the Sino-Thai for their relentless avarice, their willingness to do anything for money, their insistence on Chinese cultural superiority and their attempts to raise their children, even those by Thai wives, as Chinese.

The king accused the Chinese of being parasites on the Thai economy.¹¹ His outburst and indictment seemed rather strange given the history of Thai–Chinese relations, where the Chinese had for centuries played a vital role in the Thai trade with the outside world. Many Chinese families had become prominent members of the Thai aristocracy and been given

---

10   Asvabahu [King Vajiravudh], *Yiw haeng buraphathit* [*Jews of the Orient*] (Bangkok: Siam Observer Press, 1914). The copy I used is the cremation volume for Rear Admiral M. R. Kraithawat Sithawat, Wat Mongkutsasat, Bangkok, 7 January 1985. This nostalgic republication seems anachronistic. I suspect that Vajiravudh vilified low-class Chinese who flooded Thailand during his father's reign. Earlier, Chinese merchants were accepted as members of the Thai elite and intermarried with kings, princes and aristocracy. The Taechiu Chinese during the early Bangkok period were a privileged group known as *jin luang*, or the King's Chinese. They worked for King Taksin and lived in the vicinity of the current grand palace until they were moved to Sampheng by Rama I. These upper-class Chinese, especially those who selected a career path in the bureaucracy, quickly acquired Thai culture and values and were generally accepted as Thai. As a group, the old power elite accepted Chinese values and customs. For example, Chinese religious customs have been practised by the Thai court since the reign of Rama III (1824–51), when worship tables in Thai temples were Chinese. The worship table in front of the Siam Devathirat, the divine figure created by Rama IV to protect the country, and worship rituals are fashioned after Chinese customs; see Samnakngan Sapsin Suan Phramahakasat [Crown Property Bureau], *Pathumwan anusorn* [*Commemorating Pathumwan Temple*] (Bangkok: Amarin Printing and Publishing, 2012), 63–7. The Thai court continues to celebrate Chinese New Year with Chinese rituals, and practise Chinese funeral rites (*kong tek,* the incineration of paper replicas of worldly goods such as money, houses and cars to be used by the deceased in the afterlife) that were first performed during Rama IV's reign and later adopted as a royal ceremony by Rama V for the funeral of his queen (who drowned in 1880). This Chinese funeral tradition still takes place during the cremation of important members of the royal family, including the cremations of Queen Rambhai, the queen mother, and Princess Kalayani; see Kiti Lohpetcharat, *Tontamnan luklan jin nai sayam* [*Origins of descendants of Chinese in Siam*] (Bangkok: Kao Raek, 2011), Chapter 2. Kiti also details important royal family members who are descendants of the Chinese. For example, M.R. Seni and Kukrit Pramoj's great-grandmother (consort of Rama II) was born in China. Queen Sirikit's great-grandmother was also Sino-Thai, the daughter of a titled Chinese merchant. Rama V saw her peeking at him from a window while he was travelling by boat. Rama VII had no problem admitting publicly that he had Chinese blood in a speech during a visit to Chinese schools in 1927; Kiti, *Origins of the descendants of Chinese in Siam*, 141.
11   Prior to Vajiravudh's outburst, European advisers had warned the Thai authorities about the Chinese and their potential monopoly of the Thai economy. For example, H. Warington Smyth, the British director of the Royal Department of Mines, wrote a report in 1898 referring to the Chinese as 'Jews of Siam', see Skinner, *Chinese society in Thailand*, 160–5.

5. ARE WE THEM? THE CHINESE IN 20TH-CENTURY THAI LITERATURE AND HISTORY

royal appointments and *sakdina* (noble titles). Historical data tells us that the Chinese had intermarried with the Thai and, importantly, sired many important Thai noble families. The founder of Thonburi-Bangkok was not a Thai but a successful Chinese merchant; the hero Taksin, who liberated Thailand from Burma, had a Chinese father. The mother of the founder of the present Chakkri dynasty was Chinese and, by the mid-1800s, most of the governors of the southern provinces, such as Ranong, Songkhla, Nakhon Sithammarat, Pattani, Trang, Phuket and Chanthaburi, were Chinese merchants who had been given noble titles by the king.

From the Taksin to the early Bangkok period (up to Rama V), Thailand maintained close trade relationships with China. The Thai kings represented themselves in documents using Chinese names beginning with Taksin's Chinese clan name, Tae, such as Tae Jiew, Tae Hua, Tae Hok, Tae Huk, Tae Meng and Tae Jia.[12] Trade and foreign relations before the administrative reforms of Rama V were split between two senior titled bureaucrats who were in charge of the Port Authority. The official responsible for dealing with traders from the East was typically the richest Chinese merchant, who held the title Phraya Chodukratchasetthi. Many were tax farmers and the founders of some of the best-known families in Thailand today, to wit, Krairerk, Chotikapukkana, Chotiksawat and Laohasetthi.[13] The daughters of senior Chinese officials were also taken as concubines by Thai kings to sire princes and princesses with family ties to the Chinese. For example, M.R. Kukrit Pramoj, the famous author, critic, newspaperman and one-time prime minister, publicly acknowledged that his grandmother was Chinese and, while he was alive, he never failed to conduct rituals during important Chinese holy days.

One of the tasks of this essay is to assess whether the king's demonisation resulted in severe discrimination or lasting demonisation of the Sino-Thai, especially in Thai literary texts. Prior to the publication of *Jews of the Orient*, the Thai monarchy was not antagonistic towards the local Chinese. Vajiravudh's own father, King Chulalongkorn, emphasised in numerous speeches that the Thai and Chinese were like close relatives. In fact, several of his concubines were Chinese. Under Chulalongkorn,

---

12 Phimpraphai, *Siamese junk*, 190.
13 Many of the richest Chinese families were founded by tax farmers and merchants engaged in the junk trade with China. They made money by winning bids to collect taxes for the Thai king from people and businesses. They were also allowed to operate gambling dens and lotteries, to produce and sell liquor, and to buy and sell opium. For details on tax farming, see Suehiro, *Capital accumulation in Thailand*, 72–83; and Skinner, *Chinese society in Thailand*, 118–25.

the Thai state had maintained an open immigration policy to attract more Chinese labour. And, instead of corvée labour, the Chinese paid a very low triennial head tax to the Crown. This goodwill towards the immigrant Chinese was echoed in a speech by King Vajiravudh himself during the cremation rites for his father in December 1910. The king said:

> The Chinese people and our own people have long been of one heart; the Chinese have acted like people of the same race as our people from ancient times to the present day. I am resolved, therefore, always to assist and protect all the Chinese who come to live in this country.[14]

A few years later, however, the policy of 'protecting' the Chinese took a turn for the worse as the exigencies of world politics and new fears of rising republicanism became acute. To strengthen the position of the monarchy, Vajiravudh instituted a nationalistic campaign as a strategy to galvanise the people of Thailand to resist the spread of republican ideology, the handmaiden of incipient Han Chinese nationalism. The demise of the Manchu dynasty in China in 1911 to a republican, Kuomintang, made Vajiravudh worry that the security of his own position as absolute monarch was in jeopardy. He also resented Sun Yat-sen's visit to Thailand to raise money from the local Chinese.[15]

Two other local incidents may have also contributed to the king's ire. The first was the three-day strike of June 1910, just before the death of King Chulalongkorn and a few months before the coronation of Vajiravudh. Chinese workers went on a general strike to protest the increase in the head tax to match the amount levied against the general population following the abolition of corvée labour. The strike paralysed Bangkok, a palpable indication of the potential power of the local Chinese. The second event

---

14   Walter F. Vella, *Chaiyo! King Vajiravudh and the development of Thai nationalism* (Honolulu, University of Hawai'i Press, 1978), 191.
15   Rising Han Chinese nationalism and Sun Yat-sen's promotion of republican political ideology greatly alarmed the Thai monarchy. Sun Yat-sen visited Bangkok in 1908 and on three other occasions to recruit followers. He believed that the overseas Chinese would be the 'mother of the revolution' and the vanguard of modernisation. Another leading nationalist, Kang Youwei, was appalled by the rate of assimilation of the Chinese into their host countries. The Chinese paper *Chinosayamwarasap* also appeared in 1907, and its editor openly debated Vajiravudh on sensitive subjects such as the loyalty of the Chinese; see Phenphisut Intharaphirom, *Siew Hut Seng Sibunruang: Thatsana lae botbat khong jin sayam nai sangkhom thai* [*Siew Hut Seng Sibunruang: Perspectives and roles of the Sino-Thai in Thai Society*] (Bangkok: Faculty of Arts, Chulalongkorn University, 2004). These factors may have led to the establishment of Chinese schools in Thailand. By the time Vajiravudh became king, four Chinese language schools, a Chinese library and a lecture hall were already established; see Wasana Wongsurawat, 'Contending for a claim on civilization: The Sino-Siamese struggle to control overseas Chinese education in Siam', *Journal of Chinese overseas*, 42(2) (2008): 164–5.

was an attempted coup by young military officers in 1912. Among its leaders, several were Sino-Thai officers who protested the unfair increase of the Chinese annual head tax and the privileging of the Wild Tigers Corps over the regular army, and advocated the need for political freedom and the rejection of one-man rule.[16] The Thai monarch undoubtedly viewed these developments with alarm. To shore up his position, and influenced by his educational experience in England, Vajiravudh coined and promoted the concept 'Nation, Religion and King' as the main pillars of Thai nationalism. European anti-Semitism and the Anglophone 'God, King and Country' seemed to have inspired Vajiravudh's Thai nationalism. In this official nationalism, a good Thai is one who loves the nation, is a good Buddhist and loves the king.

Vajiravudh's articulation of official Thai nationalism contrasted the Thai people/race against a selected Internal Other, namely, the Chinese. In short, the Thai were defined by who they were not, that is, they were *not* like the Chinese. It should be kept in mind that Vajiravudh only targeted the recent arrivals from China who were mostly poor labourers from rural villages, ignoring the Chinese who had been absorbed into the bureaucracy and old merchant families that had close business and personal ties to the monarchy. Thus, the official construction of the Chinese Other in Vajiravudh's nationalism defined the Chinese as poor and desolate peasants who had come to Thailand with just 'a straw mat and a pillow [*suea phuen mon bai*]' to 'seek the protection of the king's righteous generosity [*phueng phraboromaphothisomphan*]'.

Although Vajiravudh racialised the concept of the Thai nation, he only targeted the Chinese, ignoring the other races within Thailand. Thailand was populated not only by Thai people, but by Malays, Lao, Mon, Shan, Yuan, Indians, Europeans and many others. But these other races seemed harmless to the Thai state. The Chinese, on the other hand, represented an imminent threat because of their growing numbers, especially in urban centres, their control of business and rising wealth and their propagation of subversive ideologies arising from China itself.

The nationalism initiated by Vajiravudh, and later to be enhanced by the Phibun regime in the late 1930s and early 1940s, facilitated or forced the assimilation of the Chinese into Thai society. The decree of 1913 urging the Thai to adopt family names (in contrast to Chinese clan names)

---

16   An excellent study of the 1912 coup is Atcharaporn Komutphisamai, *Kabot R.S. 130* [*The 1912 rebellion*] (Bangkok: Amarin Wichakan Press, 1997).

spilled over into the local Chinese population because some also adopted Thai surnames. In that same year, the nationality law was ameliorated to allow local-born Chinese to have Thai nationality. Paradoxically, the raising of the head tax to the level of all other citizens took away the distinction between the Chinese and the Thai, and the fall of the Manchu dynasty also led to the shearing off of Chinese pigtails to allow Chinese men to look similar to Thai men. By the 1920s, city dwellers found Western clothing and haircuts and women's hairstyles fashionable. These new developments, among others, in effect made differentiating the Chinese from the Thai more difficult.

Assimilation was intensified during the Phibun regime's nationalistic campaign from 1939 to 1942. Sino-Thai serving in the bureaucracy and the military were urged to discard their Chinese surnames and to replace them with invented Thai ones.[17] In addition, new laws that required all private schools to register with the government placed Chinese schools under the control of the state. All schools were also required to teach the Thai language (reducing Chinese language instruction to one hour each day), as well as Thai history, geography and culture (leaving no time for Chinese subjects). In 1939, Phibun closed Chinese schools but at the same time made naturalisation even easier for the Chinese. That same year, Chinese papers were banned, so news about China was filtered through the Thai-language press.

By the end of the Second World War, Chinese language schools were weakened, harassed and demoralised. Eventually, Chinese education in Thailand ended, and the Sino-Thai lost the ability to read, write and speak Chinese. This meant that they were cut off from their own culture and could only learn about it through the Thai language. By 1949, immigration of Chinese into Thailand was limited to only 200 per annum, further cutting off the supply of new Chinese to help sustain Chinese culture and language. In addition, the separate dialect groups, whose members do not necessarily speak Mandarin as a lingua franca, were soon using the Thai language to converse, which indirectly forged new common ground based on a newly shared language. Therefore, those who remained in Thailand attended Thai schools, took on Thai names, were exposed more to Thai culture and less to Chinese culture, found jobs in the bureaucracy and the military, and diversified traditional employment in the family business

---

17 Vella, *Chaiyo!*, 128–36. On the development of hypernationalism, see Scot Barmé, *Luang Wichit Wathakan and the creation of a Thai identity* (Singapore: ISEAS, 1993), Chapter 6.

into new fields.[18] In short, Vajiravudh's railing against the Chinese did not result in a purge or genocide (as suffered by the Jews in Europe) but led to political policies that began the process of forcing the Chinese to assimilate into Thai society.

Now I shall turn to discuss whether sentiments expressed in *Jews of the Orient* affected or infected how the Chinese were represented in Thai literature and other selected texts that followed. By reviewing textual representations of the Chinese by Thai and Sino-Thai authors, I will demonstrate how the Thai and the Sino-Thai negotiate identity issues, and how this process not only destabilised Chinese identity but also Thai identity in 20th-century Thailand.

Early Thai prose fiction, literary texts and the Sino-Thai (1900 – Second World War)

The introduction of prose fiction to Thailand occurred in the early 20th century. Students sent to Europe to study were exposed to the novel and to short stories that were different from traditional Thai literature, which relied heavily on formulaic plots and magical characters but lacked realism. As discussed in Chapter 1, the first novel to be published in the Thai language appeared in 1902. It was a translation of Marie Corelli's *Vendetta*. Thirteen years later, a novel written by a Thai author appeared in 1915. It was a parody of *Vendetta*, using the title *Khwam mai phayabat* [*The non-vendetta*]. This first Thai novel appeared the year after King Vajiravudh's *Jews of the Orient*, but the Chinese were not featured in the novel even though it was about the modern tastes of the middle class in Bangkok. Other early novels also failed to mention tensions between the Thai and the local Chinese. Thus, it appears that King Vajiravudh's complaint against the local Chinese was not a major social issue for early literary authors.

Interestingly, a few years after penning *Jews of the Orient*, Vajiravudh composed and published a collection of letters written by a young man returning to Thailand from England. The letters appeared around 1917 under the title *Huajai chainum* [*A young man's heart*] in the *Dusit samit* magazine, edited by the king himself. The letters are between two friends, Praphan ('Author', which suggests a reference to Vajiravudh, who is known

---

18   For details, see Wasana, 'Contending for a claim on civilization', 161–82.

as the 'Great Writer') and Prasert ('Noble', which refers to the ideal of the noble Thai), with only Praphan's letters appearing in print. Because only Praphan's thoughts are revealed to the readers, *Huajai chainum* could be interpreted as Vajiravudh speaking his mind, a soliloquy of sorts, about the kind of person he thinks the good Chinese should be.

In the first letter, Praphan tells his friend how he misses England, his English girlfriend and life in civilised Europe. He is compelled to return home because of his love for Thailand and the Thai people. His second letter is written from Singapore. He complains that he has been refused a room at the hotel because of his looks. It is only after he has pointed out to the clerk that he is Thai and not Chinese that he is given a room. Praphan tells his friend that the *jek* are everywhere and are looked down upon by the English and Europeans. He confides that being in Singapore and getting used to the *jek* again is good preparation for his reintroduction to Thailand. It is only when he complains that his own father has refused to give up Chinese ways that we learn that Praphan is also a *jek* or *luk jek* (a *jek* child). In subsequent letters, Praphan tells his friend about the Chinese girl his parents have picked for him. Fortunately, she marries someone else, a Thai who holds the bureaucratic title Luang. Praphan eventually marries an upper-class Thai woman, but soon after she runs off with another man. Praphan wants badly to become a *kharatchakan* (civil servant/servant of the king) and is eventually accepted into the Thai titled bureaucracy. He is also allowed to join the king's exclusive and controversial Wild Tigers Corps, a paramilitary group loyal only to the king.

From what is said in the 18 published letters, we could easily surmise that even Vajiravudh himself, like most Thai of that period, still considered the Chinese and their descendants as different but yet an integral part of Thai society. Praphan himself denies his Chinese heritage by making sarcastic remarks about the *jek* and by telling the hotel clerk in Singapore that he is Thai. By writing Praphan into the Thai bureaucracy and into the Wild Tigers Corps, Vajiravudh had no trouble accepting Praphan as Thai, a *jek* who loved Thailand, the Thai people and the king. It appears that his demonisation of the Chinese in his 1914 *Jews of the Orient* only singled out the 'bad' Chinese who refused to become Thai, rejecting the Thai language, the culture and service to the king.

Although we learn that Praphan is Sino-Thai and that his father is rich, we know little about him and his family. Praphan's background appears irrelevant and unimportant. It is as if he has vaulted from the condition of being part of a Chinese family to becoming Thai and being accepted as Thai.

5. ARE WE THEM? THE CHINESE IN 20TH-CENTURY THAI LITERATURE AND HISTORY

Vajiravudh was not the only person to express anxiety about the ambiguous identity of the Thai and the Sino-Thai. Contemporary with the publication of *Huajai chainum*, another Thai author, Nai But, published a poem, *A poetic appreciation of Sampheng Market*, probably in the 1920s, describing what goes on in the Chinese district of Bangkok.[19] Aside from his colourful description of the hustle and bustle of the place, he wrote the following:

> Small road is crowded by *Jek* [Chinese] and Thai,
> Unavoidably mingling, clashing with one another.
> *Jek* mix with Thai beyond recognition,
> Who is who?
> One can't help but wonder
> Modern times deviantly mess up the place.
> *Jin* [Chinese] cut off their pigtails and become Thai undetectably.
> What an unconventional abnormality,
> People surprisingly reverse their ethnicity.[20]

Although written in 1957, another popular novel, Kulap Saipradit's *Gazing at the future*, gives readers a sense of the changing values that undermined absolute monarchy in the late 1920s. In that novel, Kulap writes about social disparities present in an elite school in Bangkok, a school similar to the one that he had attended. Students in the school come from many backgrounds—the children of princes, scions of wealthy families, a few provincial students on scholarships and even Sino-Thai students. The story is told from the viewpoint of Chantha, a poor provincial student who marvels at what he sees happening at his school. The two smartest students are an outspoken Thai student, Nithat, and a humble Sino-Thai student, Seng. Seng is liked and accepted by his classmates because he is generous with his time, helping to tutor those who need it. During an incident when a student with royal background boasts about the achievements of his ancestors, Nithat reminds his classmates that Thai history should also include peasants like the ancestors of Chantha and the

---

19   Nai But, *Nirat chom talat sampheng* [*A poetic appreciation of Sampheng Market*] (Bangkok: Rongphim Phanit Supphaphon, n.d.).
20   Translated and quoted in Supang Chantavanich, 'From Siamese-Chinese to Chinese-Thai: Political conditions and identity shifts among the Chinese in Thailand' in *Ethnic Chinese as Southeast Asians*, ed. Leo Suryadinata (Singapore: ISEAS, 1997), 256. This poem is also found in Sujit Wongthes, *Kawi Sayam nam thiew krungthep* [*Siamese poets lead tours of Bangkok*] (Bangkok: Matichon, 2002), 263–96. Kasian Tejapira has also written about the slippery identification of who was Chinese and who was Thai just by looking at how men wore their hair; 'Pigtail: A pre-history of Chineseness in Siam', *Sojourn*, 7(1) (1992): 95–122.

Chinese like Seng. He says that Isan peasants and the Chinese also helped to free Thailand from the Burmese.[21] Kulap's Sino-Thai character is kind, smart, loyal, Christian and broad-minded. I suspect that Kulap and other progressives like him saw the need to reconfigure Thai identity to include non-elites who have made major contributions to the Thai state. To them, Thai historiography should also make space for the Sino-Thai.[22]

I shall turn next to a highly influential novel series in which one of its three main characters, and perhaps the most endearing, is a Sino-Thai by the name of Kim Nguan. *Phon nikon kim nguan*, by P. Intharapalit, is a serial that first appeared in 1939 and ran continuously for over 30 years. The series of comedic novels features the antics of three wealthy playboy adventurers. Not only are the stories funny and entertaining, they also highlight the important issues of the time. Taken together, the series provides a good historical record of what was happening in Thailand from 1939 to 1968. Most Thai readers are familiar with *Phon nikon kim nguan*. All in all, nearly 1,000 episodes were published.[23] Because examining all these episodes is beyond the scope of this essay, I will focus only on the significance of one of the main characters, namely, the rich Sino-Thai Kim Nguan.

---

21 Si Burapha [Kulap Saipradit], *Le pai khangna* [*Gazing at the future*] (Bangkok: Bophit Press, 1974), 182–42.
22 Seng is also berated by the aristocratic headmaster when he is caught urinating against the school fence. Seng was tutoring another student and had no time to go to the toilet when the bell rang for the next class. After the headmaster learns the truth, he asks Seng to forgive him. Unfortunately, Seng has to leave school after his father dies. Even though he is accepted by his classmates, Seng still feels like an outsider. He tells Chantha that it is because his father is Chinese and not Thai, and that, although his mother was born in Thailand, she is Sino-Thai. After leaving school, Seng becomes a journalist, perhaps an unusual profession for a Sino-Thai. Kukrit Pramoj's *Four reigns*, written in 1953, makes the distinction between the good and bad Sino-Thai. Prem, who marries the heroine, Ploy, is the son of a rich Chinese. He becomes a bureaucrat and an officer in the Wild Tigers Corps, much the same as the good Chinese in Vajiravudh's *A young man's heart*. Their daughter unfortunately marries a 'bad Chinese' who does not treat his wife's family generously; see Saichon Satayanurak, 'Si phaendin khwam pen thai lae khwam mai thang kanmueang' ['Four reigns: Thai identity and politics'] in *Chakkrawan witthaya: botkhwam phue pen kiat kae Nidhi Eoseewong* [*Universal science: Articles honouring Nidhi Eoseewong*], ed. Thanet Wongyannawa (Bangkok: Silapawatthanatham Press, 2006), 170–2.
23 Wichitwong Na Pomphetch, *Wiwatthanakan sangkhom thai kap nawaniyai chut phon nikon kim nguan* [*The evolution of Thai society and the comedic novel Phon Nikon Kim Nguan*] (Bangkok: Saeng Dao, 2001–02; 2 volumes), 1, 49. When the novel first appeared in 1939, demand was so high that 30,000 copies were printed, compared to about 2,000 copies for other publications. Considering that 25 episodes were published in 1939, the reach and popularity of *Phon nikon kim nguan* would mean that about 750,000 copies of the novel were read in that year alone. If we were to add up all the episodes in this long series, the number would be staggering. P. Intharapalit's father taught Thai in the military preparatory school. The author was also a classmate of Prince Chulachakrabongse and Field Marshal Sarit Thannarat, the prime minister from 1957 to 1963.

Similar to Praphan in Vajiravudh's short story, we know very little about Kim Nguan's background or his family. We learn that he was born in Sampheng, the Chinese district in Bangkok, that his father is the billionaire Kim Bae, and that his grandfather is the rich businessman Kim Sai. And, although his father and grandfather spoke Thai with a heavy Chinese accent, Kim Nguan is a native speaker of Thai who also knows Chinese because he studied at a local Chinese school before attending the prestigious Assumption College, where instruction is in Thai. We also know that he has been sent abroad to observe how business is conducted before returning to become manager of his father's department store, aptly named Siwilai Phanich or Civilised Commerce.[24]

To stop readers from focusing too much attention on Kim Nguan's background (in fact, we never learn his Chinese family name), P. Intharapalit tells the reader that the billionaire Kim Bae passes away at the age of 80, soon after Kim Nguan's character is introduced. We know that his mother is Thai, but she and Kim Nguan's Thai relatives are never brought into the narrative. We know that Kim Nguan is a rich *jek* who has inherited 10.5 million baht deposited in three different banks, as well as 60,000 baht buried in tin cans at home, 10 rice mills, 10 sawmills, 10 cargo ships, a bus company, and scores of rental properties. In fact, in the *Father's offspring* episode, which appeared in December 1939, Kim Nguan's daily income from his business is more than 5,000 baht a day, in a time when servants made 10 baht a month.

Kim Nguan acknowledges his Chinese ethnicity, but he usually makes lighthearted jokes about his family. When two privileged Thai girls first meet Kim Nguan, they ask him who he is and what he does. Kim Nguan replies:

> Who, me? I am *jek*, a *luk jin* [the child of Chinese born in Thailand]. My mother is Thai, her sister is Thai, but my father's elder and younger brothers are *jek*. But the Chinese and Thai are not that different; we are relatives.

Probing further, the girls ask him about his profession. Kim Nguan deflects the question by choosing instead to interpret *achip*, the Thai word for profession, as Ah Chip as 'Uncle Cheep'. He responds, 'I do not have an uncle named Chip [a Thai name], but I have one named Kim Lee

---

24 Thongchai Winichakul, 'The quest for *siwilai*: A geographical discourse of civilizational thinking in the late nineteenth and early twentieth-century Siam', *Journal of Asian studies*, 59(3) (August 2000): 528–49.

[a Chinese name]'. Exasperated, the girls explain that they already know he is *jek* but want to know what he does for a living, which in Thai translates literally as 'what do you cook to eat?' Kim Nguan replies that he does nothing because it is the duty of the chef to cook.[25] In his own mind, Kim Nguan is unequivocal about his own identity. In this case, he selects the bilateral kinship system of the Thai, siding with his Thai mother, and not the Chinese paternal kinship system on his father's side.

In the episode *State mandates* [*Ratthaniyom*], which appeared in December 1940 and is set in the period when the Phibun government campaigned to promote nationalism in order to unify and galvanise the Thai people against foreign enemies, the lead characters decide to form a sympathetic State Mandates Club in response to the government's call to resist foreign domination of the Thai economy. Thai citizens have been urged to fire foreign employees and hire Thai workers instead. Before agreeing to join this club, Kim Nguan asks for an exception. He says that there is only one Thai in his company, he himself, and all his workers are 'newly arrived Chinese' (*tueng nang*). He says that, if he fired them, it would bankrupt his company. In describing the single Thai in his company, Kim Nguan uses the Chinese term for one person, *jek kai*, which suggests that he can claim Thai identity even if he still retains aspects of Chinese culture and language. His Thai companions and readers of that episode also understand the meaning of *jek kai*.

When P. Intharapalit introduces Kim Nguan, he does not have a family name. This situation changes during the Ratthaniyom period when all Thai people are urged to take on Thai family names. Thus, Kim Nguan becomes Kim Nguan Thaithae. The word *thaithae* means authentic Thai, and this wordplay has a deeper significance than just being funny. The construction of this new name once again destabilises the notion of 'Thainess' by allowing a person with a Chinese name the option of becoming an authentic Thai. To complicate matters, Kim Nguan switches names on several occasions. At one point, he goes by Sanguan Thaithiem instead of Kim Nguan Thaithae.

By proposing these two versions of the character's name, P. Intharapalit illustrates the complexities of identity construction, especially when it is applied to the *jek*. The couplet Sanguan Thaithiem could be translated as 'keeping safe the imitation Thai', or 'preserving the imitation Thai'. The

---

25 Wichitwong, *The evolution of Thai society and the comedic novel*, 1, 215.

name uses all Thai words to proclaim that the person is a fake Thai. On the other hand, Kim Nguan Thaithae combines his given Chinese name with a Thai family name, which declares that he is *thaithae*, or an authentic Thai. In this case, Kim Nguan defiantly claims that the *jek* is also an authentic Thai. Who, one may ask, is more trustworthy in these two cases?[26] Interestingly, the cartoon drawings on the cover of the novels always show Kim Nguan wearing dark glasses. We could think of this as a way to hide his 'Chinese' facial features, especially his eyes, so he could look 'Thai' or, metaphorically, he was a Chinese looking at the world through 'Thai-tinted' glasses.

Kasian Tejapira, one of Thailand's leading scholars on the Sino-Thai, has also written about Kim Nguan's ethnicity and his business background. He analyses the episode where Kim Nguan attempts to sell his autobiography, *Born in Sampheng*. Kim Nguan is convinced that because he is revealing secrets to his success, his autobiography will become a sure bestseller. The elaborate and beautifully printed book is to be priced at 20 baht a copy with a targeted sales figure of at least 50,000 copies. But unlike the market today where Chinese and Sino-Thai business manuals sell easily, no one back then seemed interested in the autobiography. The few who buy the book curse the author and return their purchases. To sell his books, Kim Nguan resorts to inserting a 100-baht note into each copy, which costs only 20 baht. This marketing scheme allows him to sell all the books, but at a huge loss.

Although it is unclear when this episode was written, it was probably in 1950, the same year that Prince Chulachakrabongse published *Born in Parut Palace*, chronicling his life as a young boy growing up in the palace of his grandmother, the dowager queen. Perhaps P. Intharapalit was poking fun at his former military preparatory school classmate. *Born in Sampheng* makes the statement that a Sino-Thai born in Chinatown should be considered Thai if Prince Chulachakrabongse, whose mother is Russian, can be considered a Thai prince.[27]

---

26 Kasian Tejapira's interpretation of the naming issue is slightly different from mine. He asserts that the name Sanguan Thaithiem says this person is phoney and deceitful. Kim Nguan Thaithae, on the other hand, suggests that Kim Nguan feels a sense of guilt that he was not born a full Thai and has an inferiority complex. Kasian also critiques the misrepresentation of Chinese names by P. Intharapalit, which shows that the Thai author is unfamiliar with Chinese culture. Kasian points out that sharing the first part of a Chinese name such as Kim can only apply to those of the same generation. Therefore, Kim Bae's son cannot be named Kim Nguan, nor could Kim Sai's son be named Kim Bae; see his *Le lot lai mangkorn* [*Looking through the dragon design*] (Bangkok: Khopfai, 1994), 65–75.

27 Chulachakrabongse, *Koet wang parut* [*Born in Parut Palace*] (Bangkok: Khlang Witthaya, 1958). Kasian, *Looking through the dragon design*, 69.

P. Intharapalit has also made Kim Nguan more nationalistic than even his two Thai buddies. Kim Nguan is always the first to show vehement anger towards the enemies of Thailand, especially the French, who had forced King Chulalongkorn to cede territories east of the Mekong to France in 1893. When the Thai-Franco war in Indochina breaks out during the Second World War, Kim Nguan and his two Thai buddies immediately volunteer to fight the French. They enlist in the army as foot soldiers and later as fighter pilots. The three friends also receive battlefield commissions and, by the end of the Indochina conflict, Kim Nguan rises to the rank of lieutenant general. In sum, P. Intharapalit wanted to show that, in spite of his given name, Kim Nguan is indeed Thai, and that the Sino-Thai have reason to act more Thai than even the Thai and, as a corollary, can be trusted and deserving of promotion to senior military positions.

It is during Phibun's ultra-nationalistic campaign (1939–42) that the Chinese came under great pressure to assimilate. His economic nationalism also deprived the Chinese of participation in several business areas such as petroleum products, taxi driving and trade in bird's nests. Many Sino-Thai also joined the Seri Thai movement as nationalists. An example is Puey Ungphakorn, later to become governor of the Bank of Thailand and rector of Thammasat University. Puey experienced discrimination at school because both parents were Chinese and he had a Chinese name. He said that if the Thai could understand that the Sino-Thai had to face pressure from both the Chinese and Thai communities, they would be more accepting of the plight of the Sino-Thai. But his mother always told him that born in Thailand, he is Thai and must be loyal to Thailand.[28]

---

28 Puey Ungphakorn, *Santi prachatham* [*Peaceful social justice*] (Bangkok: Khled Thai Press, 1973), 7–8. Many of the most ardent anti-Chinese officials in the 1930s and 1940s who pushed for more Thai control of the economy were themselves Sino-Thai—Luang Pradit Manutham and Luang Wichit Wathakarn, for example. It should be pointed out here that most local-born Chinese had been assimilated into Thai society by the 1940s. Many joined government service and were given Thai noble titles, which made them part of the elite. Other local Chinese who were in the private sector soon realised that their future was primarily in Thailand and, therefore, to attain more prestige, status and power, they had no choice but to identify with the Thai elite, many of whom were Sino-Thai. This identification with the ruling elite may also explain why most Sino-Thai businessmen are ardent royalists, who rely on the monarchy to give them the stamp of elite status through large and frequent personal donations to the king's charitable projects. In return, the monarch gives the Sino-Thai prestige by sponsoring the weddings of their children, and by sponsoring or presiding over the funerals of prominent Sino-Thai businessmen. To be cremated by a flame that comes from the palace is highly prestigious. It is only reserved for high officials and those who have been benefactors to the country. The rich Sino-Thai have been beneficiaries of such a royal boon.

The External Chinese Other

The mid-1950s to the mid-1960s was a turbulent time for Southeast Asia. France was fighting a losing war in Vietnam, Indonesia was facing internal political problems, the Hukbalahap rebellion was still unsettled in the Philippines, and Malaya was reeling from the struggle for independence. Coming off its participation in the Korean War, the Thai government was feeling its way towards becoming a member of the 'free world' in its struggle against communism. The early 1950s was the dawn of Thailand's Cold War period. By the early 1960s, the United States was becoming more involved in Vietnam, and China under Mao was beginning to flex its muscles by supporting overseas Maoist parties. Communism, and especially communists, were demonised in the press and government pronouncements. There was also a fear that the local Chinese would become communists.

How to deal with the local Chinese was spelled out in a recently declassified secret government policy targeting the local Chinese and their descendants, formulated by the National Security Council, with detailed steps to be taken by the various government ministries and departments.[29] This document is the first I have seen that spelled out the full range of goals and policies to reinvigorate the assimilation process begun by King Vajiravudh. The document warned against using repressive measures against the local Chinese. A Thai ethno-nationalist policy aimed at eliminating Chinese influence in commerce and politics, closing Chinese schools, forming Chinese-only residential zones and shutting down Chinese associations and newspapers would only lead to unrest, resentment and friction within the country. All government agencies were urged to find ways to help make the local Chinese loyal Thai citizens. These new guidelines would prevent the spread of communism among the Chinese community by creating security for both the Thai and Chinese.

---

29   National Security Council of Thailand [Samnakngan Sapha Mankhong Haeng Chat], *Sarup ekkasan kho phitjarana khong khanakammakan wang phaen khong sapha khwam mankhong haeng chat No. 6/2508 rueang nayobai kiewkap khon jin lae luk jin in prathet Thai* [*Synopsis of the document number 6/2508 reviewed by the National Security Council on policies towards the Chinese and their descendants in Thailand*] (Bangkok: National Security Council of Thailand, 1965). This document systematically summarises past, present and future assimilation policies that would turn the local Chinese into Thai citizens.

The government should also provide just treatment for all Chinese who are loyal to Thailand; severely punish those who undermine national security; reduce drastically the number of Chinese immigrants; make sure that those who become naturalised citizens give up their former citizenship; praise the Chinese and their descendants who have done good deeds for Thai society; encourage the Chinese to change their names to Thai; provide equal rights to naturalised Chinese; and be more strict with the Chinese who retain their alien resident status. The overarching guideline is to use gentle and subtle policies to assimilate the Chinese by replacing Chinese benevolent societies with state organisations, quietly encouraging more mixed marriages, considering policies that would lower Chinese birth rates, preventing Chinese government representatives or the embassy from having influence, exerting more control over Chinese schools—their curriculum, funding and influence from abroad—and providing adequate Thai schools for new citizens and their children.

Reflecting the heightened threat of a potential spread of the political influence of Maoist China, the novel *Lep khrut* was published in 1956 by Phanom Thian, the pseudonym of Chatchai Wisetsuwannaphum, to exploit or to respond to the public's paranoia of the external (Chinese) communist threat.[30] The novel was serialised in *Ploenchit weekly magazine* and ran for 14 months. And, even though the finished novel was over 3,000 pages long, the first printing run was 100,000 copies, which, at that time (and even today), was the top figure for published novels. Parenthetically, this novel has also been reprinted numerous times. While there has been other published crime fiction, *Lep khrut* was the first of that genre circulated in huge numbers. The novel has also been made into a very successful movie.

Lep khrut involves the attempt of the Thai secret service and police to infiltrate and destroy a Chinese secret society that is extorting money from local Sino-Thai businessmen. This secret society, known as *Sing Eng* (the eagle) in the Taechiu dialect, has set up cells in Bangkok to illegally import weapons to support the fight for independence in Malaya. As we know, the struggle for Malayan independence began soon after the defeat of Japan and the return of the British, leading to the start of the Malayan Emergency in 1948. The armed insurrection was led by the Communist Party of Malaya under the leadership of Chin Peng, a Chinese born in

---

30   Phanom Thian [Chatchai Wisetsuwannaphum], *Lep khrut* [*The garuda's talons*] (Bangkok: Phanfa Witthaya, 1970; reprint edition).

5. ARE WE THEM? THE CHINESE IN 20TH-CENTURY THAI LITERATURE AND HISTORY

Malaya. The Malayan People's Anti-Japanese Army was transformed into the Malayan Races Liberation Army (MRLA) to fight the return of the British. Although most of its members were Chinese, there were also some Malays, Indonesians and Indians. In the novel, Sing Eng, which the Thai authorities have relabelled Lep Khrut, join forces with the Malayan communists to help procure weapons for the MRLA. Sing Eng assassins begin murdering prominent Sino-Thai businessmen to intimidate others into contributing to its coffers. The assassins use a large garuda or eagle's talon to kill their victims.

The Thai authorities investigating Lep Khrut are led by several young and daring police captains and detectives. Their secret weapon is a James Bond-ian figure, the army lieutenant Khom Sorakupt. Lieutenant Khom, who has seen combat in Korea, speaks English, French and several Chinese dialects fluently. In addition, he is a sharpshooter and an expert in hand-to-hand combat. He is also a well-known ladies' man, a rascal and a rogue. Lieutenant Khom assumes the character of a recently deceased criminal named Cheep Choochai, whom he resembles. As the notorious criminal Cheep Choochai, he is soon hired by Lep Khrut to help recover the pieces of an eagle sculpture that contains a secret formula it needs in its quest to dominate the world.

The novel opens with a group of 'Thai' policemen discussing the recent murder of a well-known Sino-Thai businessman. The Thai police officers make disparaging remarks about the recently assassinated man by inferring that he was not really Thai because he had just changed his name from Chinese to Thai. They also discuss the task of protecting another businessman named Wikun. Even though Wikun speaks perfect Thai and acts no different from any other Thai, the policemen still jokingly refer to him as Ma Yu Lung in Mandarin, and Bae Yu Lung in Taechiu. They also poke fun at the Chinese by speaking Thai with a Chinese accent and using common Chinese words such as *haw* to say 'yes' during their conversation. Even though Wikun refuses police protection, the authorities are compelled to protect all Thai citizens, including the Sino-Thai.

It is clear to the reader that the heroes and heroines in this novel are Thai who are tasked with protecting the local (good) Sino-Thai from bad outsiders. The villains in the novel are foreigners, mostly Chinese from Hong Kong, Singapore, Malaya and mainland China. They have names such as Peter Wong, Tunku Gustafa, Dr Hang Lee, Dr Fung Tian and Ignitius Sung. The female villains are Chinese, Ceylonese and

Malay, with exotic names like Feuy Aian, Kinaree, Euphrasia Rose and Pridahanam. The foot soldiers guarding the Lep Khrut headquarters are Chinese fighters from Hainan. Although one of the assassins is a Thai-born Chinese, he has never registered himself as a citizen, which makes him, too, an alien outsider.

The phoney Cheep Choochai works to find the pieces of the eagle sculpture, made of white gold and smuggled into Thailand. Secret agents from all over the world also descend upon Bangkok to look for these pieces but, miraculously, Cheep is the one who finds them. In doing this, he has to evade both the Thai police and crooks, kills many protagonists and seduces numerous women along the way.

Lep Khrut also establishes cells in Thailand to coordinate its weapon-smuggling operations. Heading up these cells are Chinese scientists who secretly enter Thailand—one to operate a foundry and another as chief priest of a Chinese temple. With the help of the police, Cheep destroys these Lep Khrut centres and kills the two leaders. The supreme leader of the group, on the other hand, is much craftier and more lethal than the two that Cheep eliminates.

This shadowy figure goes by the name Chang Su Liang. He is the Thai equivalent of the dreaded Dr Fu Manchu, created by the imaginative Sax Rohmer. Dr Fu Manchu achieved international notoriety when he became a cinematic character responsible for linking 'evil' with 'Chinese' permanently.[31] The description of Chang Su Liang in the novel and as a film persona is a classic imitation of Dr Fu Manchu. Both are described as a slender and tall Chinese man with a thin face, slit eyes and a mouth framed by a long moustache and a long wispy beard. In effect, the Thai Chang Su Liang reinforces the European Fu Manchu so much so that the two names have become synonymous, striking fear in the hearts of many Thai children and adults alike.

Chang Su Liang has larger intentions than merely supplying smuggled weapons to the Malayan freedom fighters. He is intent upon ruling the world and resurrecting China as a great power. Chang is obsessed with

---

31   Sax Rohmer, *The insidious Dr. Fu Manchu* (New York: A.L. Burt Co., 1917). Thai readers are familiar with Sax Rohmer because King Vajiravudh translated Rohmer's *The golden scorpion* into Thai; Ram Chitti [King Vajiravudh], *Malaengpong* thong [*The golden scorpion*] (Bangkok: Book Corner, 2004). Elaine H. Kim asserts that the cinematic character of the sinister Fu Manchu has created the stereotypical evil Chinese man; see her *Asian American literature: An introduction to the writings and their social context* (Philadelphia: Temple University Press, 1982), 4.

finding the eagle sculpture because underneath the white gold veneer is the secret formula for a weapon even more powerful than the recently exploded hydrogen or atomic bombs. The weapon is a cosmic ray that can destroy anything it is aimed at. A German Jewish scientist had invented that death ray after being abducted and taken to Russia. After the death of Stalin, the formula had been inscribed onto the eagle before it was broken up into six pieces and smuggled out, first to Hong Kong, and later to Thailand.

As dangerous outsiders, Chang Su Liang and his henchmen are able to operate freely in Thailand because they can become invisible in the large Chinese community, especially in Sampheng. The novel paints a picture of Sampheng/Yaowarat as a foreign site where even the Thai police have a hard time patrolling and controlling crime. In effect, Sampheng/Yaowarat is an alien space where the police and Chinese gangsters are engaged in fierce fights and gun battles.

To the Thai policemen, entering Chinatown is akin to entering a foreign world of restaurants, night clubs, gambling dens and bars that cater exclusively to the Chinese. In that world, Chinese is the lingua franca. The police have to disguise themselves to pass off as Chinese to operate there. Even the hoodlums and crooks in Chinatown are mostly Chinese whom the police describe disparagingly as 'fighters from the saliva-spitting nation [*nak bu chat khak thui*]', alluding to the Chinese penchant for spitting in public.[32] And because the police treat Chinatown as an alien site, its denizens are also the dangerous Other Within, who can be dispatched without any legal constraints. In one incident, police captain Krit Kamchorn, one of the leading characters in the novel, summarily hangs a Chinese gangster. In another, he also executes Peter Wong, a Lep Khrut assassin, after the latter murders a female police informant.

In the end, police brutality and the use of extrajudicial executions of external Chinese enemies allow the authorities to stamp out the threat of Chang Su Liang, his secret society and his world-conquering weapon. Chang's treachery against the Malayan freedom fighters is eventually revealed before he is dispatched. The demonisation of the external foreign

---

32 Perhaps emulating the distaste of Europeans for public spitting, especially by low-class Chinese, the Thai had also latched onto this stereotyping of the Chinese. For example, to put a stop to the Chinese penchant for public spitting, there were signs posted by the English authorities at the Hong Kong Botanical Gardens that prohibited spitting. I was surprised to see such signs also displayed on the grounds of my Anglican secondary school in Hong Kong when I visited recently.

Chinese is sufficient justification for the Thai police to use force without having to worry about legal procedures or consequences. Although we still do not learn much about the personal lives of the Sino-Thai in *Lep khrut*, the readers are exposed to Sampheng, Bangkok's Chinatown, as a community. Paradoxically, even though the Chinatown in this novel comes across as familiar, it is depicted as a zone of difference and rather foreign—a dangerous place even for the Thai police and secret service. The Chinese characters in the novel are spies, professional killers, hooligans, secret society members, multinational businessmen, informants for the police and other villainous characters. The Chinese once again become a danger to Thai society. However, the threat is from the External Chinese Other.[33]

As Thai authors, both P. Intharapalit and Phanom Thian had little familiarity with the lives and struggles of the Chinese. They had no sense of the challenges faced by the generations of Chinese who grew up in Thailand. Like most Thai, they knew many Sino-Thai and accepted them as friends, but as Thai authors they were not able to write about the Chinese qua Chinese. This condition would be rectified when the Sino-Thai began to find their voice and to feel secure enough to write about their own history as residents and citizens of Thailand. The yoke of Otherness was finally shaken off after decades of silence.

Echoing official interpellations of Chineseness

By the end of the 1960s, the Sarit-Thanom-Praphat dictatorial regime had lost its firm grip on Thai society. The war economy of the Vietnam era had brought wealth, new infrastructure and better tertiary education that

---

33 We should note that soon after this novel was published, Malaya gained its independence from Great Britain on 31 August 1957. The Malayan Races Liberation Army surrendered the following year. Ironically, Chin Peng led his forces to hide near the Thai border, and they continued fighting from 1967 until 1989, while he was based largely in Beijing from the early 1960s. From 1989, he lived in southern Thailand till his death in September 2013. The deployment of repressive police tactics in *Lep khrut* reminds us of the recent elimination of drug dealers and the harsh treatment of Muslims in southern Thailand under Prime Minister Thaksin Shinawatra. As a parallel, the south of Thailand today is usually depicted as an alien site and its Malay population still considered *khaek* (guests), and not Thai. In both cases—the External Chinese Other and the Malay Other—the use of extrajudicial force has been justified on the grounds that it occurred in alien spaces and against foreign elements.

helped to expand the ranks of the urban middle class.[34] One group which had gained much from that situation was the Sino-Thai community. It became richer and better educated. Increasingly, the presence of the descendants of the Chinese pervaded not only business and banking but also higher education, government, the military and politics. The Sino-Thai became part of the new educated middle class and the power elite, poised to take over from the old bureaucratic elite. There was new-found self confidence among the Sino-Thai together with the desire to tell the story of their successes. This new generation of educated Sino-Thai was no longer cowed or intimidated by the negative image painted by King Vajiravudh.

A major worry for the Thai state during the early 1970s was the impending withdrawal of the United States from Vietnam and the possible spread of communism into Thailand. Already, the Communist Party of Thailand (CPT) was operating internally, albeit in peripheral areas in the north, northeast and south. The Thai authorities were worried about the CPT, its Maoist philosophy and its Sino-Thai leadership. This new threat, no different from the threat King Vajiravudh felt regarding the spread of Chinese republican ideology, was centred on the loyalty of the local Chinese. The Thai state needed a way to reassure both the Thai and Sino-Thai that they were fellow citizens who should be loyal to their country.

If the novel *Lep khrut* tells us anything, it is that many Thai were anxious about the loyalty of the Sino-Thai. One strategy, as we have seen in that novel, was to clearly differentiate the external (bad) Chinese from the internal (good) Chinese. The next two novels are the first major works to focus attention on the lives, struggles and successes of the internal Chinese, the good Sino-Thai. They were quickly embraced by the Thai authorities and used as a way to educate both the Thai and the Sino-Thai to live together in peace and harmony. These two novels—narrated from the viewpoint of the immigrant Chinese who had found peace and prosperity in Thailand—were awarded prestigious literature prizes. Subsequently, they were selected as reading assignments for Thai secondary-school students. The Thai authorities wanted to neutralise possible Sinophobia and reassure the general population that the Sino-Thai were also Thai and, at the same time, remind the Sino-Thai that they also had a stake in Thailand's security and prosperity.

---

34   This argument is proposed by Benedict Anderson, 'Withdrawal symptoms', in *The spectre of comparisons: Nationalism, Southeast Asia, and the world* (London: Verso 1998), 139–73.

Letters from Thailand [*Jotmai jak mueang thai*] appeared in 1970 and immediately became a bestseller.³⁵ The novel was also awarded the SEATO prize in literature in 1970. It should be noted that SEATO, the Southeast Asia Treaty Organization, was established in 1954 as a regional anti-communist organisation to support the legitimacy of South Vietnam and to reassure US allies such as Thailand and the Philippines that, if they were attacked by a foreign enemy, the United States would come to their rescue.³⁶ *Letters from Thailand* was written by Botan, the pen name of Supha Sirisingh. Unlike the authors of the works examined earlier, who are Thai, Supha is Sino-Thai. Her father, Tian Sae Li, and her mother, Ngaw Sae Tang, were Taechiu Chinese who grew betel leaves and pomelos for sale. Supha was an excellent student who placed 13th in the national university entrance examination. She went on to study at the prestigious Faculty of Arts at Chulalongkorn University, the bastion of Thai royalist conservatism.

Notably, *Letters from Thailand* has been translated into Japanese, Chinese, Dutch, French, English, Tagalog, Polish, German and Hebrew. In 1975, which coincided with the end of the Vietnam War, the Thai Ministry of Education chose this novel for teaching social studies in all Thai schools. The stated purpose was to make sure that all Thai citizens acquired a deep appreciation and understanding of the important contributions made by the Sino-Thai to Thailand's prosperity. In contrast to Vajiravudh's *Jews of the Orient*, *Letters from Thailand* showed empathy for the struggles and hardships Chinese immigrants endured to succeed in Thailand. Perhaps the Chinese family in *Letters from Thailand* represented the type of Chinese that King Vajiravudh would have approved of, whose offspring by the second or third generation had become like Praphan, the Sino-Thai who rejected his parents' Chinese culture in the king's *Huajai chainum*. To reiterate, Vajiravudh's, and the popularly sanctioned, interpellation of the Chinese in Thailand was that they came to Thailand with *suea phuen mon bai ma phueng phraboromaphothisomphan*, that is, with only a straw mat and a pillow to seek the protection of the king's righteous generosity. And, as long as the Sino-Thai adhered to this accepted characterisation of their place in Thai society, they could be considered good and contributing members of Thai society.

---

35   Botan [Supha Sirisingh], *Jotmai jak mueang tha*i [*Letters from Thailand*] (Bangkok: Phrae Phitthaya, 1970). Translated by Susan Fulop (Bangkok: Duang Kamol, 1982).
36   On SEATO, see George McT. Kahin, *Intervention: How America became involved in Vietnam* (New York: Alfred A. Knopf 1986), 71–5.

Letters from Thailand opens with a foreword by the fictitious police general Sala Sintutawat of the Thai National Police Department. General Sala reveals that in arresting a Chinese communist who had defected from (bad) China to seek asylum in (good) Thailand, the police found a bundle of letters written by the prominent Chinese businessman Tan Suang U to his mother in China. The defector, a postal worker, never delivered the letters but pocketed the money Suang U had sent to his mother with those letters. Inexplicably, the man had kept the letters and brought them with him to Thailand. The suspicious-looking letters were confiscated and subsequently translated into Thai by the police. The first letter was written in 1945, when Suang U arrived in Thailand as a young boy. The last letter was written in 1967. All in all, 96 letters were sent to his mother. When asked by the Thai police, Suang U readily agreed to have his letters published, even though some contained unflattering remarks about Thai culture and Thai society. He only regrets that his mother never had the chance to read his letters, and that he has never received any word back from her.

General Sala explains his motives as follows:

> I am well aware that the letters are often offensive, occasionally foolish, and certain to make Thai people angry. It is even possible that they may harm the cause of Chinese integration in our society, a process which in its continuing success has marked us favorably among the nations of Southeast Asia. Nevertheless, I am convinced that our people will profit by reading them and that making them public is not only a service but a responsibility which I must not shirk … I am a Thai, a patriot, and a man concerned with the honor of the Thai people, as you surely are yourself. But I recommend that you read his letters with an open mind, and think fairly about what he has to say.[37]

The novel chronicles in detail (albeit fictionally) the daily life of a young immigrant, his acquaintances, his work, his love life, his business dealings, his thoughts about home and his new surroundings and, just as importantly, how he feels about Thai values and behaviour, both good and bad. The novel is a mirror reflecting both the images of the Chinese living and working in Thailand and also how the Thai are perceived by the Chinese. Thus the readers, both Thai and Chinese, could learn about each other and the shared society in which they live.

---

37   Botan, *Letters from Thailand*, 7.

In his letters, Suang U describes his arrival in Thailand by boat in 1945, accompanied by two other young men from his village. We learn from the letters how he is first hired as a bookkeeper because he has math and writing skills that his mother has taught him. Suang U remarks that unlike the Thai, who prefer diplomas over knowledge, the Chinese value instead substantive knowledge and real skills. He concludes that Thai children go to prestigious schools hoping to land cushy jobs afterwards, but they are not trained to work hard.[38] Suang U complains to this mother that a Thai works only half time and uses only 50 per cent of his ability. A Chinese, on the other hand, exerts himself 100 per cent in whatever he does.[39]

Because he is recognised as a learned man, Suang U is asked to teach his employer's two daughters. Eventually, he marries the elder daughter. After saving enough capital, Suang U starts his own business by exporting and importing goods. Soon after, he opens a bakery and becomes rich. His friend Gim, who works in Suang U's business, eventually marries Chaba, a Thai woman. Chaba's mother does not mind her daughter marrying a Chinese. She says being married to a Chinese means that they all 'could eat pork every day'.[40]

Not long after they are married, Chaba's drunken father falls into the *khlong* (canal) and drowns. Suang U and Gim are surprised that guests at the funeral drank, gambled and quarrelled.[41] The Thai seem to know how to live well, how to have fun, and how to live the easy life. But to the Chinese, such behaviour only means that they are lazy and irresponsible.

---

38 Botan, *Letters from Thailand*, Letter 1.
39 Botan, *Letters from Thailand*, Letter 15.
40 Botan, *Letters from Thailand*, Letter 26. The practice of Sino-Thai marrying Thai continues to this day. The poignant story of the incarceration and death of Amphon Tangnophakun, known as Ah Kong (Grandfather in the Chinese Taechiu dialect), written by Roslin, his Thai wife, is a case in point. Ah Kong was imprisoned, accused of the crime of *lèse majesté* for allegedly sending inflammatory remarks about the queen to a government official. He was sentenced to 20 years in prison and died soon after he was incarcerated. Up to the time of his death, Ah Kong maintained that he was innocent because he loved the monarchy and did not know how to send a text message. Even though Amphon and his father were born and raised in Thailand, they still spoke Thai with a strong Chinese accent. That did not prevent Amphon from marrying a Thai woman from Isan. His wife called him Ah Poh, which is his Chinese name, and when speaking to each other, they used Chinese pronouns. Even after he was arrested, he was not accused of being the ungrateful Chinese, but treated the same way as other (Thai) prisoners whose crime was disrespect for the monarchy; see Ida Aroonwong and Phiengkham Pradapkhwan, *Rak oey: Roslin Tangnophakun* [*Oh love: Roslin Tangnophakun*] (Bangkok: Aan Publications, 2012). The book was given to people who attended Amphon's cremation and later reprinted and sold to the public. Proceeds were given to the relatives of prisoners incarcerated under Article 112 of the Thai penal code, known as the *lèse majesté* law.
41 Botan, *Letters from Thailand*, Letter 28.

5. ARE WE THEM? THE CHINESE IN 20TH-CENTURY THAI LITERATURE AND HISTORY

The Thai are constantly smiling, but most of the time they drink whiskey until they become intoxicated. The Chinese are amazed that not only do the Thai like fighting with each other, they also love fighting of all sorts—fish-fighting, cock-fighting, and even bull-fighting.[42]

While King Vajiravudh accused the Chinese of being obsessed with money to the point that they would do anything to accumulate wealth, the Chinese in this novel see the Thai as overly lazy, working just enough so they can enjoy life. Suang U writes to his mother that the Thai and the Chinese have different work ethics—'The Thai could certainly work as hard as we do, but there is not anything that they want bad enough to "work like a *Jek*"'.[43]

Suang U explains to his mother why he does not like Thai officials. In one letter, he tells her that the clerks just lounge around reading the newspapers, waiting to be bribed. He laments that the district officer is never there on time because he likes to sleep late. When he appears, he always acts superior to the Chinese, and takes at least two hours off for lunch. Suang U says that he does not mind paying taxes or even bribes, but he bristles at the time wasted waiting for Thai officials.

Stereotypical jokes about the Chinese also annoy Suang U. For example, a common joke is that the Chinese were so poor and stingy that they would suspend a salted fish above the dinner table while eating porridge. The funny part to the Thai is when the Chinese mother warned the children not to stare so hard at the salted fish, or else they would become very thirsty when they slept that night. In reverse mockery of the Thai, after buying a radio in 1947, Suang U wonders why there are no programs in Chinese. 'Don't they realize those who can afford a radio are Chinese?' he asks.[44]

According to Chinese custom, Suang U is determined to have a son to carry on the family name, and to lead his funeral procession. His firstborn is indeed a boy, whom he names Weng Kim. Weng Kim grows up speaking Thai at school, but his father forces him to speak only Chinese at home. Even though Weng Kim is a Thai citizen by birth, his father wants him to retain his Chinese culture and heritage. Suang U also insists that

---

42   Botan, *Letters from Thailand*, Letter 33.
43   Botan, *Letters from Thailand*, Letter 19.
44   Botan, *Letters from Thailand*, Letter 29.

the family use chopsticks during meals and that only drinking water is allowed. He tells his children that the Thai only drink soft drinks to show others that they are not poor.

Weng Kim is pulled out of school after grade four to start work as an apprentice in his father's shop. In contrast to the Thai, who want their children to attend school so they can find a prestigious career, the Chinese usually have already predetermined what each child would do to help extend the family fortune. Weng Kim wants to become a teacher and resents his father's wishes for him to become a businessman.[45]

After living in Thailand for 16 years, Suang U realises that his Chinese identity, as well as that of his children, was slipping away. First, his only son, Weng Kim, rebels and runs off with an older Thai prostitute. Second, his youngest daughter attends a Thai school and graduates from a Thai university. She meets her husband, Winyu, a Thai, while she is at the university. To his surprise, Suang U later realises that he actually likes his Thai son-in-law, and that his negative view of Thai culture and Thai people has been based on contact with his workers. Third, as a respected businessman, he is eventually asked to be a director of the Chinese Chamber of Commerce. As a director, Suang U knows he has to use his Thai name for official purposes, even though he still feels that he is Chinese.[46] The formality of his family's assimilation into Thai society takes place in 1961 when the family goes to the District Office to change their names to Thai ones. The district officer selects Thaiyunyong ('Forever Thai') as their new family name. Suang U believes that the district officer has done it to mock the Chinese. His four children also change their names to Withya, Duen-Penh, Maliwan and Ploy-jarat, names that he finds dreadful.[47]

Soon after, tragedy strikes when his wife is killed in a car crash and a fire destroys their bakery. After the fire, Suang U goes to live with his youngest daughter and her Thai husband. When she was growing up, Suang U had ignored this daughter because he had hopes for another son. This neglect has allowed her to adjust to Thai culture and society, unimpeded by her Chinese family. After living with his Thai son-in-law and his mother, Surang, Suang U comes to realise that the two work as hard as the Chinese. Suang U's new-found respect for the common Thai person

---

45 Botan, *Letters from Thailand*, Letters 54, 58.
46 Botan, *Letters from Thailand*, Letter 61.
47 Botan, *Letters from Thailand*, Letter 68.

comes about when he addresses his son-in-law's mother as Khun Surang, using the honorific 'Khun', even though she is only a woman who made and sold candy on the streets. Khun Surang is very kind to Suang U. She also gives him insight into the Thai belief that it is possible to be happy without having much money. In the end, not only do he and his family change their names, Suang U's impression of the Thai and Thai culture also changes. Becoming more 'Thai', he decides to divide up his wealth among his children so he could live a simple life not driven by the need to acquire more and more money.[48]

Letters from Thailand is thus the rags-to-riches story of a Chinese immigrant. The novel represents a textual instrument for the Chinese to gaze back at the Thai to highlight what they perceive as weaknesses and flaws, in much the same way that Vajiravudh had done with the Chinese in *Jews of the Orient*. The novel is significant because it reveals in a serious way what Chinese immigrants have to cope with to become successful in their new home. It is not just leaving their homeland that is at stake, but they also are in danger of losing their culture and identity. This particular narrative not only reinforces the stereotypical Chinese 'straw mat and one pillow' immigrant story but is one of the first to provide a more detailed account of the life of one family. The fact that this fictitious family becomes assimilated within two generations must have been attractive to the Thai state authorities.

Unsurprisingly, *Letters from Thailand* was selected by the Ministry of Education for all secondary school students to read in their social studies classes. The novel allows young Thai to appreciate the struggles of the Chinese and their contributions to Thai society. And, perhaps just as important, it reminds the descendants of the Chinese attending Thai schools that it is alright to become Thai. The novel also contains constructive criticism of Thai culture and behaviour, chastising Thai bureaucrats, especially district officers, and reminding them not to be lazy and not to discriminate against the Chinese. The reconciliation of cultural differences and the recognition of what is good and bad in both cultures are good messages to pass on to the younger generation. Not only have the Chinese submitted to the majority culture, the Thai majority in turn also has to learn about hard work and sacrifice and to accept the local Chinese, and especially their offspring, as fellow Thai.

---

48   Botan, *Letters from Thailand*, Letter 95.

A year after the selection of *Letters from Thailand* as an official school text, another novel about the Chinese immigrant appeared. Written in 1976, *Life with Grandfather* [*Yu kap kong*] is the work of Chalerm Rodplin, who used the pseudonym Yok Burapha ('Jade of the Orient').[49] It is interesting to note that the author chose Jade of the Orient to write a novel about the Chinese in Thailand. The name reminds us of King Vajiravudh's *Yiw haeng buraphathit* [*Jews of the Orient*]. Yok Burapha's name is a play on *Jews of the Orient*. 'Jew' becomes 'Jew-el', that is 'Jade', turning a slight into something valuable and thus indicating that the Chinese are not social and economic parasites, but precious jewels to be cherished.

While not openly admitting that he is Sino-Thai, there are hints that the author has Chinese origins. Yok Burapha's family owned a rice mill (a business mostly owned by the Chinese) and, when growing up, he lived with relatives in Bangkok's Chinese district. The author graduated from Thammasat University and pursued a career as a professional writer. He has published numerous novels, including several that focus on the Sino-Thai. Most importantly, *Yu kap kong*, his first book about the Chinese, was awarded the prestigious National Committee to Develop Publications book prize in 1976. And, similar to *Letters from Thailand*, it was also selected as supplementary reading for Thai literature classes by the Ministry of Education. The novel has been made into a movie (1979) and a television series (1993), and was also published as comic books (2005) and as a collection of wise sayings (2005). This novel, perhaps even more than *Letters from Thailand*, has been used by the state to reinforce the notion of the Chinese as a 'model minority' grateful to have come to live and die in Thailand.

In this novel, the author-narrator assumes the part of Yok, the grandson of Ah Kong, a first-generation Chinese immigrant. Yok Burapha's intentions are quite clear from the beginning when he writes:

> I am confident that all Chinese in Thailand love this land, and they understand their debt and loyalty to the shade [of the king's protection] that has given them immense happiness and freedom. I can fully say that there is no other place where the Chinese are happy besides living in Thailand.

---

49   Yok Burapha [Chalerm Rodplin], *Yu kap kong* [*Life with Grandfather*] (Bangkok: Praphansarn, 1976). The author also tested the waters for interest in how to become successful businessmen using Chinese trade secrets. He also wrote *Kha baep jin* [*Business the Chinese way*] (Bangkok: Khao Fang Publications, 1980), which offers advice from ordinary Chinese merchants about how to make it from rags to riches in Thailand.

5. ARE WE THEM? THE CHINESE IN 20TH-CENTURY THAI LITERATURE AND HISTORY

At certain times there have been disturbing problems and events caused by the Chinese or their descendants that have annoyed the owners of this country, but please understand that the disturbances were caused by a small minority.

Thailand and the Thai people have never faulted the upright and trustworthy Chinese, which is a truth that is firmly stamped in the minds of the Chinese who have come to seek the righteous protection of a magnanimous king. And because of this deep and unshakeable gratefulness, the Chinese like Grandfather are plentiful.[50]

Similar to Botan's novel, *Life with Grandfather* valorises the life of a first-generation immigrant, his struggle with life, with work, with family and with the clash of cultures. What is different from *Letters from Thailand* is that the principal voice, Ah Kong, does his best to say good things about his new home and the Thai people. He always reminds Yok that love for Thailand is a paramount value to be cherished. Ah Kong becomes the model Other Within who chastises other Chinese when they criticise Thailand and Thai culture.

Addressing the concern raised in *Jews of the Orient* that the Chinese always feel superior and do not want to mix with the locals, Yok Burapha uses Ah Kong to scold the Chinese for looking down on the Thai people. Instead of maintaining racial purity, Ah Kong openly encourages Chinese men to marry Thai women. He tells the Chinese who complain about Thailand that they should go back to China. To Ah Kong, the Thai people may not be good at business but they work hard at other jobs. He says that the Thai work hard, just as hard as the Chinese, to plant rice to feed the nation, echoing official propaganda that Thai farmers are the 'backbone of the nation'.

---

50 Introduction in *Life with Grandfather*, quoted in Natthanai Prasannam, '*Yu kap kong* by Yok Burapha: The pursuit of integration ideology in the Thai social context', research project supported by the Faculty of Humanities, Naresuan University, 2007. The translation is mine. Natthanai's excellent paper uses the Gramscian notion of hegemony and Althusser's concept of interpellation as analytical tools to study Yok Burapha's *Life with Grandfather*. Natthanai cites several MA theses that focus on the Chinese in Thai literature; Jatuphorn Mahaphrom 'Kanwikhro tua lakhon chai jin nai nawaniyai thai chuang B.E. 2510–2537 2510–2537' ['An analysis of Chinese male characters in Thai novels between 1967 and 1994'], (MA thesis, Sinakharinwirot University, 1994); Nittha Chanthapanyasilp, 'Phruttikam chirayatham khong tua lakhon ek chao jin nai nawaniyai' ['Thai behaviour and ethics of lead Chinese characters in Thai novels'], (MA thesis, Chulalongkorn University, 1998); Phatcharee Warasai, 'Nawaniyai thai thi sanue phap sangkhom jin nai mueang thai' ['Thai novels that portray the Chinese community in Thailand'], (MA thesis, Chulalongkorn University, 1993). I thank Chairat Polmuk for bringing Natthanai's paper to my attention.

Although he cannot read or understand Thai well, at one point Ah Kong asks his grandson to translate the Thai national anthem into Chinese. He does not seem bothered by the opening sentence, which declares that Thailand is the land of the Thai race. In fact, he readily admits that the Chinese are guests and should always be grateful that they live in Thailand.[51] When Yok asks his grandfather about his love for Thailand, Ah Kong does not answer immediately but waits until the end of the last stanza of the national anthem playing in the background before saying, 'Kong will die here'.[52]

Writing the Chinese back into Thai historiography

In the 1980s, the prominent historian Nidhi Eoseewong and the provocative author Sujit Wongthes published several books that shook the core of official Thai historiography, which had downplayed the contributions of non-Thai actors. Taken as a whole, these radical books give the Chinese a more prominent place and role in shaping Thai history. I would like to believe that these publications and the ideas they put forth lured Sino-Thai writers out of hiding to tell stories that are closer to the truth. This intellectual shift, plus the growing influence of the Sino-Thai families in business and politics, no doubt contributed to the production of new, bold and realistic texts about the Chinese in Thailand.

In 1982, Nidhi published a long research paper, *Bourgeois culture and early Bangkok literature*, to commemorate the bicentennial of the founding of the Bangkok dynasty.[53] The paper is a serious piece of research about the rise of bourgeois culture, using literature as data to argue that bourgeois culture had already appeared before the signing of the Bowring Treaty in 1855, a date that historians have used to mark the beginning of modern Thailand. The Bowring Treaty opened Thailand to free trade and the imposition of extraterritoriality that compromised Thai sovereignty. Nidhi convincingly argues that the appearance of an indigenous bourgeoisie

---

51 Yok, *Life with Grandfather*, 104.
52 Yok, *Life with Grandfather*, 142.
53 Nidhi Eoseewong, 'Watthanatham kadumphi kap wannakam ton rattanakosin' ['Bourgeois culture and early Bangkok literature'], (Research Paper 20, 'Two centuries of Rattanakosin: The changes of Thai society' seminar, Bangkok: Thai Khadi Institute, Thammasat University, 1982); translated in Nidhi, *Pen and sail*, 1–151.

5. ARE WE THEM? THE CHINESE IN 20TH-CENTURY THAI LITERATURE AND HISTORY

predated free trade. In Nidhi's formulation, the nascent bourgeoisie was a combination of the Crown and its family, the nobles, and the rich Chinese families who had been co-opted into the king's service. This notion treats the old Chinese elite families as an 'indigenous' entity that helped form a nascent bourgeoisie.

A few years later, Nidhi dropped another bombshell by publishing *Politics during the Thonburi period*, which questions the conventional version of the heroic life and tragic death of King Taksin of the Thonburi period.[54] In the Thai chronicles, King Taksin was supposedly raised as nobility because his mother was from a noble family. Nidhi's research contradicts the official record. He argues that Taksin's mother was forced to marry a rich merchant from Swatow and that far from being a Thai noble woman she was in fact Chinese, thereby making Taksin a full-blooded Chinese. Nidhi makes a distinction between the Chinese (*jin*) and the local Sino-Thai (*jek*). A *jek* is someone brought up in a mixed culture of Thai and Chinese. It was Taksin's ethnicity as *jek* that allowed him to rally the support of the *jek* community, first in Chanthaburi and later Thonburi, to fund his fight with the Burmese and to free Thailand. Even after he became king, Taksin would use his father's clan name, Sae Tae or Tia, to conduct diplomatic relations with China. Nidhi argued that Taksin's fall from grace was not because of his religious hallucinations; he was deposed in a coup d'état by his general Jaophraya Chakkri. That general later became King Rama I, who established the current Chakkri dynasty. Scholars have also noted that Rama I's mother was also Chinese, thus reminding the Thai they owe a debt of gratitude to these two kings who were in fact *jek*.

Perhaps more effective in decentring the ethnic Thai from their own history was the slim volume published by Sujit in 1987 under the cheeky title *Jek mixed with Lao*.[55] The title had a parallel in how a Cambodian acquaintance once described a Thai as someone who looks Chinese, wears Western clothing and speaks bad Khmer. Sujit had just come back from visiting Laos and was inspired to write about the two minority groups in Thailand, which had been targets of prejudice and discrimination. In that popular book, Sujit claims that the Thai of today are really Chinese mixed with Lao. He insinuates that the Thai are no longer a well-defined race,

---

54 Nidhi Eoseewong, *Kanmueang samai phrajao krung thonburi* [*Politics during the Thonburi period*] (Bangkok: Silpawatthanatham Press, 1986).
55 Sujit Wongthes, *Jek pon lao* [*Jek mixed with Lao*] (Bangkok: Silpawatthatham Press, 1987).

but an ethnicity composed of many races and cultures. Furthermore, the various races in Thailand have also made major contributions to the modern state. If the Thai are nothing but *jek* mixed with Lao, then there should not be guilty feelings about one's family background. And even if one's family has come from China, there is no longer the need to kowtow to the officially sanctioned version of the grateful and obedient Chinese. Thailand belongs as much to the *jek* as to the Lao, the Indian, the Khmer, the Thai and others. In this reconceptualisation of race and history, the culture of the *jek* and the story of their lives in Thailand become integral to Thai culture and history.

The subaltern writes back

If we are to subscribe to the notion that the Sino-Thai were singled out as the dangerous Other Within—the foreign element in Thai society that helped defined the Thai, or the minority group that was forced to accept the role of supplicant to the generous Thai king and people—then it is possible to refer to the Sino-Thai as subalterns in mainstream Thai society. The literature that we have reviewed thus far depicts the Sino-Thai as suppressed voices. Even the last two novels, although written by Sino-Thai authors, have also accepted Chinese inferiority enforced by the official state interpellation of Chineseness. The next two novels selected for this study reject the existing stereotype of the meek and marginalised Chinese.

By the 1990s, Thai society had seen more than a decade of double-digit economic growth. The middle class had grown rapidly, following the era of Sarit's development and structural change (*kanphatthana*) policy that fuelled the economic and educational boom during and immediately following the Vietnam War. More and more young people were entering universities, and many of these students were Sino-Thai. Because government service, which used to be the standard career of university graduates, was unable to absorb the large influx of graduates, they found jobs in the private sector, jobs that paid better. The emerging well-educated Sino-Thai middle class, both in the capital and provincial cities, became more self-assured and began to question received truths about the place and social station of the Sino-Thai in Thai society and culture. The global economy penetrating into Thailand also benefited large business families active in banking, low-level manufacturing, import-and-export

5. ARE WE THEM? THE CHINESE IN 20TH-CENTURY THAI LITERATURE AND HISTORY

business, retail sales, and hotels and resorts. Most of these business families happened to be Sino-Thai families. These socio-economic changes also had an effect on the production of texts about the Chinese in Thailand.

The author of the next two novels, Praphatsorn Sewikun, tells us that he is Thai, but we also know that he has Chinese relatives. He says that his family was the only 'Thai' family living among the Chinese in the Sao Chingcha district of Bangkok.[56] He tells us that he grew up in the midst of the Chinese, which explains why he could write about their lives with great insight. He also says that he read Chinese novels to his maternal grandmother, and as a youth enjoyed studying the Thai version of *Romance of the three kingdoms*. Therefore, it is very likely that Praphatsorn represents many modern Thai with Chinese ancestry who no longer admit to being or to feeling Sino-Thai.

The first novel that we will examine, *Through the dragon design*, was written while Praphatsorn was serving in the Thai embassy in Turkey, and was published in 1990.[57] That novel won a Merit Prize at the 1990 National Book Fair. Because of its popularity, this novel, like the two examined earlier, was also made into a television drama series, thereby reaching a far greater audience compared to readers of the novel itself. The television series, however, was embraced by its Sino-Thai audience as a more realistic portrayal of the lives of their own families. They were pleased that the novel and television drama highlighted the good values of Chinese culture, and showed how the Sino-Thai lived honourable lives, different from the one insinuated in Vajiravudh's *Jews of the Orient*.

This novel is not your typical rags-to-riches story as narrated in *Letters from Thailand* and *Life with Grandfather*. Unlike those two novels, where the narrator and main character are immigrants, *Through the dragon design* is written from the viewpoint of a third-generation Sino-Thai, perhaps very

---

56   Phib Phanjan, *Praphatsorn sewikun: mangkon lot lai wannakam* [*Praphatsorn Sewikun: The dragon through the design of literature*] (Bangkok: ITN Press, 2002). When he was young, Praphatsorn's father taught him to compose Thai classical poetry and encouraged him to write. Praphatsorn joined the Ministry of Foreign Affairs and was posted abroad to places like Laos, Turkey, Germany and New Zealand. He attended several universities in between assignments abroad and finally completed a bachelor's degree. Even while working as a diplomat, Praphatsorn continued to write novels and short stories. All in all, he published more than 60 works of fiction. His success as an author was recognised when his fellow writers elected him president of the Thai Writers Association.

57   *Lot lai mangkon* [*Through the dragon design*] (Bangkok: Dokya, 1990). Praphatsorn also wrote another novel about a family who had to face bankruptcy after the 1997 Asian Contagion. That novel, *Samphao thong* [*The golden junk*] (Bangkok: Dokya, 1998), was written while he was serving in New Zealand. In 1998 alone, he wrote eight novels.

much like the book's author—someone who has grown up more steeped in Thai culture than Chinese, and is culturally Thai. It is also a novel about the contemporary. We only learn about the past from what the patriarch of the family tells his children and grandchildren. Only the patriarch and his first two wives, and the children born outside Thailand, have Chinese or Anglicised names. The rest have Thai names. Conceding to the family's Chinese roots, those with Thai names do not have nicknames. The lead character in the novel is referred to as 'Grandfather' using the Thai *Pu* and not the Chinese *Kong*, the honorific used in *Life with Grandfather*. The narrator is the child of the patriarch's eldest son by his second wife; we never hear the name or gender of the narrator, who comes across as a neutral observer, but sounding very Thai.

The novel is about the various members of the Suephanich clan. We are told that Liang Suephanich comes as a young man to Thailand in the 1920s, either during the end of the Sixth Reign or the beginning of the Seventh. He was married in China and had two sons there; they, too, are brought to Thailand after the communist victory in China. Subsequently, the China-born sons are sent to Hong Kong to study. Liang's second wife is Sino-Thai and he has three sons and two daughters with her. Later in life, he marries a young Thai woman from the north and they have a son and a daughter. The novel paints in detail intrigues, fights, tragedies, successes and lessons about how to conduct business involving the Suephanich clan—all three generations, most of whom live in the same compound.

Starting from work as a coolie, Liang eventually saves enough to open a small import business. He is successful enough to later build a textile factory using outdated machinery from Japan to mill cotton cloth for the Thai market. The Thai are partial to cotton cloth, which is also less expensive than nylon or rayon, and the Japanese have moved on to manufacturing synthetic fabrics, leaving a gap that Liang's cotton cloth fills. From manufacturing, Liang expands into finance, founding several financial and investment firms in Hong Kong and in Bangkok. Most of his children work in the family factory and various financial enterprises. The second- and third-generation Suephanich family members are sent to study in Thai schools and universities, and several are sent abroad to Hong Kong and to the United States. One son even completes a doctorate in business administration from America. We know that Liang is rich because the amounts cited in the novel concerning investments, losses and profits are in the hundreds of millions of baht.

The novel is appealing to the Thai reader because it is well written and accessible. It is especially appealing to the Sino-Thai because it portrays realistically the life history of one family, a history about the Chinese in Thailand that is not constrained by previous political or social concerns. Kasian Tejapira, the most astute scholar of Sino-Thai studies, finds this novel, and especially its television adaptation, touching in many ways. Firstly, he feels that the opening episode about Liang's impending bankruptcy is more indicative of Chinese values than the stereotype established by Vajiravudh. Liang's first business involves importing instant coffee and tea from abroad. At one point he loses the major part of a shipment because of a storm, but he is determined to meet his obligations. He first delivers what he has recovered to his closest customers; he then borrows money to buy back his goods from them so he could supply the rest of his customers. Because of his honesty, his customers appreciate what he has done and become very loyal to him. Eventually, his European suppliers pay him insurance money to cover his losses.

Kasian admits that as a Sino-Thai he had forgotten about the good Chinese values that his parents had taught him—to be *lao sik* (honest), *khiam siep* (thrifty), *nu li* (diligent) and *yuen nai* (persevering). These honourable Chinese values are represented in the novel by a large painting of an ant that is displayed prominently in the entrance hallway of the Suephanich mansion. Under the painted ant is the Chinese word *nge*, written with a brush in gold on red paper. *Nge* means 'good values', values that the ant epitomises, namely, diligence, perseverance, tirelessness and the ability to struggle against all odds without admitting defeat. Every day, members of the Suephanich family have to pass by this painting and are reminded about *nge*.[58]

Secondly, to Kasian the novel and television drama are a revolt against the traditional representation of the Chinese, especially in the popular media, as unsavoury merchants using their influence and money to cheat the public and the Thai nation. The portrayal of the Chinese in literature and the media is usually as lower-class traders selling coffee, unscrupulous money-hungry businessmen, or comedians in television variety shows who cannot speak proper Thai. In this novel, the main character and hero is an old Chinese who, in spite of his accented Thai, is able to convey important cultural lessons to his 'Thai-ified' children and grandchildren on how to live and how to operate an honest business. The hero is no

---

58 Kasian, *Looking through the dragon design*, 43.

longer an upper-class Thai male 'who gets the girl', but a Chinese man from China who wins the hand of the beautiful Khun Niam (his second wife) over Sangiam, her upper-class Thai suitor. Kasian quotes the heated exchange between the two suitors:

> Liang [speaking in accented Thai]: Every penny you have you get from your parents. How dare you come courting a woman?
>
> Sangiam: You are here as a guest of Thailand. How dare you insult a Thai like me?
>
> Liang: That is right. I have come to live in Thailand, but I do not depend on you to make a living. I am ready to kowtow to Thai people who work hard in this land, but I do not respect someone like you.[59]

Kasian remarks that the exchange, where the subaltern bourgeois Chinese talks back to his elite Thai tormentor, is revolutionary in Thai entertainment culture. Although it is unclear whether Liang speaks with a thick Chinese accent or not in the novel, he does so on television. Kasian reminds us that whether Liang speaks perfect Thai or imperfect Thai is unimportant. What is important is the fact that contemporary Thai capitalists, even those who speak perfect Thai or are portrayed as 'Thai', have historical precedents that are Chinese.

If the dynamics of Thai modernity and change rested with bourgeois and middle-class action, then the local Chinese, including those who did not 'speak perfect Thai', played an essential role in that process. The bourgeoisie that Anderson wrote about and the one identified by Kasian both had mastered and conquered the Thai capitalist market and were soon to become major players in the new global economy. The next logical step for them was to enter politics to contest the allocation of values that were still in the hands of the military and their bureaucratic and political allies. No longer were the Sino-Thai content to be supplicants of the ruling elite; they wanted to be major players in national politics.

At this point, I want to focus briefly on another novel by Praphatsorn, *Sing tueng* [*Chinese newly arrived*], which was first serialised in 1996–97 in *Si sayam* magazine.[60] This unusual novel is about Jia, a young Sino-Thai from the provinces who comes to Bangkok to search for his Thai mother. She has run away from home to escape her husband's murderer, who is

---

59 Kasian, *Looking through the dragon design*, 16–17.
60 Praphatsorn Sewikun, *Sing tueng* [*Chinese newly arrived*] (Bangkok: Nilubon, 2001).

harassing her. Jia learns that she is working as a masseuse somewhere in Yaowarat, the Chinatown of Bangkok. In his search, he is given shelter by an elderly blind Chinese woman who sells lottery tickets. Soon after his arrival, Jia falls in with a group of Thai and Chinese gangsters who work for a boss called San Pao Kung, the name synonymous with the famous Muslim eunuch Admiral Cheng Ho.

Jia, who is quite a fearless fighter, is an expert in hand-to-hand combat and the use of all types of weapons. More importantly, he soon gains the respect of the local Thai hoodlums. He is accepted into the brotherhood of gangsters because, like them, he is *nakleng*. The *nakleng* code transcends class, profession and, in this case, ethnicity to reflect the ideal type of manliness in Thai culture. The *nakleng* is a man who is not afraid to take risks, a person who likes to live dangerously. He is also a man who is loyal to his friends but cruel to his enemies; a compassionate man, a gambler, a heavy drinker and smoker, and a lady-killer.[61]

Although I will not go into the details of the novel, what is significant is this portrayal of a young Chinese from the provinces as *nakleng*. Sharing a common Thai cultural trait allowed the Chinese to become easily a part of Thai society. This depiction of Jia as a Thai *nakleng* and the epitome of Thai manliness can be seen as a subversion of the traditional concept of *luk phuchai*, or manliness, in canonical Thai prose fiction.

One of the three texts that have achieved canonical status as the first real Thai novels is Kulap Saipradit's *Luk phuchai* [*The real man*], first published in 1929.[62] The real man in that novel is a man from a working-class family who does well enough in school to win a government scholarship to study

---

61   Phaithun Khruekaew, *Laksana sangkhom Thai* [*Thai social characteristics*] (Bangkok: Liang Siang Chongcharoen Press, 1970), 84–103, identifies *nakleng* as one of nine qualities valued by the Thai—wealth, power, seniority, *nakleng* mentality, status, charity, gratitude, wisdom, and propriety in etiquette. He identifies three aspects of *nakleng* as sportsmanship, manliness and benevolence. I have also used this term to describe Sarit Thanarat in *Thailand: The politics of despotic paternalism* (Ithaca: Cornell Southeast Asia Program Publications, 2007; revised edition), 225. This concept has lost a lot of purchase in present-day Thai understanding. *Nakleng* can be both good and bad. Today, it refers generally to someone with the heart of the *nakleng*—ready for a good fight and never backing down. Chalong Soontravanich says that during the Sarit regime, many of the *nakleng* hired to protect illegal activities were Sino-Thai. These *nakleng* gave a bad connotation to the epithet. Interestingly, Sarit referred to this this group as being both *nakleng* and *anthaphan*, the latter meaning hooligans and hoodlums; Chalong Soontravanich, 'The regionalization of local Buddhist saints: Amulets, crime and violence in post-World War II Thai society', *Sojourn*, 28(2) (2013): 197–9.

62   Kulap Saipradit, *Luk phuchai* [*The real man*] (Bangkok: Dokya, 1975). This is a 'resurrected' copy I used when I taught the novel. After the political change in 14 October 1973, Kulap's novels became popular again. The original publisher is unknown to me.

abroad. But, before he leaves for Europe to study, he gives up courting a beautiful and idealistic upper-class woman so his best friend can marry her. After his return as a person who has studied abroad (*nakrian nok*), he becomes an official in the Thai bureaucracy. This narrative helps establish the ideal of the desirable modern Thai man—someone who is a good student, foreign-educated, a senior titled bureaucrat, rich and respected. At the end of that novel, his best friend and his friend's wife become aware of the sacrifice he has made. The story ends with 'the real man' getting the girl after all, except that she is the beautiful daughter of his friend and his first love.

In *Chinese newly arrived*, the hero is a Sino-Thai from a lower-class background, a *nakleng* and not a *nakrian nok*, a gangster and not a bureaucrat. His prize is a poor but good-hearted Sino-Thai girl from Chinatown whose father is a gambler and a drunk, and not the well-heeled daughter of a Thai aristocrat. The acceptance of the Sino-Thai as the epitome of the Thai *nakleng* and the embodiment of Thai manliness, neither an aberration nor alternative model, is confirmed by the fact that the novel was made into a television drama series and consumed by the Thai public of all races, ethnicities and backgrounds. Therefore, in both *Through the dragon design* and *Chinese newly arrived*, the heroes in these very Thai stories are Chinese. Their ethnicity no longer seems problematic in the discourse of Thainess in literature or on television.

In addition, the Yaowarat in *Chinese newly arrived* is no longer a foreign site; it has become a more familiar one.[63] Chinatown in this novel is treated as an integral part of Thai society, where both Thai and Chinese do business, shop, gamble, find entertainment and dine. Chinatown

---

63 Scholarly interest in Sampheng resulted in the publication of Supang Chanthavanich, *Sampheng: prawattisat chumchon chao jin nai krungthep* [*Sampheng: History of the Chinese community in Bangkok*] (Bangkok: China Studies Center, Institute of Asian Studies, Chulalongkorn University, 2006). The book is a collection of studies on specific places in Sampheng and substantive articles on the history of the arrival of the Chinese in Bangkok, roads and canals, the evolution of trade from junks to steamships, commercial and entertainment centres, and the relationship between Sampheng and the Thai monarchy. On page 131 in the chapter on the monarchy, there are two pictures of Rama IV and Rama V dressed as Chinese emperors. One can argue that Sampheng is the ghettoising of the Chinese community. But one can also posit that Sampheng is the first modern trading centre of Bangkok, where one can find gold shops, fine restaurants, the first high-rise (nine stories), and wholesale markets. This is perhaps no different than present-day Silom. Although Sampheng is mainly Chinese, it is not solely Chinese. It is frequented by Thai people and tourists from around the world.

is no longer treated as foreign and dangerous, the way it was portrayed in *Lep khrut*, where even the police were threatened and had to appear in disguise to blend into that alien place.

Excavation and recovery of lost identities: Family histories, biographies, autobiographies, handbooks and guidebooks

Although this section of my essay deviates from the analysis of fiction and turns to texts written by the Sino-Thai about themselves, their business advice and their lost culture, taken as a whole, they tell us about the mindset of contemporary Sino-Thai who now consider themselves part and parcel of Thai society. The Sino-Thai have become comfortable with their place in and contribution to Thailand and are ready to reclaim their Chinese heritage within the context of modern Thai culture.

The blurring of lines between what is Thai and what is Sino-Thai, and the significance or the necessity of the dichotomy are now less critical to understanding the dynamics of culture, politics and even the economy of contemporary Thailand. For example, when *Forbes* magazine listed Thai billionaires, such as the owner and founder of the Red Bull energy drink or the chairman of the Charoen Phokaphan international conglomerate, the magazine did not indicate that these men are Sino-Thai. Furthermore, recent Thai prime ministers such as Thanin Kraiwixien (1976) and Banharn Silapa-acha (1995) had Chinese parents, but that did not prevent them from taking on the top political position in Thailand. If the racial background of these two men has proved unproblematic in politics, then one is hard-pressed to equate Chineseness with the likes of prime ministers Chuan Leekphai, Thaksin Shinawatra or Yingluck Shinawatra.[64]

---

64 Thanin Kraiwixien's tenure lasted only a year. After his removal by a military junta, he was appointed by the king as a privy councillor. For a detailed study of Banharn's career, see Yoshinori Nishizaki, *Provincial authority and provincial identity in Thailand: The making of Banharn-buri* (Ithaca: Cornell Southeast Asia Program Publications, 2011). Two other illustrative cases come to mind. During the siege of Thammasat University on 6 October 1976, several students tried to escape but were captured by the police and armed goons. Before they were killed, their captors remarked that the students had 'pale' faces. But instead of relating the pale faces to Sino-Thai students, the murderers said that they were Vietnamese infiltrators. The other case is the attack on Thaksin for trying to usurp or undermine the king's moral authority. His accusers never said that Thaksin was behaving like an upstart Sino-Thai. Unlike politics in the United States today, where race is still

The recent production of texts about the Chinese in Thailand indicates that the Sino-Thai have shrugged off their cultural amnesia and have recovered their self-confidence to publish an endless string of books about their own history, their struggles and their successes. These authors see themselves as Thai, descendants of Chinese immigrants interested in their historical roots. Although some may exploit their connections to their Chinese origins as 'flexible citizens' in certain situations, the Sino-Thai know of no other home but Thailand.[65] They are no longer sojourners. They may visit and write about their ancestral home but only as curious tourists and as amateur historians piecing together family histories.

Although a lot can be said about the recent inundation of texts about the Sino-Thai, for the purposes of this chapter, it should suffice to highlight just a few examples.

One of the most read and talked about books about a major Chinese family history is Chamnongsi Hanchenlak's *Like a ship in the middle of the great ocean*.[66] The book developed from the cremation volume for prominent businessman Suwit Wanglee; it was first serialised in the *Sayam araya* magazine in 1996 and published as a book in 1998. The book is about the contributions of the Wanglee-Lamsam families to the development of Thai capitalism, from trading in rice to the opening of banks. The book also chronicles Chamnongsi's visit to the family's ancestral home

---

central because political parties target Hispanics, African Americans and Asian Americans to solicit their support, such is not the case in Thai politics; see Thongchai Winichakul, 'Remembering/silencing the traumatic past: The ambivalent memories of the October 1976 Massacre in Bangkok' in *Cultural crisis and social memory: Modernity and identity in Thailand and Laos*, ed. Shigeharu Tanabe and Charles F. Keyes (Honolulu: University of Hawai'i Press, 2002), 243–83. One should note that at least 12 Thai prime ministers have Chinese ancestry—Seni and Kukrit Pramoj, Pridi Phanomyong, Admiral Luang Thamrongnawasawat, Pote Sarasin, Thanin Kraiwixien, Chuan Leekphai, Banharn Silapa-acha, Thaksin and Yingluck Shinawatra, Samak Suntornvej and Abhisit Vejjajiva.

65   The term 'flexible citizenship' was first coined by Aihwa Ong, *Flexible citizenship: The cultural logics of transnationality* (Durham: Duke University Press, 1999). Efforts to compile a recent biographical dictionary of personalities of Chinese descent in Southeast Asia revealed difficulty in dealing with the Thai case. Singapore's ambassador-at-large, Tommy Koh, described talking to a Sino-Thai friend about inclusion in that book:

> But he and his family are so well assimilated into mainstream Thai society that when I asked him if they could be included in the dictionary, he said no, because he felt he has lost his Chinese heritage and could no longer read and write Chinese …

(*The Straits Times*, 2 November 2012). The dictionary includes 608 names from 10 countries; Leo Suryadinata, *Southeast Asian personalities of Chinese descent: A biographical dictionary* (Singapore: ISEAS, 2012; 2 vols), doi.org/10.1355/9789814414142.

66   Chamnongsi Hanchenlak, *Dut nawa klang mahasamut* [*Like a ship in the middle of the great ocean*] (Bangkok: Nanmee Books, 2000).

in China. Just as revealing are charts showing how intermarriage and family alliances among the Sino-Thai have created a network of relations that facilitated and enhanced major business ventures. This special ability to close ranks and to pool resources allowed the Sino-Thai business families to displace foreign competitors, especially in the banking and financial service sectors, following the conclusion of the Second World War. And, although the book is about the Sino-Thai network established by her family and its centrality to the development of Thai capitalism, the author identifies herself as a 'Thai' author. The book also features an acknowledgement from Crown Princess Sirindhorn and an introduction by Nidhi Eoseewong.

The princess endorses the notion that the Wanglee-Lamsam clan has played a pivotal role in the establishment of Thai capitalism. She agrees that the new Sino-Thai capitalists have already displaced the old Sino-Thai families absorbed into the official class under absolute monarchy. She calls that latter group the old 'bureaucratic capitalist' circle, referring to Nidhi's analysis of the birth of the bourgeoisie in the early Bangkok period. Nidhi's own introduction praises the book for succinctly telling the story of a Sino-Thai family and its 100-year history, a history that resonates with other successful Sino-Thai families. He asserts that the book allows the Chinese in Thailand, who at one time were considered outsiders, to rightfully claim that a major part of their heritage is firmly embedded in Thai society. According to Nidhi, the book encourages the descendants of the Chinese to consciously accept their rightful place in Thai society; at the same time, non-Chinese readers would be forced to consciously accept the important place the Sino-Thai have and the critical role they played in Thai history and culture.

To provide more detail about the relationship between the new Sino-Thai capitalists and the old Chinese 'bureaucratic capitalists', Phimpraphai Phisarnbut, a cousin of Chamnongsi, published *Siamese junk* in 2001 and *Mistress mother* in 2003.[67] In these books, which are about

---

67 Phimpraphai Bisalputra, *Samphao sayam: tamnan jek bangkok* [*Siamese junk: History of the Bangkok Chinese*] (Bangkok: Nanmee Books, 2005) and *Nai mae: tamnan ying keng bueanglang jesua sayam* [*Mistress mother: History of smart women behind rich Siamese Chinese*] (Bangkok: Nanmee Books, 2003). A few years after these books appeared, Charoen Tanmahaphran published *Waijao tam roithao tia* [*Father's way of worshipping*] (Bangkok: Prat Publications, 2009). Charoen's book traces the support of kings during the Ayutthaya and early Bangkok periods for Chinese Buddhist temples and Chinese shrines. The book is also a guide for both Sino-Thai and Thai worshippers at Chinese shrines about the history, meaning and importance of those shrines.

historical Chinese families who served as royal officials dating back to the Ayutthaya and early Rattanakosin periods, Phimpraphai writes about the ancestry of some of Thailand's most prominent aristocratic families, relating them back to their Chinese roots. Phimpraphai's books remind readers that wealthy Chinese merchants were appointed as court officials holding positions equivalent to cabinet ministers today. *Siamese junk* in particular traces the history of Chinese families that held the title Phraya Choduk Ratchasetthi, the title conferred by the king to the minister of the Port Authority, responsible for trade and foreign relations with the East. Phimpraphai illustrates how the relationship between the Crown and the elite Chinese families was strengthened through marriage. Thai kings frequently took the daughters of rich Chinese families as wives and concubines. Most of these families have been fully assimilated and are now an integral part of the Thai power elite.

In awakening from the long slumber and self-induced amnesia about their own cultural heritage, the Sino-Thai eagerly bought books such as Chitra Kohnanthakiat's *Children of the Chinese*.[68] The 1999 edition that I have in my personal library is the book's 19th printing. Chitra has

---

68   Chitra Kohnanthakiat, *Tung nang kia* [*Children of the Chinese*] (Bangkok: Phraew Publications, 1999). Other books by this author covering similar subjects include *Lao a kong: Khwamru rueang jin jak phuthao* [*Lao a kong: Knowledge of the Chinese from our elders*] (Bangkok: Dokya, 1993); *Thamniam ni khue kham phon: heng heng hong sok* [*This tradition is to bless: Heng heng hong sok*] (Bangkok: Phraew Publications, 1998); *Kia sung huat sai: luk lan katanyu chokdi* [*Kia sung huat sai: You will be lucky if your descendants are loyal*] (Bangkok: Phraew Publications, 2003); *Thamniam jin thi khon suanyai mai ru tae mi nai mueang Thai* [*Chinese customs not known by most Thai people but they exist in Thailand*] (Bangkok: Chitra Publications, 2010). To help the Sino-Thai excavate/recover their clan names, Chitra also published books about the origins of Chinese names and their transformation into Thai variations; *Kamnoet ton sae lae kantang namsakun jak sae khong luk jin nai thai* [*The origins of sae and the change from sae of the Sino-Thai in Thailand into family names*] (Bangkok: Chitra Publications, 2007). All of these books are so popular that they have undergone numerous printings. Caroline S. Hau argues that Chitra is no different from Amy Chua, known for promoting the idea of the Tiger Mom, who uses strict Chinese child-rearing practices to ensure the success of her children; 'Tiger mother as ethnopreneur: Amy Chua and the cultural politics of Chineseness' (paper presented at the Kyoto-Cornell Joint International Workshop on Trans-national Southeast Asia: Paradigms, Histories, Vectors, Kyoto University, 11–12 January 2013). She has also interviewed Chitra, who claims that she has sold over 600,000 copies of her books. Hau contends that such authors, including Malaysia's Lillian Too, capitalise on claims of 'Chineseness' to access local, regional and family-mediated notions of Chineseness to exploit and profit from:

> national and cultural differences within nations as well as among Southeast Asia, the U.S. and China in order to promote particular forms of hybridized (trans)national identities while eschewing the idea of mainland China as the ultimate cultural arbiter of Chineseness.

In addition, many guidebooks and manuals about worship at Chinese temples and shrines have been published, for example, Khon Yaowarat [pseud.], *Khumue wai wat jin* [*A manual for worshipping at Chinese temples*] (Bangkok: Siam Interbooks, 2007) and Bunchai Jaiyen, *Wai jao tam khwam chuea chao jin* [*Worshipping according to Chinese beliefs*] (Bangkok: Love Books, 2009). A pioneering study

written at least four other books that focus on Sino-Thai culture and, even though the books are about Chinese culture, they have received awards from national book organisations. Most of Chitra's books are full of important information about Chinese culture, the meaning of Chinese words, celebrations, rituals, opera, food, religious events and much more. They are guidebooks about how to become culturally Chinese again. Paradoxically, the books are written in Thai to explain Chinese culture to the Sino-Thai, who must now read about their ancestral culture in an adopted mother tongue whose transliteration of Chinese words is not always accurate. It is as if the Sino-Thai now speak and think Chinese with a Thai accent, unlike their ancestors who did the opposite. In addition, the wide popularity of the books indicates that Sino-Thai culture has also been embraced by the larger Thai public.

In the past decade or so, numerous biographies of Thai billionaires have also appeared in bookstores. Increased interest in the lives of the Sino-Thai encouraged others to write about themselves or to translate stories of their ancestors written in Chinese.[69] Many books about the top richest families in Thailand have been published to satisfy the curiosity of the public. Because members of this exclusive club are mostly Sino-Thai, some of these books use *Jao Sua*, the Chinese term for very rich people, in their titles. Translated texts on business practices and theories, which used to be of influential American and European authors, bankers and industrialists, have been recently replaced by business advice from prominent Sino-Thai businessmen. Instead of books revealing the secrets of an MBA, we now have books about how *Romance of the three kingdoms* and Sun Tzu's *The art*

---

of the legal status of Chinese temples and shrines, especially in Phuket, is Tatsuki Kataoka, 'Religion as non-religion: The place of Chinese temples in Phuket, Southern Thailand', *Southeast Asian studies*, 1(3) (2012): 461–85.

69   Examples are Bunchai Jaiyen, *Jaroen siriwatthanaphakdi: Burut thi ruay thi sut nai prathet thai* [*Charoen Siriwatthanaphakdi: The richest man in Thailand*] (Bangkok: Dokya, 2003) and Vikrom Kromadit, *Phom japen khon di* [*I shall be a better man*] (Bangkok: Amata Foundation, 2004). I would also like to mention two biographies of Sino-Thai doctors from southern Thailand: Banchoet Tantiwit, *Phom pen baba khon noeng pen baba Phuket* [*I am a Baba, a Phuket Baba*] (Bangkok: Watthana Lanphim, 2006) and Moh Chin Waen, *Na thap kop: ban Latiem* [*At Thap Kob: Lutiem Village*], translated by Suntharee Tantrarungrot (Bangkok: Edison Press, 1998). Banchoet's autobiography is about being a Baba, a designation used to describe the *peranakan* (locally born Chinese) in Malaysia. The Baba Chinese still maintain a cemetery on Silom Road in Bangkok, not far from the Hokkien cemetery. The second autobiography was written in Chinese and translated by Moh's children and grandchildren into Thai. For a recent study of Sino-Thai capital accumulation in southern Thailand and the Chinese community there, see Phuwadon Songprasert, *Thun jin phak tai* [*Chinese capital in southern Thailand*] (Bangkok: Thaicoon Books, 2003).

of war can be adapted for business, how to pay attention to *Tia* (Father) and *Kong* (Grandfather), whose business advice is more appropriate to the Thai situation.

In his analysis of the importance of manuals in Thai society, Craig Reynolds argues that manuals are a systematic archiving of knowledge, a 'form of cultural capital, a resource that enables people in a society to make sense of the world and to live safely, in good health, and with dignity'.[70] One can further argue that the proliferation of Sino-Thai guidebooks and manuals about rituals, practices, Chinese wisdom, business strategies, medicine, cuisine, worship, etc., written in the Thai language for consumption by the public is a clear indication that Sino-Thai culture is part and parcel of Thai cultural capital.[71]

Ironically, the change in focus from American and European business practices to practical Chinese business (and warfare!) strategies has restored the Thai appreciation of the Chinese and Chinese culture as the fountain of wisdom. Since late Ayutthaya and early Bangkok, the Thai elite have relied upon lessons imbedded in *Sam kok*, the Thai version of *Romance of the three kingdoms*, to guide their actions. In fact, literate Thai know *Sam kok* quite well because it was required reading in school. It should be noted here that in most of the novels about the Chinese, *Sam kok* is frequently invoked.[72]

---

70   Craig J. Reynolds, 'Thai manual knowledge: Theory and practice' in his *Seditious histories: Contesting Thai and Southeast Asian pasts* (Seattle: University of Washington Press, 2006), 214.
71   Examples are Thot Khanaphorn, *Sun wu son jao sua* [*Sun Tzu's lessons for tycoons*] (Bangkok: Wannasarn, 2004), Thongthaem Natchamnong, *Konlayut sam kok* [*Strategies from Romance of the three kingdoms*] (Bangkok: Dokya, 1988), and Ah Ku Khon Sae Jang, *69 khamphi jin tia son luk son lan 69* [*69 Chinese truths: Father teaches children and grandchildren the 69 Chinese truths*] (Bangkok: Good Morning, 2004) and *Ah kong son wa* [*Grandfather says*] (Bangkok: One World, 2004).
72   *Romance of the three kingdoms* [*Sam kok*] was translated into Thai during the reign of Rama I and was one of the first books to be printed by Dr Dan Bradley's press. Craig J. Reynolds has written extensively about *Sam kok* in Thai history and its popular renditions today; 'Tycoons and warlords: Modern Thai social formations and Chinese historical romance' in *Sojourners and settlers: Histories of Southeast Asia and the Chinese*, ed. Anthony Reid (Honolulu: University of Hawai'i Press, 2001), 115–47. The best analysis of the importance of *Sam kok* in Thai history, politics, and culture is Sombat Chantornwong, *Bot phichan waduay wannakam kanmueang lae prawatsat* [*An analysis of political literature and history*] (Bangkok: Kopfai, 2006), 451–550. Even today, there are numerous websites in the Thai language dedicated to this epic. Kiarti Srifuengfung's mausoleum near Phatthaya pays homage to *Sam kok* with a gallery of ceramic tiles chronicling important episodes. For the story of Kiarti, see Arunee Sopitpongsatorn *Kiarti Srifuengfung: The boy from Suphanburi* (Bangkok: Sri Yarnie Corporation, 1991). Perhaps conditioned by familiarity with *Sam kok*, Chinese literature, especially novels about Chinese martial arts, continued to be popular with the reading public. By the 1960s, most young Sino-Thai could no longer read these novels in the Chinese language. To bridge the gap, many Chinese martial arts novels were translated into Thai. One of the most prolific translators was

5. ARE WE THEM? THE CHINESE IN 20TH-CENTURY THAI LITERATURE AND HISTORY

I would like to end my analysis of this literature by highlighting two texts that prepared the way for two Sino-Thai businessmen to participate in national politics. These texts are the autobiographies of Thaksin Shinawatra, *Eyes on the stars, feet on the ground*, and Sonthi Limthongkul, *One must lose before winning*.[73] Autobiographies highlight what the authors want others to know about them and what they consider important. In these two cases, they tell us about their family roots that can be traced back to Chinese immigrants. Both became rich through the mastery of telecommunications and the media in the new global economy.

In preparing for his run in politics, Thaksin published a life story portraying himself not as a Bangkok insider but as a boy with Chinese roots from Chiangmai. He tells readers that his ancestors were Hakka who had come to Thailand from China, probably in the 1860s. His great-grandfather, like many Chinese businessmen, started out as a tax farmer.[74] He also married a Thai woman and moved to settle in Chiangmai. There, the family opened a modest coffee shop, became involved in the production and sale of silk, ran movie theatres and even operated a car dealership. Thaksin's father later ran for political office and was elected to represent Chiangmai in parliament.

Chin Bamrungphong, who used the pseudonym W. na Muang Lung. The name is derived from the initial of his first girlfriend and the place they met, Phatthalung. Chin was educated in both Chinese and Thai schools and was bilingual. He was able to translate and publish over 100 Chinese kung fu novels from 1963 to 1988. His prolific production was achieved by verbalising his translation directly into a tape recorder, which allowed him to translate 30 to 40 pages of text each day. I suspect that the eager readers of his novels were both Thai and Sino-Thai; see Pratheep Muennin, *100 nakpraphan Thai* [*100 Thai authors*] (Bangkok: Chomrom Dek, 1999), 88–90. Sitthithep Eksitthiphong argues that the Phlaphachai incident in 1974, where the Chinese attacked a police station in Sampheng, was a symptom of Sino-Thai frustration with the state. The author also argues, quite convincingly, that the popularity of Chinese martial arts novels, albeit written in Thai, was a sign of the resistance of Sino-Thai males against the oppression of the state and the depiction of them as merely weak and obedient citizens; see his *Kabot jin jon* [*Revolt of the impoverished Chinese*] (Bangkok: Silapawatthanatham Press, 2012), 166–74.

73 Wanlaya [pseud.], *Ta du dao thao tit din* [*Eyes on the stars, feet on the ground*] (Bangkok: Matichon Press, 1999) and Sonthi Limthongkul, *Tong phae kon thi chana* [*One must lose before winning*] (Bangkok: Manager Media Group, 2005).

74 As far as I can tell, no one has written a novel about the lives of tax farmers. This lacuna could perhaps be explained by the fact that the most lucrative businesses for tax farmers involved selling opium, controlling gambling dens, distributing liquor and other activities considered unsavoury by today's standards. A glimpse of the dangers involved in tax collection is the revelation that Thaksin's grandmother was shot during one of her tax-collecting forays. In addition, the experiences of radical Sino-Thai students who joined the Communist Party of Thailand after the 6 October 1976 event have yet to produce fictionalised accounts of their struggle with the Communist old guard and with the Thai armed forces.

Thaksin's great-grandfather, grandfather and father married Thai women, which makes him more Thai than Chinese. Yet he openly acknowledges his Chinese ancestry, perhaps to show that he came by his entrepreneurial talents honestly. Even though he followed a preferred Thai career path by attending the military preparatory school and the police academy, and eventually being commissioned as a police officer, Thaksin always operated a business on the side. When he eventually resigned his commission, he used his government connections to obtain concessions to supply the police department with computers. He later formed a company that sold beepers and mobile phones. Thaksin hints that because of his Chinese business background, he was able to tolerate risks and large debts and eventually turn his enterprises into successful entities. The autobiography emphasises his upbringing as a normal Thai whose father was a Member of Parliament, whose uncle and cousins were senior military officers, and whose father-in-law was a police general. For all these reasons, it is hard to consider Thaksin a Sino-Thai, in spite of his Chinese ancestry.[75]

Sonthi Limthongkul's autobiography begins with his grandfather, who came from Hainan to settle in Sukhothai. Sonthi's father was sent to China to study and eventually became an officer in Chiang Kai-shek's army, fighting the Japanese until he was summoned back to Thailand by the family. After returning from China, Sonthi's father worked for a Chinese newspaper and later opened a lumber mill. Sonthi's mother is also from Hainan; she was disowned by her family for marrying a half-Thai, half-Chinese man. Therefore, Sonthi admits that he is three-quarters Chinese, but he is unable to read or write Chinese. He studied at the Assumption School in Bangkok before going to the National University of Taiwan for a year. After Taiwan, he attended the University of California, Los Angeles, and the University of Oregon, studying history.

Although he says that he liked his one year in Taiwan more than his eight in the United States, Sonthi's intellectual leanings were formed during the anti-war hippie period of the late 1960s and early 1970s. He returned to Thailand an idealist ready to change the world and to rid Asia of Western domination. The traumatic experience of 6 October 1976, when

---

75 For additional information about Thaksin's family background, see Pasuk Phongpaichit and Chris Baker, *Thaksin: The business of politics in Thailand* (Chiangmai: Silkworm Books, 2004). The offspring of immigrant Chinese families had two main career paths to choose from: business or government service. Those choosing government service were the first to be assimilated into Thai society, discarding or cutting ties with their Chinese past. Those in business held on to their Chinese culture and connections outside of Thailand for a longer period before fully assimilating into Thai society.

left-leaning students were massacred and driven to join the CPT in the countryside, convinced Sonthi that he should focus on political change in Thailand first. He began work at *Prachathipatai* [*Democracy*], a progressive paper that was eventually closed by the reactionary Thanin government.

By the 1980s, Sonthi started his own newspaper, *Phujatkan* [*Manager*], aiming to make it the Thai equivalent of *The Wall Street journal*. He soon expanded his business into a media publishing group and eventually owned 12 newspapers and several magazines in Asia and the United States. Sonthi also was a television talk show host who supported Thaksin until a business disagreement led to their falling out. Sonthi then used his talk show to attack Thaksin at first but later took his show on the road. He helped form the People's Alliance for Democracy (the Yellow Shirts) to oppose Thaksin. Although he has been referred to as 'Jek Lim', or 'Lim, the Chink', his ethnicity as three-quarters Chinese has not been central to his identity. He is still considered a Thai royalist and conservative, a very strange trajectory for someone who was once active in the anti-war movement in the United States and who supported the cause of leftist students in the mid-1970s.[76]

We are them, and 'them' are us

From this short and discursive study of the production of Thai-language texts about the Chinese, I can conclude that targeting the local Chinese as the dangerous Other Within by King Vajiravudh had some effect on how the Sino-Thai were perceived, but not as much as one would have thought. It seems that the king was only using his admonition to remind the Chinese to be grateful and to assimilate into Thai society. We have seen how his policies and those of following governments facilitated the assimilation process.

Although Vajuravudh's nationalism predicated on race problematised Chineseness in Thai culture and society, the vilification of the local Chinese as the dangerous Other Within did not have lasting effect on the general Thai psyche. I have shown that there is minimal anti-Chinese sentiment in Thai literature and texts. If texts and literature are contextual representations of social values or reflect social perceptions,

---

76   See Chapter 6 of this volume for further discussion of these autobiographies and their place in the Thai literary landscape.

then they tell us that the Sino-Thai are seen as natural and integral to Thai society. We have witnessed how major Thai authors write about the Sino-Thai. And though he demonised the Chinese at first in *Jews of the Orient*, Vajiravudh soon ameliorated his position in *A young man's heart* [*Huajai chainum*]. In his wildly popular and enduring *Phon nikon kim nguan* series, P. Intharapalit's writing about the *jek* clearly accepted and promoted Kim Nguan as Thai. And, in the case of Phanom Thian, who demonised the Chinese as enemies of the Thai state, he identified the villains as the external Chinese and foreign secret society members. In *Lep khrut*, the police and Thai state authorities were obligated to protect Sino-Thai businessmen. Nevertheless, these Thai authors knew little and said little about the real-life stories of the Chinese.

Not until the appearance of Sino-Thai authors, like Botan and Yok Burapha, were fictionalised but realistic accounts of the Chinese experience revealed to the public. Their pioneering novels about the Chinese still seemed rather tentative in claiming a rightful space in the conscious construction of Thai history, culture and society. In fact, the two novels, *Letters from Thailand* and *Life with Grandfather*, continued to pay lip service to the official interpellation of the Sino-Thai as grateful, humble and subservient immigrants in a generous new country.

By the 1990s, however, the Sino-Thai and their offspring had become better educated and wealthier. With wealth and education came the need to exercise their right to speak out on issues important to their lives. The rise of the modern Thai middle class in the last decades of the 20th century was closely linked to the prosperity of the Sino-Thai. It was only then that the hitherto subaltern Chinese began speaking out as members of the power elite. Not only have the descendants of the Sino-Thai become prime ministers, but they have also penetrated the upper echelons of the military and civilian bureaucracies, university faculties and the banking and manufacturing sectors, and are among the wealthiest families in Thailand today. Ironically, members of the Sino-Thai middle class, like their Thai counterparts, have had very little contact with the majority of Thai, who exist in an agrarian society. It is no wonder that this middle class is a conservative one that continues to rely on the monarchy to put an official imprimatur on its status.[77] Even today, the close relationship

---

77   Sulak Sivaraksa, one of Thailand's leading public intellectuals, admits that although his family has Chinese origins, they were royalists and politically conservative. Members of his family had prospered under absolute monarchy and did not support parliamentary democracy. In his mind, they,

between rich Sino-Thai families and the Thai court is strengthened by profitable business dealings, donations to the Crown, and other royally sponsored rituals like weddings and cremations.

The production of texts written by Sino-Thai authors about themselves, their struggles, and their successes are now consumed by all Thai readers, and more than likely embraced as a natural part of Thai social and cultural history. Compared to the literature produced by other diaspora communities such as Asian Americans, the literature written by the Sino-Thai lack the edgy resentment found in early Chinese American novels and the feeling that the Sino-Thai are somehow inferior. Furthermore, Sino-Thai literature is devoid of the Filipino American lament of exile and non-acceptance by the host community.[78]

I have made the case that the exigencies and changing conditions of both local and world politics and economy, and changing social conditions have affected the representation of the Sino-Thai in textual production over the last century. The Sino-Thai are no longer considered the dangerous Other Within and, even when they were portrayed as such, that condition was short-lived. From a dangerous Other Within forced to become a meek and grateful subaltern, the Sino-Thai eventually found their voices when, as a community, they became better educated and wealthier. Assimilation helped to parry discrimination based on race to allow the Sino-Thai to easily become Thai. Thai and Sino-Thai have ceased to be critical analytical categories in contemporary Thai studies.

Before closing, we should review once again the question, 'What, then, is Thai identity?' Since Vajiravudh's time, Thai identity has been defined by the people's love of 'Nation, Religion and King'. Nation is defined by the geo-body that is Thailand, with a shared common language; religion is the tacit state religion—Buddhism; and the king is the embodiment of the glorious historical precedent, the moral present and the enduring future of the nation.

---

like other elite Sino-Thai, believed that they were smarter and better than the rest of the public. This opinion shifted after the 14 October 1973 and 6 October 1976 events; *Rueang nai pridi phanomyong tam thatsana s. siwarak* [*Pridi Phanomyong in the view of S. Sivaraksa*] (Bangkok: Komol Kheemthong Foundation, 1983), 55–79.

78   Although this discussion does not delve into comparative issues, it should suffice to point out that, unlike Asian American literature, Sino-Thai literature is not considered literature of the minority. Furthermore, Sino-Thai literature does not suffer from what Shirley Geok-lin Lim identifies as the tokenism of Asian American literature in mainstream American literature; 'The ambivalent American: Asian American literature on the cusp', in *Reading the literatures of Asian America*, ed. Shirley Geok-lin Lim and Amy Ling (Philadelphia: Temple University Press, 1992), 13–32.

Thai assimilation policies also forced the Chinese and their offspring to become Thai by giving them Thai first names and changing or masking their clan names with Thai surnames. The closing or control of Chinese schools eventually obliterated instruction of the Chinese language, history, and culture in favour of state-sanctioned Thai language and Thai classes. The various Chinese dialect groups soon spoke the new common language that is Thai, and their Chinese writing system was replaced by Thai script. The closing of open immigration eventually isolated and distanced the Sino-Thai from their ancestral home and culture. In addition, the granting of citizenship gave native-born Sino-Thai equal political rights, benefits which prompted even those born in China to become naturalised. We have already seen the success of official nationalism, which reminded the Chinese to be grateful and loyal to the king, and other reasons why the rich and successful Sino-Thai have become ardent royalists.

Furthermore, Chinese identity based on patrilineal lineage and ancestry quickly broke down because of intermarriage with the Thai, who practice a bilateral kinship system. Hence, it became easy over time for the children of the Chinese to select their Thai mother's ethnicity as their own identity. Such was the case illustrated by Kim Nguan. In terms of religion as an obstacle to assimilation, even early European travellers have noted that when the Chinese arrived in Thailand, most adapted easily to Thai Buddhism, Thai animistic beliefs and other cultural practices similar to Chinese ones.[79]

In short, the assimilation of the Chinese was a process in which the Sino-Thai became Thai citizens, assumed Thai names, spoke and wrote Thai, practised Buddhism or rituals associated with it, and professed a love for the Thai monarch and nation. We have also seen, through the evidence of literature and other textual production, that the ethnic Thai were at the same time educated through novels, texts, guidebooks and manuals to appreciate Chinese hard work, business acumen and contributions to Thai

---

79 Quoting John Crawfurd and Karl Gutzlaff, Skinner documents how immigrant Chinese became Buddhists, visited Thai temples, gave alms to monks, and readily conformed to the religious rites of the Thai. The Chinese also venerate Wat Phanangchoeng in Ayutthaya, dedicated to the great Ming admiral Cheng Ho, even though he was Muslim. Cheng Ho is known in Thailand by the name San Pao Kung, and there are shrines dedicated to him as a deity and patron saint of the Chinese in Thailand. However, instead of writing his name using the correct orthography, which means 'Three protections', the characters have been changed to 'Three treasures' to make the shrine resonate with Buddhism's 'Triple gems'—the Buddha, the Dharma and the Sangha; Skinner, *Chinese society in Thailand*, 129. Popular Chinese beliefs have also been embraced by the Thai. For example, many Thai have now given up eating beef in deference to the beliefs of devotees of the Chinese goddess Kuan Im.

national prosperity. The consumption of texts about Chinese practices, shrines and temples indicates that the Thai have also embraced Chinese religious practices and worship at Chinese temples. And, far from being treated as alien space, Sampheng is now part and parcel of Thai society, an important commercial centre and promoted as a tourist attraction.

My necessarily brief analysis suggests that accepting Sino-Thai as an aspect of Thai national identity does not diminish that identity, nor does accepting a Thai identity diminish the pride in ancestral cultural ties of the Sino-Thai. Perhaps it is this mutual consciousness that undergirds the assimilation of the Chinese into Thai society.[80] Modern Thai identity is one shared by both Thai and Sino-Thai because the category 'Thai' no longer signifies a single race but an ethnicity that gives emphasis to shared cultural and historical characteristics. Today, the idea that 'we' the Thai are gazing (down) at the Sino-Thai 'them' has been subverted to the point where the critical distinctions between the two categories are no longer clear.

The fact is, to most Thai today, we (Thai) are them (Sino-Thai), and 'them' are us.

Postscript

I hope that this foray into the subject of literary and textual representations of Chineseness will lead other colleagues to conduct similar exercises. In particular, I am interested to know how the Chinese have been represented in fiction and non-fictional texts in neighbouring countries, especially the Philippines, Indonesia, Burma, Laos and Cambodia, where the assimilation of the Chinese has also occurred.[81] Today, the

---

80 In his study of assimilation, the sociologist Bunsanong Punyodhyana asserts that the process of Chinese-Thai social assimilation is a co-operative 'two-way process which in the long run will leave Thai with something Chinese and Chinese with something Thai', *Chinese-Thai differential assimilation in Bangkok: An exploratory study* (Ithaca: Cornell Southeast Asia Program Publications, 1971), 1.
81 Leo Suryadinata, ed., *Ethnic Chinese as Southeast Asians* (Singapore: ISEAS, 1997) contains articles about how the various Chinese communities in Southeast Asia negotiate issues of identity. The articles cover Indonesia, Malaysia, Burma, Thailand, Singapore, the Philippines and Vietnam. However, the articles do not touch upon identity issues as reflected in novels and texts. Recently, Soledad S. Reyes acknowledged that although the Chinese have been present in the Philippines for centuries and Filipino culture is influenced by Chinese culture, there has not been significant study of Chinese Filipino literature. She cites the emergence of Chinese Filipino fiction writers during the last two decades who write about the experiences of their community, rejecting the stereotyping of the 'Chinese as peddlers of bottles and newspapers, with their pigtail, funny accent and costumes'; see her

interpellation of *jek* and its implied discrimination has abated in Thailand; at the same time, there has been a de-emphasis on defining 'Thai' as a race. I wonder what has happened in neighbouring countries where the distinction between the native son—*pribumi* or *bumiputera*—and the locally born Chinese—*peranakan*—still exists. As the dichotomy between the Thai and the Sino-Thai has become less distinct as inflected in textual production, will or can the *peranakan* ever become *pribumi* or *bumiputera* in Indonesia and Malaysia? Are the Philippines, Laos, Cambodia and Burma cases similar to the Thai example or are they different?

I also recognise that there are methodological issues, especially authorship and ethnic identification; debates about Chinatown as racial ghetto, privileged space or contact zone; the use of literature to illuminate social reality and values; and the linearity of my narrative that smooths over resistance and bumps along the way. How to determine who is Thai and who is Sino-Thai can also be problematic. When does a person relinquish or stop being Sino-Thai? My own designation is somewhat arbitrary, if not heuristic, based on some knowledge of their ancestral background, what they say about their familiarity with Chinese culture, and self-identification.

Narratives of note: Studies of popular forms in the twentieth century (Manila: University of Santo Tomas Publishing House, 2012), 238. The only citation she provides on the subject is an undergraduate thesis, Richard C. Uysiuseng, 'Dual heritage as a source of conflict in contemporary short fiction by Philippine-Chinese writers in English', (BA thesis, Ateneo de Manila University, 1985). Caroline S. Hau informs me that the situation is not as dire as depicted by Reyes. For example, one of the first studies of how the Chinese are portrayed in vernacular Filipino literature is Jaoquin Sy, 'Ah Tek, Pong at Chua: Ang Tsino sa panitikan' ['Ah Tek, Pong and Chua: The Chinese in literature'], *Diliman review*, 28(2) (1979): 57–65, 94–100. More recent are Lily Rose Tope, 'The Chinese margin in Philippine literature' in *Philippine post-colonial studies: Essays on language and literature*, ed. Priscelina Patajo-Legasto and Cristina Pantoja-Hidalgo (Quezon City: University of the Philippines Press, 1993), 73–81, and Shirley O. Lua, 'Dragons becoming shrimps: Toward a Chinese-Philippine poetics', (PhD dissertation, De la Salle University, 2001). Caroline Hau's *The Chinese question: Ethnicity, nation, and region in and beyond the Philippines* (Singapore: NUS Press and Kyoto: Kyoto University Press, 2014) analyses Chinese Filipino novels and short stories in English and Chinese.

6
Reading lowbrow autobiographies: The rich, the gorgeous and the comical

In the mid-1990s, Craig Reynolds gave a talk in the Kahin Center at Cornell's Southeast Asia Program about the meaning and importance of Thai manuals. I remembered how inspiring it was to listen to him talk about his fascination with Thai *khumue* (handbooks), *tamra* (manuals/texts) and *khamphi* (treatises/canons) that he had collected during his trips to Bangkok. He later wrote up his talk as a study of business manuals popular with Sino-Thai entrepreneurs during the boom years of the late 1980s and early 1990s. We can also read about his full-blown obsession with Thai manuals in his extended essay in *Seditious histories*.[1]

When I received a copy of his *Seditious histories*, I was touched to see in the hand-written inscription that Reynolds referred to me as a 'crypto-historian', perhaps parodying Michael Herzfeld's neologism

---

1   Craig J. Reynolds, *Seditious histories: Contesting Thai and Southeast Asian pasts* (Seattle: University of Washington Press, 2006), 214–42. See also his 'Sino-Thai business culture: Strategies, management and warfare', *Asia-Pacific magazine*, (6–7) (1997): 33–8. In a private email, he told me that if he were to write his intellectual autobiography it would reveal that:

> for many years I thought Buddhism was the key to understanding Thai civilization, then for a long time it was Marxism, then the *intoe* [international] globalizing Thai person with a bit of *jek* thrown in, and then manuals—absolutely the key to civilization everywhere!

Craig's latest hunch is now about risk and uncertainty and 'the sciences of prognostication that empower decision-making and the capacity to deal with tricky situations with a bit of policeman thrown in' (personal correspondence, 5 November 2013).

of crypto-colonialism to describe Thailand's colonial condition. I was honoured that he accepted me as a fellow traveller in the discipline of history and a sympathetic observer of Thai civilisation. In this chapter, I acknowledge his generous interpellation but shall steer clear of saying anything about Thai politics where I am most at home.

But instead of handbooks, manuals, texts, treatises and canons, I will focus on contemporary lowbrow pocketbook autobiographies, which are, in a loose sense, a form of manual knowledge 'that is self-consciously organised for preservation, retrieval, transmission, and consumption.'[2] To help explain the significance and relevance of the pocketbook autobiographies in this study, I am guided by the insight of Hayden White whose controversial theorising of history and literature I, nevertheless, find useful.[3] I will apply his tropes of emplotment as romance, comedy and satire to make sense of the lives of the iconic types of people who could be considered models of success or celebrities in contemporary Thai society—the filthy rich, the gorgeous women and the tragic comedians.

To begin, I offer a caveat. My discussion cannot by any means be a definitive look at all iconic models of success in contemporary Thai society. It should be seen as one example of how autobiographies can give us a glimpse of prevailing social values. I have identified only three representative models based on a research trip in 2005. The reader will see that my methodology is limited and uncomplicated.

During six months in Bangkok in that year, I made a habit of walking out of the little lane where my sister lived to the main thoroughfare to have lunch at *Nang Linchee*. After a delicious meal, usually spicy noodles, chicken rice or stir fry, I would work off unneeded calories by walking briskly down the street to the neighbourhood Tops Supermarket to pick up a newspaper and buy freshly peeled pomelo, guava, *langsat* or mango. At Tops there was also a small book stall that sold popular magazines, stationery, CDs and colourful pocketbooks. Contrary to the former Prime Minister Police Lt Colonel Thaksin Shinawatra's lament that Thais do not

---

2 Reynolds, *Seditious histories*, 214.
3 Hayden White, *Metahistory: The historical insights of a nineteenth century Europe* (Baltimore: Johns Hopkins University Press, 1973). White has been criticised by traditional historians for promoting relativism and determinism. He theorises that historical narrative falls into four large categories of emplotment—romance, comedy, satire, tragedy—which, in turn, determines how history is interpreted or narrated. His influential thinking about narrative has also affected literary analysis. In this chapter, I use White's definitions of romance, comedy and satire to analyse the life narratives of the filthy rich, the gorgeous women and the tragic comedians.

6. READING LOWBROW AUTOBIOGRAPHIES

read, implying that he is a super reader who consumes at least a book or two each week,[4] I saw many customers buying books at that small book stall. Because I was curious about what people read, every time I visited Tops, I would also buy a few of the popularly rated pocketbooks, each costing about 120–150 baht.

After reading 15 of the books, it struck me that many were autobiographies that fell into distinct categories. First, I noticed that many were written by young women telling us about their lives. Second, some were by politicians; but, on the whole, these were uninteresting. Third, many autobiographies were written (or ghostwritten) by rich and successful business tycoons. These were sold side-by-side with manuals about sure-fire ways to get rich. Lastly, I also found interesting autobiographies written by comedians.

These pocketbook autobiographies had provocative covers and even racy titles. Many had pictures to show important life-changing events. The print was usually large and easy to read. The prose style was conversational, intimate and straightforward. Several of these autobiographies apparently had sold very well, as many were into multiple printings and were affixed with stickers proclaiming the latest print run as a bestseller.

This study, a snapshot of this literary genre in pocketbook form, is my initial foray into unknown territory to see if I can catch a glimpse of changing paradigms or ideal types of successful people in these lowbrow autobiographies. I hypothesise that the high consumption of pocketbook autobiographies reflects not only public curiosity of the rich and famous, but also popular ideas of what are considered 'icons of success'. By 'public' I limit this readership to mostly upper middle–class shoppers who live in the vicinity of the *Nang Linchee* Tops Supermarket. I also assume that this particular clientele is representative of a larger readership that consumes these publications. But beyond readership, I am also assuming that publishers are market-conscious when selecting autobiographies of popular public figures, and that success is based on the sales figures of each book. At the least, the authors, in a self-affirming manner, believe they have arrived at the pinnacle of what is considered success in Thai society.

---

4   Ban Phitsanulok [pseud.], *109 Nangsue khuan an jak nayok thaksin* [*109 must-read books from Prime Minister Thaksin*] (Bangkok: Se-education Public Company Limited, 2005). Of the 109 titles, only five are in Thai.

Autobiographies differ from biographies. Biographies are usually of those already famous. In most cases, biographies are written about those who have already achieved greatness, or historical figures who are deceased. Biographies are usually well-researched, annotated and carefully constructed narratives written by scholars. They are valuable as reference texts. The value of autobiographies, on the other hand, is harder to evaluate because the genre is about self-promotion. Autobiographies are written by those who believe that they have succeeded in life (or by those who have failed utterly) and feel compelled to share their experiences with the public. Sales figures, if they are good, reinforce the notion that the writers are, in fact, celebrities admired by the public. A bestselling pocket autobiography can help make a celebrity.

As a genre, the autobiography in the West appeared in the late 18th century but did not become respectable as a literary form until much later. In 1798, the passage below appeared in one of the *Athenaeum* fragments of Friedrich Schlegel:

> Pure autobiographies are written either by neurotics who are fascinated by their own ego, as in Rousseau's case; or by authors of a robust artistic or adventuresome self-love, such as Benvenuto Cellini; or by born historians who regard themselves only as material for historic art; or by women who also coquette with posterity. Or by pedantic minds who want to bring even the most minute things in order before they die and cannot let themselves leave the world without commentaries.[5]

I assume that the egotistical Thai business tycoons fit Schlegel's first category. The autobiographies of gorgeous women may fit the description of coquettish women. In a sense, the tragi-comical have left commentaries behind for all to read. An autobiography is 'retrospective prose narrative written by a real person concerning his own experience, where the focus is his individual life, in particular the story of his own personality'.[6] They are constructed narratives that privilege some selected pivotal moments of success or failure that shape life. They are as much imagination as experience, and are representative of their time. I think that the general appeal of the autobiography is the possibility of learning about intimate, privileged and secret information known only to the author.

---

5   Quoted in Robert Folkenflik, *The culture of autobiography* (Palo Alto: Stanford University Press, 1993), 3. *The Athenaeum* is a literary journal established by Schlegel and considered to represent the German Romanticism school of literary criticism.
6   Paul John Eakin, ed., *On autobiography/Philippe Lejeune*, trans. Katherine Leary (Minneapolis: University of Minnesota Press, 1989), 4–5.

Perhaps these revelations, aside from their value as gossip, can be used as a rough guidebook for success. Although the autobiographer may have private intentions, his life story is also for public interpretive uses. The autobiography is part of a discourse on the endless possibilities in life, which explains why readers are fascinated with self-narratives especially of 'rogues, swash bucklers, and instant tycoons'.[7] It also allows for imagination and conversations about 'conceivable lives'.[8] To extrapolate from this observation, Thai pocketbook autobiographies should be able to tell us something about the kinds of conceivable or iconic lives that readers can imagine for themselves.

The filthy rich

Just prior to his first victory at the polls and becoming prime minister, Police Lt Col. Thaksin Shinawatra commissioned an autobiography called *Ta du dao thao tit din* [*Eyes on the stars, feet on the ground*], published in 2000.[9] Thaksin portrays himself as a child of an ordinary business family from Sankamphaeng, Chiangmai. He tells his readers that his family was descended from Chinese immigrants and that he is a member of the fourth generation to be born in Thailand. From 'humble' beginnings, Thaksin made it rich after gaining an education at the military prep school, the police academy and doctoral studies in the United States. He tells readers about his career in business (even while he was a police officer) and how he took many risks to sell computers, paging machines and cell phones. He tells readers about his ability to tolerate debt and high risk. Thaksin is a new kind of millionaire whose fortunes were made on the surge of global communications networks and the stock market.

In this most recent period of Thai capitalist formation, many nouveau riche families have derived their wealth from such global industries as telecommunications, multinational business conglomerates, tourism, and the service and entertainment industries. The previous generations of bureaucratic and banking capitalists resent these newly rich tycoons, and the coup that ousted Thaksin in September 2006 is said to have resulted from this tension. Fifty years ago, young people wanted to be

---

7   Folkenflik, *The culture of autobiography*, 41–3.
8   Folkenflik, *The culture of autobiography*, 41–3.
9   Thaksin Shinnawat, *Taa duu dao thao tit din* [*Eyes on the stars, feet on the ground*] (Bangkok: Matichon Press, 2000). This book was ghostwritten by 'Wallaya' (a pseudonym).

government officials; 30 years ago they wanted to be bankers; now they want to be global entrepreneurs and media tycoons. Of course Thaksin's autobiography was a clever political document that depicted him as a provincial boy who made good and became wealthy. Nonetheless, that autobiography became a prototype for self-promotion emulated by several others that followed in its wake.

Similar to Thaksin, the subjects of the two autobiographies I have selected for discussion here are also representative of the new global entrepreneur—Sonthi Limthongkul's *Tong phae siakon jueng ja chana dai* [*One has to lose before winning*], published in 2002, and Vikrom Kromadit's *Phom cha pen khon di* [*I will be a good person*], published in 2004.[10] Vikrom's book has an English title on its spine, albeit a slight mistranslation—giving the book an international character even though it is in Thai. Unlike academic texts, where one is lucky to print 3,000 copies and hope to sell these in 10 years, Sonthi's autobiography was already in its fifth printing when I bought my copy; my copy of Vikrom's autobiography is a first printing, but it enjoyed phenomenal sales of 130,000 copies. The two have since published other books detailing other aspects of their lives and achievements. Both of the authors are male, both come from Sino-Thai families, and both are listed among the top 150 wealthiest people in Thailand today. What confirmed my hunch that they are public icons of success, or celebrities, is what I was able to observe firsthand when I met each of these authors.

I met Sonthi Limthongkul for the first time in Nongkhai, a provincial capital in the Northeast of Thailand, in March 2005. He was there to give a talk to some young researchers from Laos, Vietnam and Thailand. He, Ajarn Pramote Nakornthab and I were having breakfast in a restaurant when two men approached the table to ask Sonthi to autograph his book. I found out later that they were police officers who also took the liberty of asking permission (*kho anuyat*) to pay for our breakfast that day. A similar thing happened to Vikrom when I met him at the Bira

---

10   Vikrom Kromadit, *Phom ja pen khon di* [*I will be a good person*] (Bangkok: Amata Foundation, 2004), ghostwritten by Prapatsorn Sewikun. The English title on the spine of the book is *Be a better man*. Sonthi Limthongkul, *Tong phae siakon jueng ja chana dai* [*One has to lose before winning*] (Bangkok: Manager Classic, 2005). Since its first printing in 2004, various new versions of Vikrom's book have appeared annually. Vikrom's autobiography is hagiographic and self-aggrandising. It is printed by Vikrom's Amata Foundation and mostly distributed free of charge. Another book that appeared in 2005 is Wimon Sainimnuan, *Mong lok baep wikrom* [*Seeing the world Vikrom's way*] (Bangkok: Amata Foundation, 2005). It is a compilation of Vikrom's radio show that started in 2003.

International Racing Circuit near Pattaya in February, 2004. He was testdriving a Porsche Boxster S at an exclusive introductory Porsche sports car event for potential buyers. He came in his Lamborghini, a car that sells in Thailand for almost US$1 million. Most of the invited guests to the event, who were fellow millionaires, brought along his autobiography and asked him for autographs. Everywhere I went with these two men, people appeared respectful and in awe of their presence.

Sonthi Limthongkul's paternal grandfather came from Hainan and settled in Sukhothai. Sonthi's father was sent to China to study and eventually became an officer in Chiang Kai-Shek's army. He fought the Japanese in China until summoned by Sonthi's grandfather to return to Thailand. After his return, he worked at a Chinese newspaper and later started a lumber business. He was closely tied to the clique of Police General Phao and Field Marshal Phin and became bankrupt after Phao was ousted by the Sarit coup in 1957.[11] Sonthi's mother is from Hainan as well. She was disowned by her own father when he learned that she was marrying a half-Thai, half-Chinese man. Sonthi says, therefore, that he is three-fourths Chinese but he is unable to read or write Chinese. He attended Assumption School before he was sent in 1965 to study in Taiwan for a year at the National Taiwan University through his father's KMT (Kuomintang) army connections. Although he says he is Thai, he acknowledges his Chinese roots and says that he cherishes his one year in Taiwan over his eight years in America.

Although to his father the world was either black or white, Sonthi's experience abroad and his love for history made him realise that the world exists in many shades of grey. From Taipei, he enrolled at UCLA and later Oregon to study history. His stay in America coincided with the antiwar movement. At UCLA, Sonthi worked as a reporter for the student paper, writing anti-war articles. He returned to Thailand in 1974 as an idealist, determined to succeed and to do good for society. He says that he is a child of the 1960s. His original goal was to change the world and to rid Asia of Western domination. However, after the 6 October 1976 suppression of university activists at Thammasat University, he decided to limit his ambition to changing only Thailand.

---

11 For details about this period see Thak Chaloemtiarana, *Thailand: The politics of despotic paternalism* (Ithaca: Cornell Southeast Asia Program Publications, 2007; revised edition), Chapter 2; in the Thai translation of a previous edition, *Kanmueang rabob phokhun uppatham baep phadetkan* (Bangkok: Munnithi Khrongkan Tamra, 2005), 86–139.

His first job was with the Paul Sitthi Amnuay (PSA) group, which had interests in publishing and investments. He was assigned to oversee the progressive newspaper, *Prachathipatai* [*Democracy*], which was a favourite of the radical students. However, he was disillusioned when he was asked by his conservative bosses to fire reporters who were writing anti-government articles. This was one of his first brushes with the realities of business. After the 6 October 1976 incident, the paper was closed by the Thanin government. Following that experience, Sonthi was assigned to manage the magazine *Business times, Who's who in Thailand* and the PSA group's pocketbook publications company. He learned to think big and strategically from his work with the PSA group. To launch *Business times*, the company allocated 20 million baht, with the stipulation that it should be spent in two years. Although the enterprise failed, he learned that it is better to lose 20 million baht in two years rather than in five years because time and opportunity are more important than money.

By the 1980s, Sonthi had his own newspaper called *Phujatkan* [*Manager*]. It caught the fancy of the public, which was increasingly tuned to trade and business. It became the equivalent of *The Wall Street journal* in Thailand, a serious newspaper that did not tolerate the tabloid sensationalism of the other major Thai papers. Before long, the paper had a circulation of 400,000 a day. By 1991, as Thailand's economy boomed, Sonthi had visions of becoming Asia's leading media tycoon. He organised Asia Inc. to expand his media network into other parts of Asia and Europe. His company quickly acquired many newspapers abroad and, by 1993, *The Asian Wall Street journal* featured Sonthi on page one touting him as the future Rupert Murdoch of Asia. By that time he owned 12 newspapers in Asia and *Buzz* in the United States. A few years later he launched a satellite costing US$200 million, aiming to broadcast news directly to clients in Laos and elsewhere.

With the Thai stock market booming and foreign loans cheap, he expanded his business into hotels, land holdings and publishing. In an interview he gave to *Asiaweek*, he said that he wanted to be known as a pioneer, the first Asian to rise against the 'repression of the West'. He felt that information and the news industry was a monopoly of the West, and he vowed to break that monopoly. He revealed that he had made three promises to himself when he was still in college: to help expel the US from Vietnam; to become an Asian nationalist; and to destroy the Western monopoly of news in Asia.

At its height, Sonthi's company, the M Group, had total assets of US$500 million. But, after the Asian economic contagion hit in 1997, the M Group found itself holding debt of US$235 million. Sonthi was forced to sell off assets at a loss, and he soon retired from running his newspaper. He is not a pauper by any means and is still considered one of Thailand's wealthiest men. He regularly appeared on TV talk shows and at one time supported Prime Minister Thaksin. He has strong opinions and is privy to a lot of inside political information that makes him a popular political and economic commentator on TV and radio. He is one of the most recognisable public figures in Thailand, especially after his successful campaign to topple Thaksin. Even today, Sonthi remains a controversial public figure. He survived an assassination attempt in 2009 and, more recently, he has been sentenced to serve time for securities fraud and for committing *lèse majesté*.

Vikrom Kromadit's family is Hakka Chinese, who migrated to Thailand in 1850. They settled in Kanchanaburi and traded tobacco with China. His father was born in Thailand, the youngest of seven children. The eldest was sent back to study in China, but his father studied Chinese in Thailand. Vikrom's maternal grandfather is also Hakka but his maternal grandmother is Thai-Mon-Chinese. His mother did business with the Japanese during the Second World War and later continued to do business with the Japanese. Vikrom is the eldest of 10 children by the same mother. He also has 10 other siblings from several of his father's wives.

His childhood was rough because his promiscuous father was also a tyrant, who would beat up his children and who always carried a gun and was not afraid to use it. His mother would eventually leave his father because of the womanising. Vikrom himself would leave home after a fight with his father. The quarrel occurred after Vikrom's mother ordered him to go fetch one of his father's mistresses for a confrontation. But, before he could leave, his father dragged Vikrom from the family car. During the struggle, Vikrom struck his father. As punishment, his father's men held him down while his father beat him up. He apologised for hitting his father and left home. His family life was also dysfunctional in other ways. In another violent incident, his father and his younger brother shot at each other to settle a disagreement. His brother missed and was shot in the head by his father. Although he survived, he is seriously disabled. His brother's injury at the hands of their father made Vikrom think about killing his father. To this day, Vikrom has yet to forgive him.

According to family tradition, Vikrom was sent to study Chinese in Taiwan in 1969. After some tutoring, he was able to gain entrance to National Taiwan University. His father only gave him enough money to study for a year, but Vikrom was able to secure a scholarship from the Taiwanese government. He was a good student and a good athlete. He was also the first president of the Thai Student Association at the university. Even as a student, he was always looking for business opportunities. When he returned to Bangkok for visits, he would introduce himself to shop owners as a student from Taiwan and ask if they would be interested in doing business with Taiwan or whether they wanted to buy some goods he brought back with him.

After graduation, he had to forgo dreams of MA studies in Australia for lack of funds. He returned to Thailand and immediately started a small business with borrowed capital to export black onyx. He also helped manage a paper mill that had connections with Taiwan. He married his Chinese college sweetheart and received some help from his Taiwanese in-laws. His familiarity with Taiwan was put to good use. His early business ventures included management of a paper mill, partly owned by a Taiwanese company, and trade in tapioca and animal feed with clients in Taiwan. His first major break was marketing Thai canned tuna. The Chicken of the Sea Company began importing his canned tuna in 1980. Four years later, his company became the largest exporter of canned good to the United States.

The novel idea of constructing an industrial park was suggested to him during a visit to Taiwan in 1987. With the help of a large loan from the Thai Farmer's Bank (Lamsam family), he started the Bang Pakong Company. His first 300-*rai* (about 118 acres) industrial park immediately sold out, giving Vikrom a profit of 100 million baht. He followed that success by building a 1,400-*rai* (about 553 acres) estate. The Amata Group was soon formed to build another gigantic industrial park in Rayong. In 2005, the Amata Nakorn industrial estate housed 300 factories with an investment of 1 trillion baht (about US$25 billion) and sales of 2 trillion baht (US$50 billion). He also opened a branch of his company in Vietnam.

These two men represent the successful entrepreneur, the hard-working Sino-Thai who had parlayed family business acuity, a foreign education, risk-taking and successful forays into global enterprises— telecommunications, media, export industry—to make their millions. Their rise to wealth was also driven by their large egos, wanting to share their political, economic, and social ideas with the public. Both Sonthi and Vikrom had their own talk shows, and they appeared frequently on radio and television to express their strong opinions about domestic and foreign affairs. If future Thai politics is to be led by another leader similar to Thaksin, there appears to be others like him among the 'filthy rich', waiting in the wings to lead another charge.

Another indication of public interest in how to make money and how to become a business tycoon is the large selection of business manuals sold at Tops. Although there are still books about American tycoons (Lee Iacocca is a favourite), most of the business handbooks are based on Chinese business practices. I believe that the readers think—and this belief is no different from the World Bank study touting Confucian Culture—that the Sino-Thai tycoons made it rich because they know about Chinese business practices. The business manuals range from *A gong son wa* [*Lessons from a Chinese grandfather*], *69 khamphi jin* [*69 lessons from the Chinese bible*], *Sun wu son jao sua* [*Sun Tzu teaches the tycoon*], and a translation of *Sun Tzu's The art of war* where the Thai script is ingeniously made to look like Chinese characters.[12]

For example, the first story in *Lessons from a Chinese grandfather* teaches the reader how to 'spend money in order to accumulate money'. The advice is to buy gold ornaments for women because these are easily transportable and can be readily converted to cash when needed. This observation faults Thai people for buying jewellery as decoration and as markers of social status. Jewellery does not easily convert to cash and, in most cases, one loses money in such transactions. Therefore, to the Chinese, gold ornaments are not for decoration but are ways to accumulate capital. There are other gems of advice like this one that celebrate Chinese acumen and deride the Thai for their poor financial habits.

In *Sun Tzu teaches the tycoon*, each of Sun Tzu's five conditions (legitimacy, environment, battlefield, commander and military discipline), and 64 victorious strategies are illustrated with examples of real business transactions in Thailand.

---

12   Ah Koo Khon Sae Chang, *Ah kong sorn wa* [*Lessons from a Chinese grandfather*] (Bangkok: One World Press, 2004); Ah Koo Khon Sae Chang, *69 khamphi jin* [*69 lessons from the Chinese bible*] (Bangkok: Good Morning Publishing, 2004); Thot Khanaphorn, *Sun wu son jao sua* [*Sun Tzu teaches the tycoon*] (Bangkok: Samnakphim Wannasan, 2004); *Tamra phichai songkhram khong sun wu* [*Sun Tzu's The art of war*] (Bangkok: A.R. Business Press, 2004). When I purchased these manuals in 2005, most were in their fifth or sixth printings. This is the genre of business manuals discussed by Reynolds, 'Sino-Thai business culture'.

The incredibly gorgeous

The icon for female success is harder to construct because it emerges as a composite. In general, autobiographies of the Thai women are stories of family survival, struggle against social conventions, living abroad, defying the odds, self-affirmation, agency and the attention to their physical assets. None of the women in the autobiographies I read fixate on material wealth or power. Their stories are of survival. Although the stories these women tell differ in the scale of risk-taking in business, they do take risks by challenging established social conventions. These autobiographies appear to be declarations of independence from traditional normative behaviour, and from male exploitation and abuse.

I have concentrated on five autobiographies: Suntharee Wechanon, *Yindi jao* [Pleased to meet you]; Jidapha Na Lamliang, *Rak khong jina* [*Jina's love*]; Wae Soul, *Wae Soul*; Prisna Phraisaeng, *Pooki no tom*; and Khemika Na Songkhla, *Ok hak rueang lek ok lek rueang yai* [*A broken heart is a small matter, a small breast is a big matter*].[13] All of these autobiographies have striking pictures of the women on the covers. The women are shown provocatively, and everyone is smiling. Three are by themselves; one is shown hugging her daughter; one is naked and clearly pregnant à la Demi Moore. The titles of the last two autobiographies are also suggestive. *Pooki no tom* is immediately recognisable by the Thai reader to be *Pooki nom to*, a reversal of consonants that gives it a different meaning. *No tom*, which means 'no filth' or 'no more suffering', whereas *nom to* means 'large breasts'. Indeed, Pookie, who appears on the front page, is quite well-endowed by Asian standards. The other title, *Ok hak rueang lek ok lek rueang yai*, contains rhymes in Thai that again pander to men's fixation with women's breasts. In addition, the subtitle says that the author is known as 'Phi Kung: the originator of the breast slapping formula' (*phi kung jaokhong sut top nom*).

Suntharee's story resonates with many Thai women, especially those from the north or northeast who end up marrying *farang*. At a very young and vulnerable age, Suntharee, who is from Chiangmai, found work with

---

13   Suntharee Wechanon, *Yindi jao* [*Pleased to meet you*] (Bangkok: Amarin Book Center, 2004); Jidapha Na Lamliang, *Rak khong jina* [*Jina's love*] (Bangkok: Samnakphim Sai Jai, 2004); Wae Soul, *Wae Soul: I am proud to be mom* (Bangkok: Samnakphim To Be Love, 2005); Prisna Phraisaeng, *Pooki no tom* [*Pookie Big Tits*] (Bangkok: Samnakphim Baanphot, 2005); Khemika Na Songkhla, *Ok hak rueang lek ok lek rueang yai* [*A broken heart is a small matter, a small breast is a big matter*] (Bangkok: Anit Publishing, 2004).

an Australian government project constructing roads. She had worked in a hotel before and even started a singing career with the late singer and songwriter Charan Manophet. At 23, she married Terry Anderson, an Australian Foreign Service officer, who helped her find work. After his assignment in Thailand, Terry took his wife to live in Australia, Malaysia and the Philippines. Life in Australia was tough for Suntharee, who had two children by Terry, and she suffered abuse and loneliness. After Terry resigned from the Foreign Service, they moved back to live in Bangkok. Suntharee eventually divorced her alcoholic husband and returned to live in Chiangmai where she bought a small house, converted it into a restaurant and began to sing again.

Suntharee's book is full of romantic poems and stories about her failed love life. The only thing that saved her from self-destruction were her children, Lanna and Andrew. While Andrew lives in Australia, Lanna has become a popular Thai singer with many CDs to her credit. As a Eurasian (*luk khrueng*), Lanna fits the contemporary Thai model of a beautiful woman who combines Asian and Western features. Suntharee does not reveal much about herself except that she comes from a poor family. Her father was a primary school teacher, but her grandfather served King Rama VI as a soldier in the palace. Her life is about being a mother trying to survive a broken marriage to a foreigner.

It is not uncommon today in Bangkok to see Thai women with Caucasian men. Many in fact do marry and move abroad. One only has to look at the long lines of people seeking visas to go to Italy, Germany and the United States to witness Caucasian men with their Thai wives and children in tow. But there are also those who live in Thailand, or who have returned to live in Thailand with their Eurasian children. Nowadays, young women from villages in the north and northeast actively seek out older white men to marry and to have their children. There are villages where these men have built new homes for their Thai wives and children.[14] I assume that young Thai women, who desire financial security if they are from less affluent families, want Eurasian children for three reasons: they want to have children; they want to have Eurasian children who can find

---

14   For example, Andrew Hicks, *My Thai girl and I* (Bangkok: Konstrukt Books, 2008). The author is a retired English lawyer who married a Thai woman and moved to live in Isan. He writes about the clash of cultures but enjoys his new life.

good jobs in the entertainment business so they can rely on these children in their old age; and they want the children to have legal rights to claim their foreign father's estate when he dies.

Suntharee's life reflects the danger, pitfalls and possibilities of success for many Thai women. The internet is full of sites advertising romantic relationships with young Thai women. The copy of Suntharee's autobiography that I bought had been on sale for less than a year, but it was already affixed with a label declaring it a bestseller in its twelfth printing.

Two of the autobiographies in my sample are about very beautiful women intent on becoming single mothers. Unlike Suntharee, who married a *farang* and became a single mother after her divorce, Jindapha Na Lamliang and Wae Soul wanted to have children but without marrying their children's Thai fathers.

Jindapha, or Jina, is a Eurasian whose father is Thai and whose mother is American. Her Thai father moved to the United States when he was just 16 years old. He married an American woman whom he later divorced. Jina grew up in the United States and started a career as a model while she was still in high school. On a whim, she was asked to enter Thammasat University's Thida Dome Beauty Contest and easily won. Following that success, she was entered in the Miss Thailand Beauty Pageant where she was first runner-up. Many thought that she should have won, except that the Miss Universe competition was to be held in Bangkok that year, and nationalistic considerations demanded that Miss Thailand should be a 'real' Thai and not a 'half-Thai'. Jina returned to the United States, enrolled at Cornell University, and continued her modelling career.

In today's beauty business, which is now global in scope, Jina continued to work in New York and in Bangkok. She met a man in Bangkok who fathered her daughter Jeda. In her book, she never mentions his name, only that he was well-known in the entertainment business. Jina returned to the United States to give birth to her daughter. She reveals that her daughter's father came to see the baby when she was born and then left. Jina tells us of her determination to be a good single mother. It is interesting that her autobiography is in Thai and not English. The book is about the meaning of life, a woman's life. It is a declaration of sorts, because it celebrates the independence of a professional woman who also wants to be a mother. If she married, it is possible that her husband would not have allowed her to work.

6. READING LOWBROW AUTOBIOGRAPHIES

Wae Soul's story is similar. Her autobiography, published in 2005, was also advertised as a 'bestseller'. My own copy, purchased soon after the book was published, is in its third printing; a total of 10,500 copies have been sold. Wae's father is a Chinese man who fenced pilfered and stolen goods. Her mother, who is illiterate, is a Thai from Chiang Mai. Wae's early life was hard, especially after her mother abandoned her and two other siblings. Living with an abusive father was not that easy either. Sometime later, Wae reconciled with her mother and even went to live with her. The family was quite poor, and Wae even tried to commit suicide but survived. As a young girl, because of her good looks, she was hired to model clothes at the Jatujak Sunday Market. An advertising agency spotted her and gave her a job. She became a model and eventually tried her hand at acting.

Her book tells her life story, but only superficially. She writes about her friends and her suitors. One particular suitor even ran off with her money and left her pregnant. Like Jina, she too never mentions the name of her child's father. Instead of getting an abortion, she decided to keep the baby. She believes that she herself was almost aborted because her father did not want to have another mouth to feed. Only her mother's determination saved her.

In defiance of social convention, Wae made public her pregnancy and told the press that she had decided to keep the baby. She made pictures of herself during the various stages of her pregnancy and published them unabashedly in magazines and in her autobiography. Wae gave birth to a baby girl on 22 March 2005 and, as she was wheeled out of the delivery room, she gave a quick interview about how great it was to become a mother. Wae's autobiography declares once again a woman's emancipation from both husband and the nuclear family. Similar to Jina's autobiography, it valorises motherhood. Motherhood is a woman's right even if she is unmarried. Wae's success exploits her physical beauty, which she flaunts by showing the public that a pregnant woman is also a beautiful woman. She is an individual, a model, an actress, a mother and a survivor.

Two other autobiographies focus mainly on modifying a woman's body to make it fit conventional ideals of Thai beauty. They mainly focus on a woman's breasts and how to manage them. As we have seen, the titles of the books are rather scandalous at two extremes, one proclaiming that bosoms that are too large can be reduced, the other promising a way to enhance breasts that are too small. The two autobiographies deal with what is traditionally a woman's private issue in an open and matter-of-fact manner. That is to say, there is no need to feel ashamed of one's physical shortcomings when there is help on the way. It is interesting to note that both authors say little about their family backgrounds, but focus mainly on breast treatment techniques that are rather unusual and based on Thai herbal medicine. Both involve massaging but, in the latter case, the term used is *top*, which means to slap.

Prisna Phraisaeng, or Pookie, is a Thai Australian who returned to work in Thailand when she turned 15. The account of her life was written in response to an unfortunate incident that occurred on 28 February 2005, when Pookie, as PR director of a cosmetics company, arranged a private demonstration for specially invited guests of how to apply a breast-enhancing cream. Reporters got wind of it and appeared at the demonstration. Although Pookie, as emcee, asked the photographers not to take pictures, her requests were ignored. The following day, pictures of beautiful models having their bare breasts massaged were splashed on the front pages of the morning dailies. The police were called, and charges of public lewdness were levelled against the organisers and the emcee.

The book is her way of countering the accusations and explaining her role in the scandal. Pookie begins by telling readers about her youth in Australia and the 'problem' she had even as a child. She was troubled with ample breasts. By the time she was a teenager, she was wearing a C cup bra. She believes that she inherited that trait from both her mother and her grandmother who also had large breasts. Her autobiography focuses mainly on her breasts and her flabby stomach, whose appearance worsened after she gave birth to her first child when she was only 18. She admits that her bra size jumped to an E cup. But, in spite of her ample endowment, Pookie was another *luk khrueng* who became active in the entertainment business as a model and a singer.

In her book, Pookie tells about the surgery she underwent to reduce the flab on her tummy and eventually the operation to reduce the size of her breasts. She even described, in some detail, what was involved in the procedures. And, in a very strange but matter-of-fact manner, she launches into an elaborate discourse of the merits and drawbacks of different types of nipples. She tells her readers that it is their right to go under the knife if they want to alter the appearance of their bodies.

Because she believes in the principle that women can manage their own bodies without being ashamed, she agreed to help promote a special cream that promises to enhance a woman's breasts. The cream was made with secret Thai herbal medicine that has been marketed successfully abroad. The cream did not directly enlarge breasts, but it made the tissue firmer and tauter. Pookie wanted Thai woman to have the benefits of that cream, and she also wanted to sell it in Thailand.

The second autobiography about breast enhancement is by Khemika Na Songkhla, or Phi Kung, who invented the *top nom* 'slapping' method. I think that the *top nom* method would not be suitable for mass marketing, unlike Pookie's herbal cream marketed by a company with an impressive foreign name. Phi Kung's herbs and the method of application was at first limited to advertising by word-of-mouth. Phi Kung's *top nom* service received national attention when it was featured in the mass circulating *Thai Rat* newspaper on 2 June 2001. From that moment her phone rang off the hook. She even appeared on several TV shows. The title of her book comes from a popular bumper sticker found on commercial trucks.

When she was young, she says that she was flat-chested until she found the courage to ask if she could inspect the beautiful breasts of her 74-year-old grandmother. Apparently her grandmother had a secret formula she was willing to pass along to Phi Kung. She tells us that her apprenticeship was serious and strenuous. She had to spend 15 days bending her fingers to make them strong and supple. That exercise was followed by daily exercises where she had to hold on to the foundation post of her grandmother's house while using the other free arm and hand to massage the side of her body and eventually to move up to her massage her own breasts. She performed 500 of these movements a day. Following the exercise, some herbal concoction was massaged onto the breasts, and a long strip of cloth was used to wrap around the breasts. Apparently, her grandmother had no conception of the modern bra. Phi Kung later designed a special bra for this purpose.

Although she learned this supposedly ancient method from her grandmother, she was able to use it only on herself. She made a living doing odd jobs to save money to go to school. She eventually opened her own beauty salon. The autobiography also revealed that she found other ways to make more money than cutting hair, which brought 50 baht a head. She tells the reader of a service she provided called 'maintaining one's private preserved forest' (*du lae pa sanguan suan tua*). For this delicate service she was able to charge 500 baht, equivalent to 10 times the price of a haircut.

Phi Kung says that her clients talked only about three things: their eyes, their noses and their breasts. Most were unhappy with the way their breasts looked or 'performed'. Because she had been taking good care of her own breasts using her grandmother's method, many of her clients often asked if they could inspect her breasts. Soon she was offering a service to enhance breasts using her grandmother's formula. At first, she only charged 70 baht and called it *phok nom*, which referred to applying a special cream to the breast. As a marketing ploy, she would stop cutting a client's hair and excuse herself to look into the condition of another client who is in the process of *phok nom*. Phi Kung says that 10 out of 10 women wanted to know about that procedure.

In no time, her breast enhancement service became the main service she offered, even though the sign outside her shop said that it was a hair salon. From *phok nom*, the terminology used among the women became cruder, and *top nom* was coined, that is, to slap one's breast around. From a fee of 300 baht, she soon decided to charge an exorbitant 16,000 baht for the procedure. In spite of the high fee charged, she continued to draw customers. One even sent her a ticket to fly to Chiang Mai to perform her magic treatment. Having never flown before and unaware that she was in the first-class cabin, she hid in the toilet the entire flight because the cabin was full of *farang*. According to Phi Kung, the procedure is good for three years and can increase the size of a woman's breast by one to three inches.

The tragically comical

The last example of an icon for social success is the Thai comedian. At first glance, such a person could hardly be considered an icon. But the fact that there are several autobiographies of these performers suggests that, in the minds of some readers, they are heroes and models of success. My sense is that, to the lower classes, most of whom are Thai (here I include those from Isan, the north and the south but do not include the ethnic Chinese who are also successful comedians), the comedians appearing on TV and in movies represent a kind of indigenous lower-class success story popular in the mass-mediated entertainment business.

The two examples are Thep Pho-ngarm, *Kho tok din thao tit khlon* [*Head bowed to the ground, feet stuck in mud*]; and Note Chern-yim, *Chiwit khot talok* [*Life is damn funny*].¹⁵ The title of the first book no doubt parodies the title of Thaksin's autobiography. It sold well, because the copy I bought was the book's fifth printing within a year. The second book was in its fourth printing. Both comedians felt compelled to share the story of their humble beginnings, their rise to fame, and how, in spite of the opportunities they had, they failed to make it rich in the entertainment industry. Unlike the 'filthy rich' who were from somewhat humble beginnings but were able to climb into the higher echelons of Thai society, the comedians came from the lowliest class and have made it too, in a sense, but not quite as big nor as lasting.

Thep Pho-ngarm's family lived in the basement of a hotel in Hat Yai, Songkhla, in southern Thailand. His father was a carpenter who built schools. Thep noted the irony that his father built schools for others but had no home for his own family. The family washed clothes for a living, charging 1 baht per item. It was not a lucrative business and most of the time they had little to eat. To get by and put food on the table, his mother resorted to cooking rice mixed with yams, potatoes or taro roots. Many times Thep had to sell their clothes for cash to buy food. As a young boy of 11, he even made money sleeping in the same room with newly initiated prostitutes who were afraid of sleeping alone at night and who paid him to stay with them as company.

Thep's big chance came when a travelling outdoor movie company adopted him as a gofer, paying him 5 baht a day. When time permitted, he would practise dubbing live Thai voiceovers when the movies were shown. After the movie company folded, he found work in a charcoal factory. For entertainment, he bought a cheap radio to listen to his favourite Thai country folk songs. He practised singing the songs so he could enter singing contests, which were popular with the country folks. Many singers are discovered in this way: for rural folks, becoming a successful folk singer was a coveted avenue of social mobility. On one occasion, Thep bought beer for the leader of a famous band, got him

---

15   Thep Pho-ngarm, *Kho tok din thao tit khlon* [*Head bowed to the ground, feet stuck in mud*] (Bangkok: Samnakphim Aksorn Khao Suay, 2004); Note Chern-yim, *Chiwit khot talok* [*Life is damn funny*] (Bangkok: Anit Publishing, 2004).

drunk and then proceeded to sing for him. The band leader was too drunk to know if the singing was good or bad and, out of pity, he hired Thep to cook for the band.

Thep wanted only to sing, but all country folk bands had a comedy team to fill in time between sets. The comedy team also needed someone they could use as the butt of their jokes, and they soon dragged Thep onto the stage. Because of his funny looks, anything he did on stage drew laughter. He decided, after failing as a tricycle noodle vendor, to return to perform comedy at small cafes. He subsequently formed the comedy team of Den, Doeh, Thep, who were funny enough to be invited to perform on television.

Thai comedy is mostly based on crass jokes, slapstick and the innocence or gullibility of the country bumpkin. The role of the comedian is thus easily assumed by lower-class Thai (mostly men), especially those with physical deformities. These performers are not seen as tragic figures, but their odd physical features are regarded as comedic. In some instances, many comedians who are far from good-looking are asked to play romantic leading roles with beautiful women. Many comedians are dwarfs or men with deformed faces who somehow are seen as funny, although in the West this would be politically incorrect and seen as humiliating. Thep finally made it to the big time when he was cast in a Thai movie where the comedian was one of the lead characters. He made a handsome 15,000 baht (about US$500) in his first movie, and his career in the national entertainment business began to take off.

Thep's use of language in his autobiography is raw and vulgar. He has no trouble using obscenities, nor does he have qualms about admitting to adultery. He said that it was the way of life for people like him, and that his wife accepted it. Thep admitted to wanting to have a successful business, but he said that he did not want to be a businessman. The reason was partly that he had no idea about running a business, and the many attempts to start one failed. Like many in the entertainment world, he opened a restaurant but went bankrupt when the clientele he drew was too rowdy or friends would eat and then not pay. Thep also tried his hand at building and selling properties but, without a background in real estate, his buildings cost more than they sold for, and he went bankrupt again. In spite of being a well-known comedian, his background, education and family experience had not prepared him for any success beyond his ability to make people laugh. Nevertheless, as an icon of success for lower-class Thai, he is a model to emulate.

This observation is reinforced by the autobiography of Note Chern-yim, who admitted to emulating the 'success' of Thep and other successful comedians. Note, whose real name is Bamroeh Phong-insi, was born in the middle of a Thai folk opera known as *likae*. The performance was interrupted briefly so the lead actor could cut Note's umbilical cord. His mother was the lead actress of the troupe and his father was its comedian and set painter. He was born in Nong Mon, Siracha Province. The family was poor and became poorer when Note's father left to find work in the South. Note was left to live with his grandmother in a lean-to next to a fence. His grandmother had once been a slave and mistress of an ageing nobleman.

Unfortunately, his grandmother was caught selling drugs and was sent to prison, leaving Note to fend for himself as a street person. His one favourite pastime was to watch public television in front of the municipal building. He liked watching *McHale's navy* starring Earnest Borgnine. As a street urchin, he would steal food to eat and betel to give to his grandmother in prison. He would try to sneak on board buses and passing boats to find his uncle, who had a *likae* troupe in Bangkok. Eventually, he found his uncle and began apprenticing to be a *likae* performer until his uncle escaped from his debtors by ordaining as a monk.

Note continued to perform *likae* but could hardly make ends meet. He made a hut out of some billboards and shared the hut with a fellow actor. At one time, they had but one pair of trousers to share. One had to stay home if the other wanted to go out. Even though he was poor, he eloped with a nice woman he had met. But he admits shamelessly to sleeping with a *likae* fan from Hong Kong who gave him a garland and 5,000 baht (about US$160) after one of his performances. This woman also showed up unexpectedly at his apartment. Note convinced his poor wife to go hide in the toilet while he and his *likae* fan had sex. After she left, Note found his wife had passed out on the toilet floor.

He later formed his own comedy team that performed at a disco nightclub. The comedy team got lots of laughs because they were different from the clients. The comedians were from a lower class, they spoke in provincial accents, they dressed outlandishly, and they behaved differently. Their jokes were also crass, irreverent and indecent, but people found them funny.

Like his hero Thep Pho-ngarm, Note also performed in movies and became famous. He also opened a restaurant and failed for the same reasons that Thep's business failed. Note, more than Thep, retained his roots in the lower class and was ready to pick fights with his clients and audience when they became disrespectful or rowdy. When he had money, he would gamble and drink with his friends. He tried his hand at starting a company called Comedy Line and made himself managing director. With no background in management or accounting, the company went bankrupt in no time.

Like Thep's autobiography, the language in Note's book is also raw and vulgar. He is not shy about revealing his roots. He even asks his readers to read his book aloud with a country bumpkin's accent for effect. Even though he and other comedians made a name for themselves in the entertainment business, they were never successful as entrepreneurs. All their attempts to start businesses failed.

Conclusion

To be sure, there are other examples of autobiographies that might suggest other iconic success stories. For example, we can imagine the iconic Thai professor, the iconic soldier or the iconic politician, but never the iconic noodle vendor or the iconic street walker. This short review of lowbrow, high-consumption pocketbook autobiographies suggests that, for those who aspire to be rich businessmen, the path to success can be had by emulating the likes of Thaksin, Sonthi and Vikrom. Thais should learn from the experience of the Sino-Thai tycoons whose business success was the result of some indeterminate connection to Chinese culture that emphasises hard work, capital accumulation, good education, internationalism, risk-taking and thinking big. There is also much to be learned by reading Chinese business manuals and war treatises. The autobiographies of rich men are written in the romantic mode which, according to Hayden White, is 'symbolized by the hero's transcendence of the world of experience, his victory over it, and his final liberation from it.'[16]

---

16   White, *Metahistory*, 8.

For modern Thai women, the provocative, seductive and empowering autobiographies encourage them to free themselves from stifling social conventions. These autobiographies are written in a comedy mode where there are occasional victories and reconciliations with the forces at play in the social and natural worlds. Thai women can and should exercise new roles to become respectable single mothers and entertainers on the international stage, and to exercise management of their physical assets. The autobiographies also propose that it is alright to be Eurasian, to marry non-Thai men or not to marry at all. In fact, a recent study shows that, among middle-class women of marrying age, an alarming 25 per cent resist marriage. They would rather remain single 'than giving up their autonomy for a patriarchal family life'.[17] For women, fulfilment in life does not depend on the kind of financial success represented by the filthy rich. Filthy rich men want to conquer the world; the women are content to be masters of their lives.

Tragically, the icon for lower-class Thai is the comedian who may have risen above their collective poverty to taste success and a modicum of wealth, but because of their class background, limited education and social upbringing, their participation and success in business and commerce is limited. The narrative mode for these autobiographies is satire, where a person is a captive of the world rather than its master: 'ultimately, human consciousness and will are always inadequate'.[18] Perhaps those from the countryside understand that even though the comedian represents their 'conceivable lives', they and their parochial heroes and icons will never become filthy rich because they are not equipped to master the intricacies of the business world, the global media and the entertainment industry. Their education, family background and horizons restrict and constrain them.

It occurs to me that even though the filthy rich strongly identify themselves as Thai, they learned about business early in life from their Sino-Thai families. The women all seem to share a common characteristic that is not tied to ethnicity. What binds them together is an ideal based on universal standards of beauty that cut across class and race. It is easier to make it in life if they can liberate themselves from social conventions and to manage and

---

17 Darunee Tantiwiramanond and Shashi Ranjan Pandey, 'New opportunities or new inequalities: Development issues and women's lives in Thailand', in *Women, gender relations and development in Thai society*, ed. Virada Somswasi and Sally Theobald (Bangkok: Women's Studies Center, Faculty of Social Sciences, Chiangmai University, 1997), 82.
18 White, *Metahistory*, 9.

improve their physical appearances. The comedians signify the larger mass of lower-class 'ethnic Thai', country bumpkins from the provinces. Their success is limited by their lack of education and experience in business, and class stereotyping. The comedians' continued success depended on how they portrayed themselves as crude but lovable country bumpkins. On the basis of the two autobiographies in my sample, life imitates art and, on this point, Note Chern-yim's autobiography is instructive: *Life is damn funny* [*Chiwit khot talok*].

Previously published works

Chapter 1, 'The first Thai novels and the Thai literary canon', is an edited, consolidated version of the following previously published works:

- 'Khru Liam's *Khwam mai phayabat* (1915) and the problematics of Thai modernity', originally published in *Southeast Asia research*, 17(3) (November 2009), 457–88, doi.org/10.5367/000000009789838477.
- 'Khru Liam's *Nang neramid*: Siamese fantasy, Rider Harggard's *She* and the divine Egyptian nymph', originally published in *Southeast Asia research*, 15(1) (March 2007), 29–52. The final, definitive versions of these two papers have been published by SAGE Publishing. All rights reserved.
- 'Making new space in the Thai literary canon', originally published in *Journal of Southeast Asian studies*, 40(1) (February 2009), 87–110.

Chapter 2, 'Racing and the construction of Thai nationalism', was originally published as 'Through racing goggles: Modernity, the West, ambiguous Siamese alterities and the construction of Thai nationalism' in *Sojourn*, 31(2) (July 2016), 532–74. This work is reproduced here with the kind permission of the publisher, ISEAS-Yusof Ishak Institute, Singapore (bookshop.iseas.edu.sg).

Chapter 3, 'Adventures of a dangerous Thai woman: *Huang rak haew luk* (1949)', was originally published as Thak Chaloemtiarana, 'Move over, Madonna: Luang Wichit Wathakan's *Huang rak haew luk*', in *Southeast Asia over three generations: Essays presented to Benedict R. O'G Anderson*, edited by James T. Siegel and Audrey R. Kahin, 145–64. Copyright 2003 Cornell Southeast Asia Program Publications. Used by permission of the publisher, Cornell University Press.

Chapter 4, 'A civilized woman: M.L. Boonlua Debhayasuwan', was originally published as a book review in *New mandala*, 22 November 2013: www.newmandala.org/book-review/review-of-a-civilized-woman-tlc-nmrev-lxiv/.

Chapter 5, 'Are we them? The Chinese in 20th-century Thai literature and history', was originally published as 'Are we them? Textual and literary representations of the Chinese in twentieth-century Thailand' in *Southeast Asian studies*, 3(3) (December 2014), 473–526.

Chapter 6, 'Reading lowbrow autobiographies: The rich, the gorgeous and the comical', was originally a lecture titled 'Autobiographies of the rich, the gorgeous, and the comical: Iconic achievers in contemporary Thai Society', given at the Center for Southeast Asian Studies, University of Wisconsin-Madison, 30 November 2007. Not previously published.

Index

Where a text has both a Thai title and an English translation, both are included, with the version used most commonly in the text listed first.

A locator containing 'n' indicates a reference appearing in a footnote on that page (e.g. '26n28' indicates a reference on page 26, footnote 28).

adaptation
  as cultural survival, 13–14
  literature, 17–18
adultery, 28, 37–38
appropriation
  as control, 14–16, 18, 24, 41, 73
  Ramakian, 18, 65, 69, 118, 153
  through translation, 65–68
  Western grammar, 26, 26n28
  Western technology, 96, 103–105
authenticity, 62, 71, 170
  in literature, 60
autobiography, 213–215
  beauty, 222–228, 233
  Chiwit khot talok [*Life is damn funny*], 231–232
  humour, 228–232
  Kho tok din thao tit khlon [*Head bowed to the ground, feet in the mud*], 229–230
  Ok hak rueang lek ok lek rueang yai [*A broken heart is a small matter, a small breast is a big matter*], 222, 227–228
  Phom cha pen khon di [*I will be a good person*], 216
  Pooki no tom, 222, 226–227
  popularity of, 213, 216, 232
  Rak khong jina [*Jina's love*], 224–225
  Successes and failures [*Khwam samret lae khwam lom laeo*], 139–140
  Ta du dao thao tit din [*Eyes on the stars, feet on the ground*], 203–204, 215–216
  Tong phae siakon jueng ja chana dai [*One has to lose before winning*], 216
  wealth and success, 215–222, 232
  Yindi jao [*Pleased to meet you*], 222–224

Bangkok Grand Prix International Motor Race *see* racing
Birabongse, Prince 'Bira' Bhanudej, 75, 88–89
  in books, 94–95
  death, 109
  education, 97–98
  Gold Star award, 90, 92–93, 95, 97, 98
  racing, 90–93

relationships, 99, 103
success, 98, 105, 108–109
visit to Thailand, 99–103, 104
Boonlua. *see* Mom Luang Boonlua Debhayasuwan
Bowring Treaty of 1855, 13, 107, 188
Buddhism, 41n48
   influence on literature, 21n16, 23n19, 28, 43, 47–48, 133
   masculinity, 38
   and modernity, 41
   namatham and *rupatham* (subjective and objective truth), 47, 52–53, 57, 74
   Thai nationalism, 28n32, 207
   values, 16n9, 24, 38

canonical literature, 44, 56, 56n62, 68–69, 74
   contruction of canon, 59–63
   tension with modern literature, 58n63, 149, 153
capitalism, 198–199, 215–216
censorship, xi, 3–4, 58–59
Chinese newly arrived [Sing tueng], 194–197
Chinese-Thai *see* Sino-Thai
Chiwit khot talok [Life is damn funny], 231–232
Chula Chakrabongse, Prince, 75, 171
   books, 94–95
   and English royalty, 89, 98, 106
   parents, 86
   politics, 96–97, 102
   relationships, 99, 103
   royal title, 89
   visit to Thailand, 99–103, 104
   wealth, 89–90
Chulalongkorn, King (r. 1868–1910), 11, 25, 42, 66, 86, 160n10
   and Chinese-Thai, 161–162
   and European royalty, 13n4
   and literature, 15
   polygamy, 142

colonialism, 72, 114n8
   crypto-colonialism, 14, 16n9, 66
   hybridity, 72
   independence of Thailand, 104–105, 127
   in literature, 45–46
   postcolonial perceptions of novels, 15, 73n87
   Thailand as semi-colonial state, 107
   translation, 65–66
comedy
   autobiography, 228–232
   comic relief, 48
conceivable lives, 117, 215, 233
Corelli, Marie, 19, 22, 43
crypto-colonialism, 14, 16n9, 66
cultural strategy, 17
   consumption, 35–36
   democracy, 106, 108
   People's Alliance for Democracy, 205
   Prachathipatai [Democracy], 218
Don Quixote, 12

education. *see also nakrian nok* (Thai students educated overseas)
   elite, 14, 85n31, 88, 89, 148–149
   women, 144
elite, 77, 105–106
   education, 14, 85n31, 88, 89, 148–149
   lifestyle, 94
   possessions and modernity, 85, 86–87
   ruling power, 108
Europe
   dominance of, 12, 41–42, 85
   education of Thai youth, 14
   glamour of, 35–36
   Thai relationship with, 98

INDEX

farang (foreign, Western), 15–16, 26, 73, 94, 228
   novels, 42–43, 46
Four reigns [*Si phaedin*], 3, 168n22
   and *A civilized woman*, 147–148

guidebooks, 201–202, 221
   Lessons from a Chinese grandfather [*A gong son wa*], 221
   Sun Tzu teaches the tycoon [*Sun wu son jao sua*], 221

Haggard, H. Rider, 43
   translation, 28
historical revisionism, 113–117
Huang rak haew luk [*Sea of love, chasm of death*], 152
   plot summary, 121–133
   role of women, 133–135
   title, 111n1

Jidapha 'Jina' Na Lamliang, 224–225

Kepner, Susan Fulop, 144
   A civilized woman, 140
   translations, 137–138
Kho tok din thao tit khlon [*Head bowed to the ground, feet in the mud*], 229–230
Khru Liam, 25–27, 42–43, 71, 72–73
   themes, 50
   translation of *She*, 28, 39–40
Khwam mai phayabat [*The non-vendetta*], 19
   author's postscript to, 25–28
   as first Thai novel, 39, 70–71
   and *Nang neramit*, 55–56
   plot summary, 29–32, 39
   print history, 23n19
   publication, 24–25
   reception of, 39–41, 55–57
   and *Vendetta!*, 23–24
   women in, 36–38

Khwam phayabat [*The vendetta*]
   changes in translation, 20–21
   as first novel in Thai language, 22, 64, 69
   influence, 19–21, 22
   print history, 21

Lakhon haeng chiwit [*Circus of life*], 56n62. see also canonical literature
Lep khrut, 174–178, 179
Lessons from a Chinese grandfather [*A gong son wa*], 221
Letters from Thailand [*Jotmai jak mueang thai*], 180, 181–185
Life with Grandfather [*Yu kap kong*], 186–188
Like a ship in the middle of the great ocean [*Dut nawa klang mahasamut*], 198–199
Literary Act 1914, 25, 26n26
literature, 56–57, 157–158. see also autobiography; novels; theatre
   adaptation, 17–18
   and history, 158–159
   magazines, 18
   Royal Society of Literature, ix
Luk phuchai [*The real man*], 28n33, 195–196. see also canonical literature

Mae Wan, 19, 20–21
masculinity, 33–34, 33n41
   male sexuality, 38, 49, 51–52, 53–54
   nakleng, 195, 195n61, 196
   suphap burut (brave gentleman), 28, 28n33
modernity, 11–12, 14
   cars, 86–88
   consumption, 86–87
   criticism of, 33, 34–36, 41
   novels, 18, 20, 22–23
   as sophistication, 45
   Thai attitude towards, 17

in Thai society, 42, 194
than samai (modern), 16, 85
women, 34, 37, 41, 118–119
Mom Luang Boonlua Debhayasuwan
   background, 140–143
   bureacracy, 145–148
   Dok Mai Sot, 138–139
   education, 144
   educator, 148–149, 153
   literary criticism, 138–139, 153
   nobility, 141
   novelist, 138, 148, 149–151, 152–153
   personality, 146
   Successes and failures [*Khwam samret lae khwam lom laeo*], 139–140
Mongkut, King, 12
morality
   Buddhism, 16n9, 24, 38
   corruption, 23, 33–34, 37

nakrian nok (Thai students educated overseas), 34, 36n43, 40, 73, 196
Nang neramit [*Divine nymphs*], 71–72
   and *Khwam mai phayabat*, 55–56
   plot summary, 46, 48–51
   as second Thai novel, 43
   and *She*, 46–47
   women, 47
nobility
   decline, 143, 148
   descended from royalty, 140–141
   employment, 144–145
   marriage, 142–143, 143–144, 151
Note Chern-yim, 231–232
novels, 17n10, 23n19, 70. see also *Khwam mai phayabat* [*The non-vendetta*]; *Khwam phayabat* [*The vendetta*]; *Nang neramit* [*Divine nymphs*]
   canon, 60–62
   canonical literature, 44, 56, 56n62, 68–69, 74
   crime fiction, 174–178

European tradition, 14–15
exoticism, 56–57, 71
Four reigns [*Si phaedin*], 3, 168n22
historic, 147–148
history of, 12
Huang rak haew luk [*Sea of love, chasm of death*], 111n1, 121–133, 133–135, 152
Lakhon haeng chiwit [*Circus of life*], 56n62
The land of women [*Suratnari*], 150–151
Letters from Thailand [*Jotmai jak mueang thai*], 180, 181–185
Luk phuchai [*The real man*], 28n33, 195–196
Phon nikon kim nguan, 168–172
as resistance, 26n27, 40, 58n63
Sanuk nuek [*Fun-filled thoughts*], 27, 27n29
Sao song phan phi [*The two-thousand-year-old maiden*], 44–45, 152
Sattru khong jao lon [*Her enemy*], 138n6
as social critique, 58–59
Thai characters, 40, 56, 57
themes, 22–23
Through the dragon design [*Lot lai mangkorn*], 191–194

occult, 52–57
Ok hak rueang lek ok lek rueang yai [*A broken heart is a small matter, a small breast is a big matter*], 222, 227–228
Other, 103
   Chinese, 167–168, 187
   Internal Other, 163, 190, 205
   in novels, 41, 42–43, 44, 55, 178
   racial, 48–52 (see also race)
   sexual, 48 (see also sexuality; women)
   Thai Other, 107

phi (ghosts, spirits), 52–53
Phi Kung, 227–228
Phibun, Phibunsongkhram, 102, 107–108, 112–113, 172
  foreword to Prince Chula's book, 95–96
Phom cha pen khon di [*I will be a good person*], 216
Phon nikon kim nguan, 168–172
  nationalism, 172
plagiarism
  Lak witthaya magazine, 18
  as virtue, 16
Pooki no tom, 222, 226–227
Prisna 'Pookie' Phraisaeng, 226–227
publishing industry, 61, 69

race
  in fiction, 48, 49–50, 52, 127
  marriage, 130
racing
  Bangkok Grand Prix International Motor Race, 76, 78–85, 102
  background, 78–80
  Bangkok time trials, 99–100
  books, 93–96
  cars, 80–81, 82–84, 86–88, 102
  display, 84–85, 99, 102
  and national pride, 92, 95, 96–103, 105
  White Mouse Racing Team, 80, 90, 91, 92
Rak khong jina [*Jina's love*], 224–225
Rama V. *see* King Chulalongkorn (r. 1868–1910)
Rama VI. *see* King Vajiravudh (r. 1910–1925)
Ramakian [*Ramayana*], 18, 65, 69, 118, 153
Ratchadamnoen (Royal Boulevard), 87, 87n38, 88, 99, 102
royalty, 13n4, 106. *see also* nobility
  Chinese heritage, 189
  'good royals', 98–99
  in literature, 113–114, 128–129

military service, 97
polygamy, 142–143
public attitude to, 108
titles, 89
use of Chinese names, 161
Sanuk nuek [*Fun-filled thoughts*], 27, 27n29
Sao song phan phi [*The two-thousand-year-old maiden*], 44–45, 152
Sattru khong jao lon [*Her enemy*], 138n6. *see also* canonical literature
sexuality, 22–23, 31–33, 31n37, 33n40, 48–52. *see also* adultery; masculinity; women
She, 45
  and *Nang neramit* [*Divine nymphs*], 46–47
Siam, 116
Siamese junk [*Samphao Sayam*], 199–200
Sino-Thai, 156–157, 207
  acceptance, 206
  assimilation, 163–164, 173–174, 205, 208–209
  Buddhism, 208, 208n79
  capitalism, 198–199
  Chinatown, 177, 178, 196–197, 210
  Chinese language, 164
  and communism, 173, 179
  demonisation, 177–178
  discrimination, 172
  elite, 200
  'good' and 'bad', 179
  in historiography, 188–190
  history of, 160–161
  Huajai chainum [*A young man's heart*], 165–167
  Jews of the Orient [*Yiw haeng buraphathit*], 160–161, 160n10, 165, 166, 206
  labour, 162
  in literature, 159, 167–168, 179, 193, 206–207

masculinity, 196
middle class, 179, 190–191, 194, 206
  stereotypes, 185, 193
  use of Chinese names, 156n2, 161, 170–171
  wealth, 201, 206, 216, 233
Sino-Thai literature, 197–198
  autobiography, 201, 203–205
  Chinese newly arrived [*Sing tueng*], 194–197
  guidebooks, 201–202, 221
  Lep khrut, 174–178, 179
  Life with Grandfather [*Yu kap kong*], 186–188
  Like a ship in the middle of the great ocean [*Dut nawa klang mahasamut*], 198–199
  Phon nikon kim nguan, 168–172
  Siamese junk [*Samphao Sayam*], 199–200
  Through the dragon design [*Lot lai mangkorn*], 191–194
siwilai (civilised, especially Western-influenced), 11n1, 16, 21, 142–143, 146–147, 152
Sonthi Limthongkul, 203, 204–205
  background, 216–217
  career, 218–219
Successes and failures [*Khwam samret lae khwam lom laeo*], 139–140
Sun Tzu teaches the tycoon [*Sun wu son jao sua*], 221
Suntharee Wechanon, 222–223

Ta du dao thao tit din [*Eyes on the stars, feet on the ground*], 203–204, 215–216
Taksin, King (r. 1767–82), 161, 189
Thai culture, 27n30, 114–115
  adaptation, 41–42
  attire, 11n1, 100, 101
  autobiography, 213–214
  bureaucracy, 145–148

canonised literature, 44, 59–63, 68
class, 126n31, 233, 234
comedy, 228–232
impact of nationalism, 101
influence of Western culture, 15–16, 56–57, 104
literature, 56–57, 157–158
perceptions of, 183
reading, 212–213
Thai identity, 155, 170, 189–190, 207–209
Thai language, 22, 24, 26, 62, 74, 103
  as assimilation practice, 164, 208
Thai nationalism, 63, 75, 77, 106, 108
  Buddhism, 28n31, 207
  and Europe, 98
  literature, 25–26, 172
  'Nation, Religion and King', 163, 207
  promotion, 116
  racing, 79, 81, 84, 91, 92, 96–103
  royal support, 102
  and *siwilai*, 146–147
Thailand, 93
  flag, 91n50, 92, 93, 96
  name change, 116
  political change, 62–63, 89, 108, 147–148, 173
  trade, 13n4, 42, 160
Thaksin Shinawatra, 203–204, 215–216
Thammasat University suppression, xi, 3, 197n64, 217
The land of women [*Suratnari*], 150–151
The non-vendetta. see *Khwam mai phayabat* [*The non-vendetta*]
theatre, 114–115, 117n14
  building, 115n10
  and nationalism, 114n7
Thelma and Louise, 132, 132n40
Thep Pho-ngarm, 229–230

Through the dragon design [*Lot lai mangkorn*], 191–194
Tong phae siakon jueng ja chana dai [*One has to lose before winning*], 216
translation, x, 16n8, 64
    as control, 65–66, 68, 73
    literature, 18
    Ramakian [*Ramayana*], 18, 65, 69, 118, 153
    vernacularisation, 67, 68n81, 69

Vajiravudh, King (r. 1910–25), 86, 89
    and Buddhism, 28n32
    and Chinese-Thai, 159–160, 162–163
    flag design, 91n50
    Huajai chainum [*A young man's heart*], 165–167
    Jews of the Orient [*Yiw haeng buraphathit*], 160–161, 160n10, 165, 166, 206
    nationalism, 26n26, 114n7, 115n10
    Royal Society of Literature, ix
Vendetta!, 19
    and *Khwam mai phayabat*, 23–24, 28
    role in Thai literature, 22
    Thai translation (*see Khwam phayabat* [*The vendetta*])
Vikrom Kromadit, 216
    background, 219–220
    career, 220
virtue, 34, 38

Wae Soul, 225
Western culture, 107
    appropriation of, 18, 66–69
    dominance, 14
    influence on Thai culture, 15–16, 56–57, 104
    Thai adaptation of, 66–67, 108
    Thai mastery of, 77, 82, 90, 147
    Thai perception of, 105

Wichitwatthakan, Luang, 14n6.
    see also *Huang rak haew luk* [*Sea of love, chasm of death*]
    background, 112
    criticism of legal system, 134
    historian, 113
    and literature, 117n14
    novelist, 117, 128–129
    playwright, 111, 113–117, 113n5, 114n6, 127n33, 133
    political actions, 98, 101, 105, 107
    women, 117–118, 120, 126
women
    'a neatly folded piece of cloth', 118
    autobiography, 222–228
    beauty, 225–228, 233
    dangerous, 120–121, 122, 134–135
    as display, 36–37
    education, 144
    European women, 103
    female identity, 119
    ideal, 38n45, 135
    justice, 134
    Madonna/Whore dichotomy, 119–120, 119n20
    marriage, 143–144, 151, 222–223
    military, 111–112, 115, 127, 133–134
    modernity, 34, 37, 41, 118–119
    motherhood, 39, 223–225
    novels, 144, 151–152
    privilege, 143–145
    roles, 51n58, 117, 124, 131, 135, 233
    sexuality, 35–36, 51–52, 54
    traditional roles, 34, 36
    upbringing, 141

Yindi jao [*Pleased to meet you*], 222–224

www.ingramcontent.com/pod-product-compliance
Lightning Source LLC
Chambersburg PA
CBHW061254230426
43665CB00027B/2941